SUMMER JOBS BRITAIN 1992

EDITOR EMILY HATCHWELL

Assistant Editor Sara Rafferty

Distributed in the U.S.A. by Peterson's Guides, Inc.,
202 Carnegie Center, Princeton, N.J. 08543

Published annually by
Vacation Work, 9 Park End Street, Oxford.

Twenty-third edition
THE DIRECTORY OF SUMMER JOBS IN BRITAIN
Copyright © Vacation Work 1992
ISBN 1 85458 058 2 (hardback)
ISBN 1 85458 057 4 (softback)
ISSN 0143 3490

Statement for the purposes of
The Employment Agencies Act 1973:
The price of *The Directory of Summer Jobs in Britain*
is £9.95 (hardback) or £6.95 (softback) and is for the book and the information contained therein; it is not refundable.

Cover design by Miller Craig & Cocking Design Partnership

Printed by William Gibbons & Sons, Wolverhampton, England

Preface

Following a steady fall in unemployment during the 1980s — a period when the temporary employment market remained comparatively buoyant — unemployment figures have risen steadily in recent years. The economic recession has hit a large number of industries, and the decreased number of job vacancies has made it harder for those looking for summer work. Nevertheless, the majority of temporary labour is still employed on a seasonal basis, so there remains scope for those who wish to earn some extra money during the summer vacation in 1992.

Summer Jobs in Britain is intended for people who do not wish to mope around at home this summer, and for those keen to find interesting work, whether locally or further afield. In the Directory we have collected details of job vacancies supplied to us by employers in England, Scotland, Wales and Northern Ireland. The jobs have been arranged under the headings Business & Industry, Children, Holiday Centres & Amusements, Hotels & Catering, Medical, Outdoor, Sport, and Language Schools, in the geographical locations shown on the next page.

We have put an (O) after those employers who will consider applications from Canadian, American and Australian job-seekers with permission to work in the UK, and from EC nationals who speak English to a reasonable standard. It should be noted that nationals from other countries will find it extremely difficult to take up employment in Britain unless they enter under one of the special schemes operated by the Department of Employment, details of which are given under the Visa and Work Permit Requirements section.

The companies and individuals listed in *Summer Jobs in Britain* are for job-seekers to apply to directly; the publishers cannot undertake to contact individual employers or to offer assistance in arranging specific jobs.

The Directory is an annual publication and is VALID FOR 1992 ONLY. A thoroughly revised edition will be published early in 1993.

Emily Hatchwell

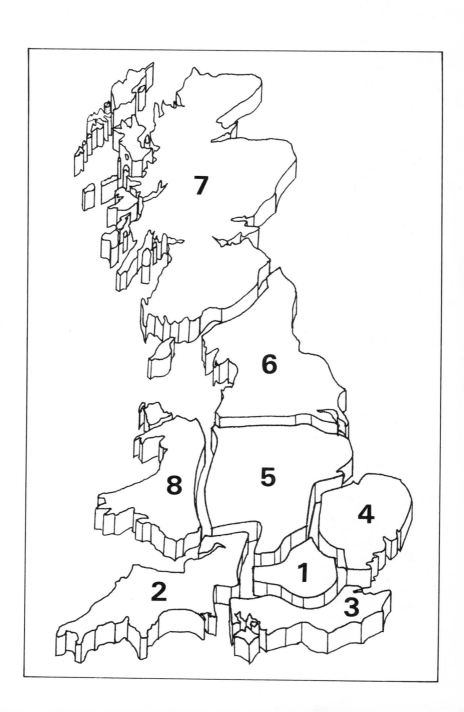

Contents

Working this Summer

The range of summer jobs on the market is extremely varied, and not restricted simply to the perennial fields of tourism and fruit picking. For example, jobs are available in pubs, hotels and shops — to cover for staff holidays or cope with the seasonal rush — and it is also possible to find more unusual summer work, such as modelling or working as a clown on a holiday camp.

There are many ways of going about the search for a job. You can, for example, sign up with an employment agency which handles secretarial, catering or warehouse work, or apply to the local council for work on playschemes or in parks and leisure centres. Alternatively, you can approach employers direct from addresses in the Yellow Pages or Local Directory, stressing your availability for work. Local papers can be a good source of information as they display adverts for jobs of all kinds, and also give news of local events, etc. which may need short term helpers. Below are some of the various areas which can offer temporary summer work.

Business and Industry. Temping is one of the most widely available and most lucrative summer jobs. All major towns have a number of agencies specializing in temps, but it is also worthwhile looking in Jobcentres for further vacancies. Many employers are looking for people with clerical skills, and it is worth investing in a typing course. This type of work is available at any time of year. If you have some clerical experience and a good telephone manner, and especially if you can speak a European language, it is a good idea to contact major holiday tour operators in the spring for seasonal jobs.

There are opportunities in the retail industry in large stores such as Boots, Comet, Our Price Records, and department stores, etc. The recent trend, however, is to offer sophisticated training and staff promotion schemes rather than take on short-term casual work. Supermarket chains also recruit extra staff for the season. For full time work preference is often given to those wanting to pursue a career in the retail trade, but with an increasing number of shops opening late and on Sundays, there is a steady demand for part-time workers.

It may be worth wandering around the commercial and shopping area of your local town looking out for job notices. Turf accountants in particular regularly display part-time and temporary vacancies. Your chances of getting work this way are always improved if you do your best to look tidy and presentable.

Office and Industrial cleaning is another area that can offer temporary vacancies. Most cleaning companies generally employ staff over a longer period, but they will occasionally take people on temporarily for jobs such as cleaning newly-built or refurbished office blocks, and factory units. This kind of opportunity occurs more frequently in New Towns or overspill and relocation areas such as Milton Keynes, Welwyn Garden City, Telford, Crawley, Stevenage and Harlow.

Summer is the time when factories and food processing centres prepare for the Christmas sales rush or compensate for staff holidays. Many have an urgent need for line workers, packers and delivery van drivers.

The building and construction industry offers some opportunities for labouring jobs, but these are not as numerous as they were a few years ago. The work is very hard physically and, unless you have any specific skills, will be of the most menial kind. Most jobs are filled by word of mouth or by visiting sites. Asking someone in the industry is the best way of finding out where jobs are likely to occur.

Children. There is a real demand for people to occupy children over the long summer holiday, either on playschemes, at specifically run centres, or within the family. No specific qualifications are usually required, but most employers are looking for people with energy and some sort of experience of working with children.

Most local councils offer playschemes throughout the school holidays and they need dozens of play leaders and assistants to organize activities for groups of children of all ages.

Children's summer camps and activity holidays are now very popular and employ large numbers of activity instructors and monitors. There are also openings for more senior supervisors (preferably trainee or qualified teachers) and nurses. Staff are rarely highly paid, but food and accommodation is often provided, and the work can be fun since a high degree of participation in activities and sport is expected.

Anyone preferring closer contact with children should consider working in a family. There are a number of agencies, the majority of which are in London, that specialize in placing nannies and mother's helps. Jobs can also be found in magazines such as *The Lady*, which advertises this kind of work. Details of agencies and au pair opportunities are listed in the final chapter of the book.

Holiday Centres and Resorts. Holiday companies, such as Pontins and Butlins, are among the largest seasonal employers in the country. They recruit bar staff, waiting staff, cleaners, and clerical staff to man their holiday camps and centres all over Britain. They usually want people to work for the whole season which is longer than college holidays, and they need early applications around February or March.

There is a growing number of specialist sports and activity centres which are also seasonal employers. They usually centre around sea, river or mountain activities, so are often found in remote places and need to recruit live-in staff. These centres require sports instructors and teachers, and there are plenty of opportunities for those with professional training and qualifications in activities such as sailing, canoeing, windsurfing, climbing, archery, etc. Riding schools and trekking centres, which are particularly common in Wales, also take on experienced riders. Since a lot of the work will be dealing with groups, the ability to get on well with people is just as important as experience of sports.

Tourist resorts and amusement parks are a great source of summer employment. There is a large number of leisure complexes, theme parks and tourist attractions that take on staff for swimming pools, bars and cafés, gift shops, car parks, rides, and maintenance. It is advisable to apply early to these places because they need to recruit a full staff ready for their peak season, but it is possible to get jobs fairly late on as they usually take on extras for bank holidays and particularly busy weeks.

There are temporary jobs to be found at any sort of tourist attraction, and it is worthwhile asking at country houses or castles, zoos, parks, nature reserves, etc.

Hotels and Catering. Tourist resorts and seaside towns are often a good source of work over the summer because their many hotels, guest houses and restaurants all need extra staff. The work can be fairly hard and tiring, and you are usually expected to work in shifts, sometimes at fairly unsociable hours. Although there are vacancies for kitchen, chamber, restaurant and bar staff, many hotels tend to employ general assistants for duties that can range from washing up to working at reception. Finding a job that offers free board and lodging or provides meals while you are on duty can also help you to save your money.

The big hotel chains, such as Trust House Forte and Thistle Hotels, tend to be located away from the more popular holiday spots and are often found in or around big cities. Work in this kind of hotel is less likely to include accomodation and they are more likely to want trained staff for particular duties.

Hotel and catering work has a reputation for being low paid, and the Wages Council exists to combat possible exploitation in the trade. The majority of hotels will abide by their minimum wage regulations, but unfortunately these only apply to those aged 21 or over; under that age the wage is an agreement between the employer and employee only. The hourly rate for licensed hotel and restaurant work is £2.56 per hour and £3.84 overtime rate, although this is currently under review. For further information contact the Officer of Wages

Council (Catering), Steel House, 11 Tothill Street, London SW1H 9NF.
It is easier to save money by working in remote areas such as the Scottish
Highlands or the Welsh Mountains. The other advantage with these isolated
hotels is that they often have facilities, such as swimming pools, horses,
windsurfers, which they may allow you to use in your free time.

Agriculture. Despite increased mechanism, summer farm work is still available
in some areas of the country. In more populous areas and those which attract
holiday makers, 'pick your own' farms have meant that fewer jobs are available
However, because a substantial part of the crop is needed for processing, pickers
and packers will always be required. In the main agricultural areas of Britain
(East Anglia, Evesham, and Perthshire, for example) fruit such as strawberries,
raspberries, plums and apples are still picked by hand; therefore large numbers
of pickers are needed, although the work can be fairly short term. Picking fruit
is extremely hard work, and the accommodation provided by farmers is often
extremely basic; some require you to take your own tent and you must usually
prepare your own meals.

Many farmers pay for piece work, which means that you are paid according
to the quantity you pick. In the height of the season this method can be very
satisfactory, but when fruit is more scarce, earnings can be pitifully low. You
can be paid as little as 10p for picking a pound of strawberries. To combat
exploitation, the Agricultural Wages Board (3-8 Whitehall Place, London SW1A
2HH) sets miniimum hourly wages, e.g. £2.69 for seasonal workers over 20,
and £4.03 overtime. Many farmers calculate wages by a combination of piece
work and hourly rates of pay. A piece work rate can be paid as long as an
'average' worker could not earn less than the minimum hourly rate. To avoid
being caught out, remember to ask exactly how much you will be paid before
accepting a job.

Language Schools. The teaching of English as a Foreign Language (TEFL)
has been a major growth industry over the last decade. Particularly during the
summer months, people of all nationalities and ages come to spend time in
Britain to pick up or polish their English. The language schools that cater for
them tend to be concentrated in popular tourist areas in the south — mainly
in London, along the south coast and in towns such as Oxford and Cambridge.
Teaching jobs are few and far between in the northern parts of the country,
Wales and Scotland.

Although it is still possible to find teaching posts abroad without qualifications,
most British language schools require a TEFL qualification. Some, however,
will take on graduates with an English or modern language degree, or PGCE
and teacher training students. Teachers are employed either for a complete

holiday course for both classroom work and social and recreational activities (such courses are usually residential), or on an hourly basis for classroom teaching only.

Language schools that run residential courses often take on staff to supervise day trips, visits and the more social side of the school's programme. There are also opportunities for sports instructors of all types as many of the schools offer a wide range of sporting activities.

Local Government. Councils often hire temporary staff during the summer, although cuts have meant a reduction in the number of positions available. The most readily available summer vacancies are usually as playscheme leaders and assistants. Jobs as gardeners, litter collectors and ground staff are often available annually through the city works department, and Leisure Services and Recreation Departments take on swimming pool attendants, lifeguards and recreational assistants of various descriptions.

Area Health authorities have been known to recruit nursing assistants and auxiliaries for the summer, but the more frequent vacancies in hospitals are for laundry workers and cleaners. Other departments may need people for clerical or information duties, cleaning, maintenance or various other types of work, but vacancies of this sort do not usually occur on a regular basis.

Most councils advertise in the local press and display vacancies in Jobcentres.

Jobcentres and Agencies. In large towns, and places near holiday areas, Jobcentres hold details of temporary summer work and recruit for a number of major companies. Most Jobcentres have a display for temporary work, but distinguish between the skilled and unskilled. If you have a specific skill to offer you can be put on a register, but for any kind of unskilled work you are best off simply checking the boards regularly to see what is available. It is possible to ring either your local Jobcentre or one further afield for general information on whether any temporary employment is available; but unless you have a skill, they cannot give you details of specific jobs. It may be a good idea to apply earlier in the year, as some firms keep waiting lists or want to recruit early; but many jobs are available on the spot and regular enquiries are always advisable.

It is worth finding employment agencies that specialize in the type of job you are looking for e.g. word processing, catering or driving. Under the Employment Agencies Act it is illegal to charge a fee for finding someone a job, and the agencies make their money by charging the employers.

Voluntary Work. There are many organizations that need volunteers over the summer (and often all year round) for conservation or archaeological work, care of the disabled or elderly, social projects with children or the homeless, and so on. This kind of work can be very demanding; you are often expected to work hard physically, give a lot of time and commitment, and the people you work with usually expect a lot from you or may be reliant on you. This of course can be very challenging, and working as a volunteer is often quoted as a rewarding and maturing experience.

Some voluntary projects, especially conservation or work camps, ask for a contribution from the volunteer; most volunteers, however, are given some kind of renumeration, whether in the form of free board and lodging or a small amount of pocket money.

Voluntary work is dealt with in a separate chapter near the end of the book.

A NOTE ON TAX

Students looking for employment over the summer should be aware of their position as regards tax. The annual personal allowance for students is £3,295, and few people are likely to earn this much over the vacation. To avoid paying tax you should present your employer with a completed form P38(S), which can be picked up at your local tax office. If you neglect to do this in advance, you will have to pay tax (at 25%) and claim it back later, which can be a time-consuming business.

Anyone who earns more than £52 per week must pay National Insurance, and this is not refundable.

Creating Your Own Job

There is no reason why you should not create a job for yourself. If others can set themselves up as car-washers, gardeners, shirt pressers, dog exercisers or granny minders, there is no reason why you should not do so as well. The questions to ask yourself are:

1. What do people want?
You can find out by asking neighbours, reading local papers and enquiring at local shops (especially newsagents, tobacconists and grocers) and at your local Jobcentre. You will then have obtained a general picture of what sort of thing local people want done — window cleaning, grass-cutting and gardening, painting and decorating, housework, babysitting, etc.

2. What can I offer?
It is surprising how many different things most of us can turn our hands or minds to. It may well be that a hobby or spare-time activity can be turned towards earning money: walking — dog exercising, tourist guiding or shopping; sewing — dressmaking, repairs and alterations, cushion making, patchwork quilts or costume making; knitting — jerseys and commissions; cooking — lunch and dinner party catering, sandwich-making; cycling — bicycle repairs (highly recommended).

3. What do I need?
It is no good embarking on a career as a window-cleaner without a bucket. An assessment of your requirements will give you an idea of how much the initial setting-up of your operation is going to cost and may narrow down your field of options. Most householders will have a lawn mower of sorts, but if you have one of your own which is easy for you to handle and maintain, the job becomes easier for you and a better service to your clients.

4. Who wants me?
After you have identified the job you can do and for which you think there will be a demand, you need to publicize your services as widely as possible in the area you are able to cover. The best way to start is with advertisements in local shops, which are free or very cheap, and, if you can afford it, in your local newspaper (especially the free papers). It will also be useful to run off

a handbill and distribute it locally. Considerable care should be taken with this and you should ask a friend to comment on what you produce. It is surprising how often people advertising their services neglect to mention vital details. When distributing leaflets it is worth taking care who gets them; there is no point in advertising a grass-cutting service to a house surrounded by gravel.

5. What should I charge?

It is as easy to undercharge as it is to overcharge. You will need to take into account all the expenses you will incur (i.e. advertising, replacement of equipment) if you wish to make any money. The one thing you must try to avoid is having to put up your prices, as this is a sure way of losing recently gained customers. You should also find out what the professionals are charging for a similar service so that you can undercut them substantially.

The principal feature of successfully creating a job for yourself is your reputation. If you impress someone with your hard work, promptness and efficiency, they will tell others; recommendations are not only free but guarantee future business.

Notes on Applying for a Job

1. Remember that employers generally prefer to take on one person for the whole season rather than several people for short periods. If you are able to work for longer than the minimum period quoted, you are most likely to be offered the job.

2. Most employers like to make their staff arrangements in good time. Therefore try to apply early, but never earlier than the date mentioned in the job details. If you decide to look for a job late in the season, and have missed most of the application deadlines, ring round a number of hotels or farms, or write a letter explaining that you are prepared to start work immediately. Positions continue to become vacant as people cancel at the last minute or leave for various reasons. The more employers you approach, the better are your chances of finding one with a suitable vacancy.

3. Before applying for a position check that you fulfil all the requirements as to a period of work, age and qualifications. In a time of high unemployment, employers are normally able to find someone who meets all their needs, so you are wasting your time (and the employer's) if you apply without fulfilling the requirements. It is particularly important to note whether or not accommodation is provided, especially for those who are coming from abroad. In many parts of Britain, above all those which attract a lot of tourists over the summer, temporary rented accommodation is virtually impossible to find. If rooms are available the rent is likely to be extremely expensive. Some employers can recommend lodgings in the area or be of more positive help, but often they are reluctant to recruit those who have no pre-arranged accommodation.

4. Compose a short letter, explaining which position interests you, why you think you are suitable for it and the maximum time you are available. It would also be worth mentioning that you are available for interview, if such is the case. Hotel managers, for example, are quite likely to wish to interview their prospective employees. Those applying from overseas should also make it clear that they are eligible for a work permit if one is necessary. (See under *Visa and Work Permit Requirements*.) If possible, type this letter; if not, make sure that it is legible. Remember that first impressions are very important. If an

employer receives a lot of applications for a certain position, he or she may be forced to make use of small omissions or mistakes to help the process of elimination.

5. Enclose with your letter a standard resumé or c.v. covering the following points and any others you consider relevant:
    i.   Personal details (name, address, telephone number, nationality, age, marital status).
    ii. Subject studied if you are a student, otherwise your present occupation.
    iii. Relevant qualifications and previous work experience (possession of driving licence, etc.).

6. Enclose a small recent photograph of yourself.

7. **Always** enclose a stamped addressed envelope or, if you are applying from abroad, an international reply coupon. It can be both expensive and inconvenient for employers to reply to a large number of applicants, especially once the positions have been filled. Some employers are so inundated with applications that they are simply unable to reply to many of them.

8. When a job is offered to you check details of wages, hours and the conditions of work. The details in the Directory are supplied by the employer and are normally correct, but it is wise to obtain confirmation of them before accepting the position.

9. If you are offered more than one job, decide quickly which one you prefer and inform all employers of your decision as soon as possible.

10. One further point needs to be stressed. Many young people regard their summer job as their summer holiday. However, this is very seldom the attitude taken by the employer. If the job details indicate that a hotel needs an assistant to serve three meals a day six days a week, or a hop farmer needs pickers to work seven days a week in all weathers, then you should be warned that there will be far more work than holiday.

N.B. the authors and publishers have every reason to believe in the authenticity and correct practices of all organizations, companies, agencies, etc. mentioned in this book; however, they strongly advise readers to check credentials for themselves.

Visa and Work Permit Requirements

Visa Requirements. Citizens of European countries, most Commonwealth countries and the United States do not need a tourist visa to enter the UK. Nationals of Eastern Europe and most Asian and African countries require a visa. Exceptions include Israel, Japan, Turkey and South Africa. For details check with the UK Consul in your country.

Work Permits. Britain has been a member of the European Community since 1973. This means that nationals of EC countries (excluding Spanish and Portuguese citizens until 1993) are free to enter Britain to seek employment without a work permit. If an EC national intends to stay longer than the six months normally given, then he or she should apply for a residence permit upon arrival.

The situation for non-EC citizens, however, is more difficult. Since 1980, the Department of Employment has ceased issuing permits to all unskilled and semi-skilled workers, including those that come to find seasonal work in the hotel and catering industry. There are a few exceptions to the rule, however. For example, citizens of Commonwealth countries between the ages of 17 and 27 may visit the UK as a 'Working Holiday Maker' to take up casual employment which will be incidental to their travelling. Before leaving their home countries they can obtain the appropriate passport endorsement from the British High Commission, or they can show the Immigration Officer a letter offering employment or sufficient funds and ask for the Working Holiday Maker stamp at point of entry. The total period which can be spent in the UK as a working holiday maker is two years, whether aggregated or in one continuous spell. Commonwealth citizens with at least one British-born grandparent may wish to apply for entry clearance from the British High Commission, which eliminates the need for work permits altogether.

Farm camps are the main hope for non-EC and non-Commonwealth workers. These camps, authorized by the Home Office, are permitted to issue entrance authorization cards to a certain number of non-EC nationals each year. Most of the recruitment is handled by Concordia Youth Service Volunteers (Recruitment Secretary, Concordia (YSV) Ltd, Brunswick Place, Hove, East Susssex BN3 1ET) and the Harvesting Opportunity Permit Scheme or HOPS (YFC Centre, NAC, Stoneleigh Park, Kenilworth, Warwickshire CV8 24G). For further information write to either of these two organizations, enclosing a stamped addressed envelope. Both have entries in the Nationwide section of this book: see page 29.

American students seeking temporary work in the UK can benefit from an exchange scheme operated by CIEE (Council on International Educational Exchange), 205 East 42nd Street, New York, NY 10017, USA (tel 212-661-1414). They can issue a blue card to students which allows the holder to work for a maximum of 6 months at any time of the year. Extensions are never granted.

For details of regulations affecting au pairs please see the chapter *Au Pair, Home Help and Paying Guest.*

Further information about work permits can be obtained from the Department of Employment, Overseas Labour Section, Caxton House, Tothill street, London SW1H 0NF. Any non-EC or non-Commonwealth nationals who believe themselves eligible for a work permit, must apply to the Department of Employment before they arrive in the UK. The employee must present the permit to the Immigration Officer on arrival. The absence of such a permit in one who cannot prove that he or she has sufficient funds to be self-supprting may result in refusal to leave or enter.

ABBREVIATIONS

approx.	approximately	o/t	overtime
a.s.a.p.	as soon as possible	pce.wk.	piece work (i.e.
ave.	average		payment according to quantity
B.&.L.	board and lodging		of produce picked
c.v.	curriculum vitae	p.w.	per week
h.p.w.	hours per week	s.a.e.	stamped addressed
IRC	International Reply Coupon	TEFL	envelope Teaching English as a
min.	minimum		Foreign Language
m.p.w.	minimum period of work	w.p.m.	words per minute

Employers willing to consider applications from English-speaking EC nationals and from North Americans and Antipodeans with permission to work in the UK are marked with an (O) at the end of their entries which stands for Overseas.

NATIONWIDE

Organisations which have branches in various parts of Britain

Business and Industry

CHRISTIAN SALVESEN FOOD SERVICES PLC: see below for addresses. Large frozen food company, with branches in various parts of the UK. FACTORY PRODUCTION WORKERS. Wages by arrangement. Hours according to Continental shift pattern: 4 days on, 2 days off. Hours may also vary according to ripening dates of vegetable crops. Ave. 10-hour shifts, 5 days p.w. including weekends. No accommodation is available. Min. age 16 years. M.p.w. 8 weeks between June and end of September, although period of work may vary from region to region. Send applications a.s.a.p. to the Personnel Manager at one of the addresses listed below:
Tunnel Bank, Bourne, Lincolnshire PE10 0DJ.
Gourdie Estate, Kingsway West, Dundee DD2 4TD.
Easton, nr Grantham, Lincolnshire NG33 5AU.
West Harbour Road, Granton, Edinburgh EH5 1PS.
Eyemouth Industrial Estate, Eyemouth, Berwickshire TD14 5AN.
Ladysmith Road, Grimsby, South Humberside DN32 9SL.
Salvesen Way, Hull, North Humberside HU2 4XN.
Dalcross Industrial Estate, Inverness IV1 2JB.
Gorleston Road, Lowestoft, Suffolk NR32 3BN.
Shrewsbury Avenue, Woodston Industrial Estate, Peterborough PE2 1LB.
West Marsh Road, Spalding, Lincolnshire PE11 2BE.(O)

KENTUCKY FRIED CHICKEN (GREAT BRITAIN) LIMITED: Colonel Sanders House, 88-97 High Street, Brentford, Middlesex TW8 8BG (tel 081-569 7070).
CUSTOMER/FOOD SERVICE WORKERS. Min. £122-120 p.w. Hours are flexible. Normal shifts 10am-6pm and 6pm-midnight, Monday to Sunday. Min. age 16. Should have a polite and friendly manner and be able to do basic mental arithmetic. M.p.w. 2 months between June and September. Accommodation is not available. Free uniform, meals provided and training given. Positions

available in London, Birmingham, Newcastle, Leicester, Nottingham, Oxford. Applicants should contact the Personnel & Training Officers from June onwards at one of the following District Offices:
Christine Webb or Jaqui Grace at Kentucky Fried Chicken, 96-102 Uxbridge Road, Shepherds Bush, London W12 8AL.
Rose Kudarenko at Kentucky Fried Chicken, 498a Hagley Road West, Quinton, Warley, West Midlands.

Children

ACTION HOLIDAYS LTD: 'Windrush', Bexton Lane, Knutsford, Cheshire WA1 69BP (tel 0565-654775: 24 hours). Approx 200 staff needed to run multi-activity centres for children aged 3-15 in Greater London, Hampshire and Cheshire.
ACTIVITY CENTRE DIRECTORS and DEPUTY DIRECTORS (10). £200 p.w. Considerable experience of working with children and managing teams of staff is necessary.
SENIOR SUPERVISORS (20). £120 p.w. Responsible for co-ordinating and overseeing the care, welfare and instruction of children.
SUPERVISORS (70). £45-75 p.w. To look after general care, welfare and instruction of the children.
SPECIALIST INSTRUCTORS (70). £60 p.w. To teach archery, rifle shooting, arts & crafts, computing, football, golf, go-karting, gymnastics, judo, performing arts, squash, swimming, tennis, trampolining, outdoor pursuits and watersports.
OFFICE MANAGERS (8). £85 p.w. General administration and timetabling responsibilities.
EQUIPMENT MANAGERS (4). £75 p.w. To maintain equipment and run tuck shop.

NURSES (8). £100 p.w. Responsible for general and medical care, and welfare of children.
DOMESTIC SUPERVISORS (4). £75 p.w. In charge of cleaning, laundry, lost property and general domestic responsibilities.
GENERAL ASSISTANTS (10). £45 p.w. Responsible for equipment, domestic and general supervisory duties.
Staff get 1 full day and additional sessions off p.w. B.& L. provided. M.p.w. 3 weeks during July and August. Enthusiasm and good sense of humour important. Min. age 19. Preference given to those with relevant qualifications and experience with children. For full details and application form contact Mr Martin Vasey, Director of Personnel, at the above address.

ARDMORE ADVENTURE LTD: 11-15 High Street, Marlow, Buckinghamshire SL7 1AU (tel 0628-890060). Adventure camps for 5-14 year olds (both residential and day camps) located throughout Britain.
GENERAL MONITORS (100). £25-60 p.w. Hours of work at day camps: 9am-5pm Mondays to Fridays; hours at residential camps (which run Saturday-Saturday): 8am-9pm at least. Staff lunch provided at day camps, full B.& L. at residential camps. Experience with children and familiarity with sports preferred. M.p.w. 1-9 weeks between April and August. Applications a.s.a.p. to Ardmore Adventure Ltd. (O)

CAMP BEAUMONT: 9 West Street, Godmanchester, Huntingdon, Cambridgeshire PE18 8HG (tel 0480-456123). Ten residential and day camps throughout England and Wales.
GROUP LEADERS (200). £60 + p.w. To co-ordinate children's activities. Experience preferable. Free B. & L.
MONITORS for day camps. £45 p.w. To accompany children from one of over 500 pick-up points in England to nearby camp. Must live locally.
MONITORS for residential camps. £45 p.w. To work 6 days p.w. Free B. & L.
CATERING SUPERVISOR/HEAD COOK. £100+ p.w.
CATERING ASSISTANTS also required.
To work 5 days p.w. Ages: 18-35 years. M.p.w. 3-9 weeks between 1 July and 30 August. Attendance at 1- or 2-day orientation compulsory. Free uniform (T-shirt and sweat shirt) provided. Interviews held between February and May. Applications a.s.a.p. to the Personnel Department, Camp Beaumont. (O)

EF LANGUAGE TRAVEL: EF House, 1-3 Farman Street, Hove, Sussex BN3 1AL (tel 0273-723651). Residential courses held for European students aged 9-18 in locations around Britain.
COURSE DIRECTORS. Wages by arrangement. To work 6 days p.w. Ages:

23-35 years. Previous administrative and staff management experience essential. Period of work 8/9 weeks from 22 June.
ASSISTANT COURSE DIRECTORS. Wages and hours as above. Min. age 23 years. Good organizational skills, imagination and a sense of humour needed. Period of work 6-8 weeks from 22 June.
COURSE LEADERS. Wages from £105 p.w. Time off on rostered basis. Young, energetic and committed persons to work with foreign children. Teaching experience an advantage. Period of work 6-8 weeks from end of June.
All positions include free B. & L. Full training will be given. M.p.w. 3 weeks. Applications a.s.a.p. to the Residential Courses Manager, EF Language Travel. (O)

FREETIME SUMMER CAMPS: 149-151 Goldsworth Road, Woking, Surrey GU21 1LS (tel 0483-740242). Multi-activity and sports coaching holidays for children aged 7-15. Day and Residential Centres in Surrey, Sussex and Somerset.
SPORTS INSTRUCTORS AND COUNSELLORS (100 +) From £50-100 p.w. 5-7 days p.w. Free B. & L. at residential centres. Activities include archery, arts & crafts, canoeing, computing, rifle-shooting, tennis and windsurfing. M.p.w. 3 weeks during July and August. Applications from January to the Personnel Manager, Freetime Leisure Limited. (O)

HF HOLIDAYS LIMITED: Redhills, Skirsgill Park, Penrith, Cumbria CA11 0DT (tel 0768-899988).
CHILDRENS ACTIVITY LEADERS. £46 p.w. plus free B. & L. Work involves organizing games, joining walks, etc. Applicants should enjoy the countryside and have empathy with children. Leaders required for 1-6 weeks in July and August at numerous locations throughout the UK. Applications to the Staffing Department, at the above address.

PGL YOUNG ADVENTURE LTD: Alton Court, Penyard Lane (874), Ross-on-Wye, Herefordshire HR9 5NR (tel 0989-764211). Over 2,500 staff needed to assist in the running of activity centres throughout the UK.
GROUP LEADERS to take responsibility for small groups of children and ensure that they get the most out of their holiday. Pocket money from £30 p.w. Free B. & L. Min. age 20 years. Previous experience of working with children necessary. Vacancies available for short or long periods between February and October. Requests for application forms to the Personnel Deprtment, PGL. (O)

PRIME LEISURE: The Old Mill, Mill Street, Wantage, Oxfordshire OX12 9AB (tel 0235-770261). Runs multi-activity holidays and day camps for children in 10 centres in Oxfordshire, Hampshire, Berkshire and Surrey.

CENTRE LEADERS (10). Wages £175-200 p.w. Preferably qualified teachers, 25+ years, with camp experience.
SECOND IN CHARGE (10). Wages £125+ p.w. Preferably third year trainee teachers, 21+ with coaching qualifications and camp experience.
INSTRUCTORS (75). Wages £85+ p.w. Should have experience/qualifications in LTA tennis, swimming ASA Bronze Medallion, trampolining BTF, firearms experience, first aid, art, etc. Trainee teachers/sports students welcome. Min. age 18.
ASSISTANT INSTRUCTORS (20). Wages £55 p.w. Applicants should be interested in sports and/or arts and crafts. Min. age 16.
All the above staff work from Sunday evening to mid-day Saturday.
GENERAL ASSISTANTS (15). Wages £30 p.w. To work from 9am-4pm, Monday-Friday. Age: 14-16. There may also be positions available for nurses/student nurses. Staff needed from March to April, and from the end of July to the end of August. Free B. & L. Interview sometimes necessary. Applications from January to the above address. (O)

Holiday Centres and Amusements

BOURNE LEISURE GROUP LTD: 51-55 Bridge Street, Hemel Hempstead, Hertfordshire HP1 1LX (tel 0442-69257). Over 20 holiday parks in resorts in the UK.
BAR STAFF, RECEPTIONISTS, SITE WORKERS and SALES ASSISTANTS. For further information contact Mr Steve Mullings, at the above address.
CHILD MINDERS, LIFEGUARDS, DJs and ENTERTAINERS. For further information contact Mr Malcolm Murray, Suite 11, 3 Quay Walls, Berwick upon Tweed TD15 1HB (tel 0289-330148/9).
500 staff needed in all. Competitive wages and full training provided. Accommodation is available, where appropriate, for which a small charge may be made. Previous experience is not essential. Applicants should be prepared to work flexible hours and have an outgoing personality and smart appearance. Min. age 18. Vacancies are available between March and October, for long and short periods, although a m.p.w. of 8 weeks is preferred. (O)

EUROCAMP: Edmundson House, Tatton Street, Knutsford WA16 6BG. Campsites in the Lake District and Cornwall.
CAMPSITE REPRESENTATIVES, CHILDREN'S COURIERS, WATERSPORTS COURIERS. Wages £350 per month. To erect and dismantle tents, and to see to the welfare of clients, provide local information and solve any problems which may arise. Variable hours, up to 7 days a week. Free accommodation on site. Period of work April to mid-July, July to late September,

 # BOURNE LEISURE GROUP

The Bourne Leisure Group is a fast growing Company, with over 20 holiday Parks situated in resorts in the U.K., Canada and America, require the following seasonal staff:

BAR PERSONS

RECEPTIONISTS

CHILDRENS' AUNTIES & UNCLES

SITE WORKERS

LIFEGUARDS (Bronze Medallion Level)

SALES ASSISTANTS

Vacancies are available for both short and long periods between March – October.

Previous experience is not essential, however you should possess an outgoing personality, smart appearance and be prepared to work flexible hours in a holiday environment. In return we offer a competitive wage, full training and where appropriate seasonal bonus, uniform, accommodation and the chance to gain nationally recognised qualifications and staff awards.

Minimum age 18.

The possibility of full time employment and the opportunity to progress into sales, bar and general management also exists.

Write or telephone for an application form, stating your preferred area of work to:

Steve Mullings
Personnel and Training Officer
Bourne Leisure Group Ltd
51–55 Bridge Street
Hemel Hempstead
Herts HP1 1LX
Tel: 0442 69257

or the full season. Children's couriers must be available mid-May to early September. Applications from October.

HF HOLIDAYS LIMITED: Redhills, Skirsgill Park, Penrith, Cumbria CA11 0DT (tel 0768-899988). Operates many guest houses throughout England, Scotland and Wales.
ASSISTANT MANAGERS. Responsible to management for efficient organization and smooth function of all household duties. Experience essential.
GENERAL ASSISTANTS. For domestic work in household and dining room. Training provided.
KITCHEN PORTERS. To assist cooks with the cleaning of utensils and maintaining cleanliness of kitchen. Involves the preparation of vegetables and salads. Training given.
ASSISTANT COOKS. Previous experience preferable though positions are suitable for students undertaking first appointments after college.
DEPUTY COOKS. Practical experience required. Responsible for kitchen in Head Cook's absence.
HEAD COOKS. Practical experience of catering for up to 100 covers is essential. Wage according to qualifications and experience.
Rates of pay vary from £50-160 p.w. according to position. Free B. & L. Guests' social and walking programme available to staff in off-duty hours. Season lasts from March to November. Applications to Staffing Department, HF Holidays Limited. (O)

PGL YOUNG ADVENTURE LTD: Alton Court, Penyard Lane (874), Ross-on-Wye, Herefordshire HR9 5NR (tel 0989-764211). Over 2,500 staff needed to assist in the running of activity centres throughout the UK.

Would you like to work with the Leading Activity Holiday Specialists in Europe?

POSITIONS IN THE UK EXIST FOR:

 INSTRUCTORS in canoeing, sailing, windsurfing, waterskiing, pony trekking, hill walking, archery, fencing, judo, rifle shooting, fishing, motor-sports, arts and crafts, drama, English language and many other activities. Minimum age 18.

 GROUP LEADERS to take responsibility for small groups of children and ensure they get the most out of their holiday. Minimum age 20, plus previous experience of working with children necessary.

 GENERAL STAFF to help with stores, site cleaning, kitchen, driving (car, LGV or PCV), administration, coffee bar, nurses (RGN or EGN), etc. Minimum age 18.

WE WILL RECRUIT OVER 3,000 STAFF FOR '92!! CAN WE COUNT ON YOU?

We'll provide you with full board & accommodation, a lively environment and pocket money from £30 per week. Vacancies are available for short or long periods between February and October.

For full details and an application form simply 'phone or send your address on a postcard to:

PERSONNEL DEPARTMENT, PGL YOUNG ADVENTURE LTD., ALTON COURT, PENYARD LANE (874), ROSS-ON-WYE, HR9 5NR. TEL: (0989) 764211.

GENERAL STAFF. To help with stores, site cleaning, kitchen, driving (car, PCV or LGV), administration, coffee bar, nurses (RGN or SEN), etc. B. & L. provided. Pocket money from £30 p.w. Min. age 18 years. Staff required from February to October for long or short periods. Requests for application forms to the Personnel Department, PGL. (O)

PONTIN'S HOLIDAY CENTRES:
Barton Hall Chalet Hotel, Torquay, Devon TQ2 8JY.
Blackpool Holiday Centre, Lytham St. Anne's, Lancs FY8 2SX.
Brean Sands Holiday Village, Burnham-on-Sea, Somerset TA8 2RJ.
Camber Holiday Village, nr Rye, Sussex TN31 7RL.
Dolphin Holiday Centre, Brixham, Devon TQ5 9NZ.
Hemsby Holiday Village, Hemsby-on-Sea, Norfolk NR29 4HL.
Little Canada Holiday Village, Wooton, Isle of Wight PQ33 4JP.
Middleton Tower Holiday Centre, nr Morecombe, Lancs LA3 3LJ.
Osmington Bay Holiday Village, Weymouth, Dorset DT3 6EG.
Pakefield Holiday Centre, nr Lowestoft, Suffolk NR33 7PF.
Prestatyn Holiday Village, Prestatyn, Clywd, N. Wales LL19 7LA.
Riviera Holiday Centre, Bowleaze Cove, Weymouth, Dorset DT3 6PR.
Sand Bay Holiday Centre, Kewstoke, Weston-super-Mare, Avon BS22 9UR.
Seacroft Holiday Centre, Hemsby-on-Sea, Norfolk NR29 4HR.
South Downs Holiday Centre, Bracklesham Bay, nr Chichester, Sussex
    PO20 8JE.
Southport Holiday Village, Southport, Merseyside PR8 2PZ.
St. Mary's Bay Holiday Village, Brixham, Devon TQ5 9UG.
Torbay Chalet Hotel, Paignton, South Devon TQ3 1LZ.
Wall Park Holiday Village, Brixham, Devon TQ5 9UG.
Wick Ferry Holiday Centre, Christchurch, Dorset BH23 1HY.

COOKS, KITCHEN STAFF, WAITING STAFF, CAFE/RESTAURANT ASSISTANTS, BAR STAFF, CHALET STAFF, SHOP ASSISTANTS, CLEANERS, NURSERY NURSES (NNEB/NTC), ADMINISTRATION, etc. Some positions include full B. & L. The amenities of the Centre are available for use in off-duty periods. Applicants should be over 18 years of age. Preference will be given to applicants who are available for the whole season from Easter to 20 September or later. M.p.w. 8 weeks. Further details of vacancies and wage rates available on request to the Manager at the Centre of your choice (see above).

Hotels and Catering

ANGLIA AGENCY: 70 Southsea Avenue, Leigh-on-Sea, Essex SS9 2BT (tel 0702-471648). Places people all over Britain.
HOTEL AND CATERING POSITIONS. Wages and hours by arrangement. Short-term placements, mainly for qualified or experienced staff. Applications to Jill Corbet, Anglia Agency, at the above address. (O)

FRIENDLY HOTELS PLC: Premier House, 10 Greycoat Place, London SW1P 1SB (tel 071-222 8866). Hotels in London, Birmingham, Hull, Burnley, Glasgow, Perth, Falkirk, Milton Keynes, Walsall, Nottingham, Newcastle, Northwich, Edinburgh, Ayr, Norwich, and the New Connaught Rooms, London.
ROOM ATTENDANTS (50), WAITERS/WAITRESSES (40), BAR STAFF (15), HOUSE AND KITCHEN STEWARDS (30). Ave. basic wage £97 + p.w. To work 39 h.p.w. with opportunities for o/t. Min. age 18. Should have a good personal appearance and personality. M.p.w. 3 months. B. & L. often available. Foreign applicants must have work permits. Applications at any time of year to Mr Brian Worthing, Personnel Director, at Friendly Hotels Plc. (O)

LITTLE CHEF: Cartel Business Centre, Unit 2, Stroudley Road, Basingstoke, Hampshire RG24 0FW.
GENERAL CATERING ASSISTANTS. For 350 units throughout the UK. Wages specified on application, dependent on hours, etc. To work on a shift basis to cover opening hours of units: 7am-10pm, 7 days p.w. Min. age 16 and no experience necessary. Accommodation is not available. All candidates must be available for interview, including those from abroad. Applications from Easter to Mrs V. Hayday, Personnel Director, at the above address. (O)

McDONALDS: consult the telephone directory for addresses of local restaurants.
STAFF needed for all types of work in quick service restaurants around the country. Full and part-time work available at any time of year. Wages dependent

on experience. Paid holidays, life assurance scheme after qualifying period, private medical care after 3 years service, education assistance schemes, free meals and uniform provided. No previous experience needed: training given. Applications should be made direct to restaurants.

MONTPELIER EMPLOYMENT AGENCY: 34 Montpelier Road, Brighton, Sussex BN1 2LQ (tel 0273-778686).
ALL TYPES OF CATERING STAFF (male and female) required for positions in hotels and restaurants throughout Britain. Wages negotiable. Usually $5\frac{1}{2}$ days per week. Previous hotel and catering experience essential. Applicants must be resident in the UK. M.p.w. 12 weeks from May/June to September/October. Applications from April/May to the Montpelier Employment Agency. (O)

PIZZA HUT (UK) LTD.
KITCHEN STAFF, RECEPTIONISTS, WAITING STAFF and DRIVERS required for the summer period. Wage rates vary according to location, age, and experience. Hours vary but staff should be as flexible as possible since the Pizza Huts are staffed between 8am and 1am every day. Applicants should be bright, energetic and over 18 years old, and take a personal pride in delivering a high quality service to customers. Foreign applicants are welcome to apply providing they have a current work permit and can demonstrate a good command of both written and verbal English. Applications should be sent to the Manager or Delivery Unit of your nearest Pizza Hut. (O)

WELCOME BREAK: Head Office, 2 Vantage Court, Tickford Street, Newport Pagnell, Bucks MK16 9EZ (tel 0908-617766). Welcome Break, part of Forte Restaurants, operate Service Areas throughout the UK.
CATERING, RETAIL and FORECOURT STAFF to work over the summer period. Wages by arrangement plus free meals on duty, free uniform and discounts in Forte shops, hotels and restaurants. Transport to and from work can be provided. Shift work over a 24-hour period. Period of work by arrangement. Staff are expected to maintain a high standard of service to customers. Applications to Mrs Kathie Kinton at the above address.

Medical

CAMP BEAUMONT: 9 West Street, Godmanchester, Huntingdon, Cambridgeshire PE18 8HG (tel 0480-456123).
NURSES (25). £100 + p.w. To work 5/6 days p.w. Free B. & L. Ages: 18-35 years. Must be qualified RGN or SEN. Usually nursing combined with administrative role assisting the Director. M.p.w. 1 week, though longer

preferred. Applications a.s.a.p. to the Personnel Department, Camp Beaumont. (O)

PGL YOUNG ADVENTURE LTD: Alton Court, Penyard Lane (874), Ross-on-Wye, Herefordshire HR9 5NR (tel 0989-764211).
NURSES (RGN, SEN or equivalent) to work at residential Children's Activity Holiday centres throughout the UK. Vacancies can be for as little as one week or as long as eight months. Free B. & L. supplied plus £75 p.w. Full details and an application form can be obtained from the Personnel Department at the above address.

Outdoor

CONCORDIA (YOUTH SERVICE VOLUNTEERS) LTD: 8 Brunswick Place, Hove, East Sussex BN3 1ET (tel 0273-772086).
FRUIT/HOP PICKERS & AGRICULTURAL WORKERS are recruited by Concordia between May and October for over sixty growers throughout the United Kingdon. Accommodation varies from full B. & L. to camp sites. Pce. wk. or weekly rates of pay as laid down by Ministry of Agricuture. A registration fee of £25 (1991 figure) is charged, plus a returnable deposit of £25 for overseas students. For further details send an s.a.e. or IRC to the above address. (O)

HARVESTING OPPORTUNITY PERMIT SCHEME [GB]: YFC Centre, NAC, Stoneleigh Park, Kenilworth, Warwickshire CV8 2LG (tel 0203-696589). Issues workcards to Central and Eastern European university students between 19 and 25 years of age, who are not in their final year of studies. Also finds placements for them on HOPS [GB] registered farms.
FRUIT/VEGETABLE PICKERS needed between May and November. Self-catering B. & L. provided, e.g. camping, caravans, dormitories, etc. Wages pce. wk. or weekly rates as laid down by the Agricultural Wages Board. HOPS [GB] charges an administration fee of £35. Applicants must apply the summer of the year before the planned visit. Application forms from the above address.

SPORTSMARK LTD: Sportsmark House, Ealing Road, Brentford, Middlesex TW8 0LH (tel 081-560 2010). Work available mainly in Home Counties but also throughout the country.
ASSISTANT SPORTSGROUND MARKERS/DRIVERS. £120 p.w. basic plus o/t. Hours: 9.30am-5.30pm, 5 days p.w. No accommodation available. Duties include setting out and marking courts at playgrounds and sports centres. Must have a clean driving licence. Period of work normal vacation breaks, but

employment available throughout the year. M.p.w. 1 month. Applications to Employment Dept, Sportsmark Ltd.

Sport

ARDMORE ADVENTURE LTD: 11-15 High Street, Marlow, Buckinghamshire SL7 1AU (tel 0628-890060). Adventure camps (both residential and day camps) located in rural areas throughout Britain.
SPECIALIST INSTRUCTORS (20) in tennis, swimming, canoeing, TEFL, archery, judo, etc. Wages £25-100 p.w. depending on qualifications. Hours of work at day camps: 9am-5pm Monday-Friday. Hours at residential camps (which run Saturday-Saturday): 8am-9am at least. Staff lunch provided at day camps; full B. & L. at residential camps. Must have experience in chosen field and preferably with children aged 4-16. M.p.w. 1-9 weeks between April and August. Applications a.s.a.p. to Ardmore Adventure Ltd.(O)

CAMP BEAUMONT: 9 West Street, Godmanchester, Huntingdon, Cambridgeshire PE18 8HG (tel 0480-456123). 10 residential camps throughout England and Wales.
SPECIALIST INSTRUCTORS and MONITORS (600). Wages £50-100 p.w. for instructors and £45-60 p.w. for monitors. To work 6 days p.w. Free B. & L. Ages: 18-35 years. Activities include canoeing, sailing, windsurfing, swimming, sub aqua, archery, rifle shooting, riding, tennis, judo, dance, gymnastics, fencing, arts & crafts and computing. M.p.w. 5-9 weeks between 1 July and 30 August. Attendance at 1- or 2-day orientation compulsory. Free uniform (T-shirt and sweat shirt) provided. Interviews held between January and May. Applications a.s.a.p. to the Personnel Department, Camp Beaumont.

HF HOLIDAYS LIMITED: Redhills, Skirsgill Park, Penrith, Cumbria CA11 0DT (tel 0768-67670).
WALKING LEADERS are required by one of Britain's leading walking holiday companies that caters for all types of walkers. They need enthusiastic people to lead their walking holidays. Applicants may choose how often and when they want to lead (from 2-12 weeks) and training will be given. Accommodation, travel expenses and approx. £15 p.w. equipment allowance will be provided. Students can be employed for the Easter or Summer periods at a higher rate of pay. Candidates should be experienced walkers with leadership potential, fully competent in the use of map and compass, considerate and tactful. Training courses are held during the winter so early application is essential. For an information pack contact Mr Chris Bagshawe, Walking Department, at the above address.

OUTWARD BOUND TRUST: Chestnut Field, Rugby CV21 2PJ (tel 0788-560423). A registered charity with six residential centres in Wales, the Lake District, Scotland and on Merseyside.
TUTORS required to encourage people of all ages and backgrounds to examine themselves and to take responsibility for their own development. Wages specified on application. Applicants must have developmental skills such as identifying training needs, designing training programmes, managing the learning process, and assessing the results of the training. Staff are required all year round. For an application form write to the Director, The Outward Bound Trust, at the above address.

PGL YOUNG ADVENTURE LTD: Alton Court, Penyard Lane (874), Ross-on-Wye, Herefordshire HR9 5NR (tel 0989-764211). Over 2,500 staff needed to assist in the running of activity centres throughout the UK.
INSTRUCTORS in canoeing, sailing, windsurfing, pony trekking, hill walking, fencing, archery, judo, rifle-shooting, fishing, motorsports, arts and crafts, drama, English language and many other activities. Pocket money from £30 p.w. Full B. & L. provided. Min. age 18 years. Vacancies available for short or long periods between February and October. Requests for application forms to the Personnel Department, PGL. (O)

Language Schools

CAMP BEAUMONT: 9 West Street, Godmanchester, Huntingdon, Cambridgeshire PE18 8HG (tel 0480-456123). Ten residential and day camps throughout England and Wales.
ENGLISH TEACHERS (20). £120-140 p.w. To work 6 days p.w. Free B. & L. Ages: 18-35 years. Should have RSA or TEFL certification. Period of work June to August. Applications a.s.a.p. to the Personnel Department, Camp Beaumont. (O)

EF LANGUAGE TRAVEL: EF House 1-3 Farman Street, Hove, Sussex BN3 1AL. Residential courses for French, Italian and Spanish groups, all aged over 16, held in Brighton and London, etc.
COURSE LEADERS to teach English and organize leisure activities. Wages from £120-140 p.w. depending on experience. To work a 7-day working week. Time off by arrangement with foreign leaders. Applicants need to be lively, inventive and enthusiastic, with some knowlege of the local area and the ability to control and organize young foreign students. Min. age 21 years. All applicants should have completed at least 1 year of a relevant degree course or have experience of teacher training. TEFL/teaching experience desirable. M.p.w.

3-4 weeks between mid-June and end of August. Applications to EF Language Travel.

EURO-ACADEMY LTD: 77A George Street, Croydon CR0 1LD (tel 081-681 2905). Runs 15 summer language schools throughout England. TEACHERS (100-130) of English as a foreign language. From £145-180 p.w. depending on qualifications and experience. To work full time Monday to Saturday, with one afternoon off p.w. Applicants should have a degree or teaching certificate, or be graduates with EFL experience. Teachers must be prepared to work on Saturdays and supervise evening activities once a week. Afternoon activities include sports and local visits/excursions. No accommodation available except for some residential posts in London. M.p.w. 3 weeks between 25 June and 25 August. All applicants must be of smart appearance and responsible: the work is very demanding, and adaptability is essential. The positions are suitable for native English-speakers. Applications to the Director of Studies, Euro-Academy Ltd.

INTERNATIONAL STUDY PROGRAMMES: The Manor, Hazleton, nr Cheltenham, Gloucestershire GL54 4EB (tel 0451-60379). Runs about 50 EFL courses for European teenagers aged 11-18.
TEACHERS OF ENGLISH (50). Wages from £160-210 depending on experience. Free B. & L. with local families. To teach 4 mornings and 1 afternoon per week plus supervise full social programme of sports, excursions and evening activities. Min. age 21 years. Tutors are normally either PGCE students (in English or modern languages), or final-year modern linguists who have had a year of teaching abroad, or experienced teaching of TEFL. M.p.w. 3 weeks between June and August.
TEACHERS OF FRENCH also required to work on Fun With French courses for 5-12 year old British children, at 20 UK locations. Teaching through activities — drama, language games, cookery, art and craft, sport, music, etc. Tutors are normally experienced teachers of French, PGCE students of French, graduates who have worked in France, or else native-speakers of the language with teaching experience. Experience at primary levels especially useful. To work during Easter and August. Period of work 1-4 weeks.
Applications to International Study Programmes, at the above address. (O)

K.S.I. KOMPASS INTERNATIONAL LANGUAGE COURSES: c/o 15 Carew Close, Crafthole, Cornwall PL11 3EB (tel 0503-30583; fax 0503-30906). Runs courses in Edinburgh, Weston-super-Mare, Margate, Oxford, Plymouth, Dublin, Colwyn Bay and Cardiff.
COURSE DIRECTORS (4) for residential courses only. Required to run

centres, appoint and oversee teaching staff, and ensure the successful operation of leisure programmes. Substantial renumeration given, plus bonus, in line with responsibilities and workload. B. & L. provided free. Applicants should be well qualified TEFL teachers, active and with varied interests.
COURSE TUUTORS (30). Well qualified, active TEFL teachers required for contracts in all centres. £120-160 p.w., depending on qualifications and experience. B. & L, for residential courses arranged if required.
All staff to work 6 or 7 days p.w. including overtime. Contracts available for the month of July and/or August. Applicants must be available for interview. Applications, from 1 January, to the above address.

NORD-ANGLIA INTERNATIONAL LTD: 10 Eden Place, Cheadle, Stockport, Cheshire (tel 061-491 4191). Courses held throughout the UK and Ireland, but particularly in the North-West, Yorkshire, Edinburgh, London, Oxford, Cambridge and Kent.
TEACHERS OF ENGLISH as a foreign language (550). Wages £135 p.w. Approx. 15 hours of teaching p.w. Duties include teaching and assisting with sports and social activites. Applicants should be graduates with suitable degrees and preferably have TEFL qualifications and/or experience. Min. age 20 years.
COURSE DIRECTORS (50). £160 p.w. Must take responsibility for course content. Must be experienced TEFL graduates. Min. age 25 years. M.p.w. 3 weeks between mid-June and mid-September. Applications from 1 March to the Recruitment Department, Nord-Anglia International. (O)

THE OISE YOUTH LANGUAGE CENTRES: 1 Kings Meadow, Ferry Hinksey Road, Oxford OX2 0DP (tel 0865-792702). Work available in England and Wales.
TUTORS to teach English as a foreign language to small groups of foreign students. Must be qualified teachers or graduates with language background.
COURSE LEADERS. Qualified EFL teachers with organisational ability.
SOCIAL TUTORS to run a pre-planned leisure programme for foreign students and teach 15 periods a week.
Some residential courses available. Period of work Easter and July/August. Details from the Director of Studies, OISE.

PGL YOUNG ADVENTURE: Alton Court, Penyard Lane (874), Ross-on-Wye, Herefordshire HR9 5NR (tel 0989-764211).
EFL TEACHERS required during July and August to work at Children's Activity Holiday centres throughout the UK. Free B. & L. is supplied plus a wage of between £65 and £90 p.w. Full details and application forms from the Personnel Department at the above address.

YOUTH FOREIGN HOLIDAY SERVICE: Manor Chambers, School Lane, Welwyn, Herts AL6 9EB (tel 043871-6421).
TEFL TEACHERS (2-3 per centre) to work in Broadstairs, Ramsgate, Margate, Brighton, Shoreham, Worthing, Lancing, Canterbury, Poole, Great Yarmouth and Ryde. £7.80 per hour plus some expenses. To work $2\frac{1}{2}/3$ hours four mornings p.w. plus some additional hours for excursions. Period of work from 16 June-27 August. Applicants should preferably have an RSA TEFL diploma; otherwise experience in TEFL, RSA practitionary certificate, degree or teaching certificte is necessary. Applications to the Personnel Department at the above address.

LONDON AND HOME COUNTIES

Berkshire
Buckinghamshire
Hertfordshire

London
Surrey

Milton
• Keynes
•
Buckingham
Letchworth

Hertford
•
High
Wycombe • St. Albans
•

Maidenhead   LONDON
•
• Windsor
Newbury • Reading
•

Guildford
•
Reigate•

Jobs in and around London are fairly plentiful, but you will probably find that it is only worth looking if you already have somewhere to live. Temporary accommodation is hard to find and rents are very high. Magazines such as *TNT* carry classified advertisements which may be a source of cheap accommodation. These and other magazines and papers also carry job advertisements. Many are for secretarial and clerical work, but there are also opportunities for less skilled work, including hotel and restaurant work, domestic work, etc.

The Jobcentre at 33-35 Mortimer Street (tel 071-323 9190) deals with temporary jobs of all kinds, including hotel and catering vacancies. There are also hundreds of private employment agencies (especially along Oxford Street) which place people with office skills in temporary positions. Some useful addresses include the Hammersmith Jobcentre, 73 King Street, W6 (tel 071-741 9010) which recruits people for the Olympia Exhibition; South of the River Agency, 128c Northcote Road, SW11 (tel 071-228 5086) which handles cleaning jobs; Industrial Overload, 8 Little Turnstile, WC1 (tel 071-242 5376) and Office Overload, 225 Regent Street, W1 (tel 071-734 0911), or Plantation House, 31-35 Fenchurch Street, EC3 (tel 071-621 0495), which are part of Drake International and cover a range of fields, including office cleaning, packing, catering, and so on, as well as more skilled jobs.

The scope for jobs in the Home Counties is less broad, although arguably more interesting. The area surrounding the M4 is a fairly good source of vacation work. In Reading vacancies occur in cleaning, canteen work, van driving and packing. Labouring jobs can also e found, as can work for semi-skilled machine operators, and there are vacancies for general clerical and promotional sales work. The Thames Valley Authority (headquarters in Reading) sometimes advertises for summer lock keepers. Car park attendants and catering staff are needed for the Henley Regatta in June, and the Chelsea Flower Show in May is also likely to create temporary jobs.

Windsor is a busy tourist town all year round, but especially over the summer. Temporary work may be available at the Leisure Pool, the Royalty and Empire Exhibition (similar to Madame Tussauds), as well as at the local hotels and river boat companies. McDonalds and the Windsor Safari Park are among the largest employers of temporary staff.

There are several racecourses in the area: at Epsom, Newbury, Ascot and Windsor, some of which hold shows (such as the Windsor Show in May), and these would be worth contacting at anytime of year.

In Luton, north of London, there is a high demand for temporary office workers. Catering staff are sometimes required at the airport, and the Vauxhall factory occasionally has vacancies for warehouse staff and packers.

Business and Industry

THE AIR TRAVEL GROUP: 227 Shepherds Bush Road, London W6 7AS (tel 081-748 4999).
OFFICE CLERKS (4). Wages approx. £6,500 per annum. Min. age 19. Work comprises office duties, preparation of post and issue of travel documents. No accommodation is available. Period of work May to September, although permanent positions may also be offered. Please apply as early as possible to Mario Pozzati-Tiepolo, at the above address. (O)

ANGEL INTERNATIONAL RECRUITMENT: 50 Fleet Street (Head Office), London EC4 (tel 071-583 1661). Work may be arranged for WP operators, catering staff and trained nurses. Appointments and arrangements for work can only be made after arrival in London. It is not necessary to write in beforehand, but if you do, enclose an s.a.e. Help cannot be given to aliens without a work permit. Recruitment takes place all year round.

BONAVENTURE HOLIDAYS: The Mews, 6 Putney Common, London SW15 1HL (tel 081-780 1600).
RESERVATION STAFF (2) to take holiday reservations over the telephone for a tour operator. Involves typing, collecting and delivering holiday documents

in London and at Gatwick and Heathrow airports. To work 9am-6pm, 6 days p.w. Longer hours may occasionally be necessary. No B. & L. available. M.p.w. from July to October. Applicants should be aged over 17, bright and literate with an articulate telephone manner, and be able to type. Applications from Easter to the Manager, Bonaventure Holidays.

CATCH 22 EMPLOYMENT AGENCY LTD: 199 Victoria Street, London SW1E 5NE (tel 071-821 1133). Four branches covering central and greater London.
GENERAL INDUSTRIAL STAFF for temporary jobs such as furniture moving, driving, warehouse and message-running. Min. £120 per 40-hour week. Flexible hours but usually 8 hours per day and preferably 5 days p.w. Possiblity of o/t.
OFFICE STAFF for general secretarial duties, including word processing, filing, accounts, etc. Usually $7\frac{1}{2}$ hours per day, 5 days p.w. No B. & L. available. Min. age 18 years. Must be adaptable to different environments. M.p.w. 2 months all year round but especially from March to April, and from June to October. Applications anytime to the above address, from where applications will be directed to the nearest branch.

COMPUTER APPLICATION CONSULTANTS LTD: Pharmacia House, Prince Regent Street, Hounslow, Middlesex TW3 1NE.
MARKET RESEARCH TELEPHONE INTERVIEWERS (5-10). Wages approx. £4 per hour. Full-time $37\frac{1}{2}$ h.p.w. No accommodation available. Min. age 18 years. No experience needed, but must be confident on the telephone. Positions available for fluent speakers of French, German, Italian and other European languages as well as English. M.p.w. 1 month throughout the year. Applications by letter only to Cathy Ham, Company Secretary, Computer Application Consultants Ltd. (O)

DRIVERS BUREAU: 221 Streatham High Road, London SW16 6L (tel 081-677 9655).
VAN DRIVERS required for temporary delivery work. Wages £3.25 per hour, with o/t rates available. Applicants should have a clean driving licence and be aged over 21.
LABOURERS/WAREHOUSE PERSONS required for temporary work. Wages £3 per hour plus o/t. Age: over 18. Applicants must be on the telephone. Accommodation is not available. Period of work June to October. Applications to the above address.

GISELA GRAHAM LIMITED: 12 Colworth Grove, London SE17 1LR (tel 071-708 4956). Warehouse: 2 Juno Way (Elizabeth Industrial Estate), London SE14 (tel 081-691 9488).
PACKING STAFF — PICKERS AND PACKERS, DRIVERS, SHELF STACKERS, AISLE CAPTAINS, CLERKS, TALLYPERSON. Required by leading Christmas decorations company for its warehouse during despatch season 27 July-21 November. Hourly wages, according to grade/responsibility/shift/day of week — but above local average rates for comparable jobs, plus weekly performance bonuses. Hours 8am-6pm, plus some Saturdays. Deptford location with good local rail and bus services. Frenetic but friendly atmosphere (mostly student workforce). Must be fit. Write or phone for application forms in early July.

HARRODS LTD: Knightsbridge, London SW1X 7XL (tel 071-730 1234, ext 2211).
SALES STAFF, CLERICAL ASSISANTS, MANUAL WORKERS to cover the July sales, and from August to December/January to cover the Christmas and New Year sales. To work 5 days p.w. Monday to Saturday, with 1 week-day off. Min. age 17 years. Applicants must be based in London. Applications from May to The Recruitment Department, Harrods. (O)

JET TOURS & FRENCH TRAVEL LTD: 69 Boston Manor Road, Brentford, Middlesex TW8 9JQ (tel 081-750 4251).
CLERICAL STAFF (2). Wages £60 p.w. For work in the operations department dealing with ticketing and invoicing. Should be accurate and good-spirited and have knowledge of English and French. To work from 9am-5.30pm, 5 days p.w. Staff needed from June to October. M.p.w. 6 weeks. No accommodation available. Applications from May to the above address. (O)

MISON RECRUITMENT SERVICES: Ludgate House, 107-111 Fleet Street, London EC4A 2AB (tel 071-583 4749).

TEMPORARY SECRETARIAL/CLERICAL STAFF for central London area. Hours and wages vary with assignment. Applications anytime (but especially June onwards) to the Temporary Division, Mison Recruitment Services. (O)

O.V. SELECTION AGENCY: Abford House, 15 Wilton Road, London SW1V 1LT (tel 071-828 8345). Located opposite Victoria Station.
OFFICE WORKERS recruited for shorthand, typing, filing and occasional messenger work. Wages by arrangement. For secretarial work min. typing speed 40 w.p.m., shorthand speed 80 w.p.m. Work available at any time. Applications to Mrs Odette Veazey, O.V. Selection Agency.

PLEXUS STAFF SERVICES LTD: 131 Curtain Road, London EC2A 3BX (tel 071-828 8345). Located opposite Victoria Station.
PORTERS, PACKERS, WAREHOUSE STAFF, LABOURERS. Wages £3.50-4.00 per hour. To work approx. 8 hours per day. Period of work all year round. M.p.w. 1 day. B. & L. is not available. Applications at any time to Plexus Staff Services Ltd.

POLY-CONTACT INTERNATIONAL LTD: PO Box 53, Isleworth TW7 4EU. GENERAL ASSISTANTS (1 or 2) to help a small training and research company. Work includes escorting clients to activities, airport transfers, serving in the canteen, delivering messages and some book-keeping, etc. The work will be at various venues in central and greater London. Wages by arrangement, plus lunch allowance, with fares in the course of work paid. Variable working hours: $3\frac{1}{2}$-$5\frac{1}{2}$ day week including some Saturdays. A good knowledge of London is absolutely essential. Candidates should be London born and bred, or resident for several years in the capital. Applicants must live within easy reach of Hounslow, and all candidates must provide their own accommodation. Applicants should be aged 19-24 with at least some basic knowlege of a foreign language and reasonable maths, common sense and the ability to get on with people. Due to the nature of Poly-Contact International Ltd's work, only people with fluent English should apply. Previous experience of at least 8 weeks holiday work or a year of Saturday jobs necessary. References are required, and possession of a bike is an advantage. Applications in writing with c.v. to Administration, Poly-Contact International Ltd.

TASK FORCE PRO LIBRA LTD: 22 Peter's Lane, London EC1M 6DS (tel 071-251 5522).
LIBRARIANS/INFORMATION OFFICERS for company libraries. Positions often involve the use of computers and online services as well as more traditional library resources such as books and journals. Wages £5-7 per hour, depending

on experience. Vacancies occur all year round. Applicants with qualifications in, or studying, librarianship/information science preferred. Applicants from abroad must have librarianship/information science/documentauste qualifications. (O)

TIE RACK: Capital Interchange Way, Brentford, Middlesex TW8 0EX. SALES ASSISANTS (20) required to work in shops based in Central London. Wages at basic rate of £4 per hour. To work full or part-time, including shifts and some Saturdays and Sundays. No qualifications necessary but selling experience desirable. Full training provided. On-the-job training and courses offered to all staff. Accommodation is not provided. M.p.w. 6 weeks between June and October. Applications, enclosing an s.a.e., from April onwards to the Personnel Department, Tie Rack, at the above address. (O)

UNIVERSAL AUNTS LTD: PO Box 304, SW4 0NN (tel 071-738 8937). CLEANERS required for families, in both residential, and non-residential positions. Must be available to sign on with the agency for min. of 2 months. Applications anytime to Universal Aunts Ltd.

WETHERBY STUDIOS: 23 Wetherby Mansions, Earls Court Square, London SW5 9BH (tel 071-373 1107). MALE PHOTOGRAPHIC MODELS. Wages £75-100 cash for 3 hour sessions. Dozens needed throughout the year. No B. & L. available. Should be aged 18-40 years, but physique is more important than age. Men who have worked on their arms and chests preferred, as look more effective in leisure wear. Moustaches and beards permissable. No modelling experience necessary. Applicants must supply snapshots or test shots (if possible) to show how they photograph facially and physically. Follow-ups are frequent, depending on the photographers' reactions to the first session of pictures. Foreign applicants must speak fluent English. Applications to Mr Mike Arlen, Director, Wetherby Studios. (O)

THE WILLIAM HILL ORGANIZATION LTD: 5 Clifton House, Clifton Terrace, Finsbury Park, London N4 3JP (tel 071-281 5292). CASHIERS. To work various hours during the summer. Also Saturday jobs available. Duties include general cashiering work in betting shops. Min. age 18 years. Training will be given. Period of work approx. 10 weeks between June and September. Applications from June to the Recruitment Office, The William Hill Organization.

WORKSHOP SHIRTMAKERS LTD: 2 Lawrence Street, Cheyne Walk, London SW3 5NB (tel 071-351 5538). A direct marketing and mail order company.

SALES STAFF. Salary based on commission, but there is a guaranteed minimum of £150 p.w. after the first two weeks. Young people, mainly women, aged 18-30, are required to promote the company's range of ladies' and men's high quality shirts, primarily through cold calling. No experience or qualifications necessary but applicants must be out-going, well-spoken and energetic. The company also stresses that applicants must be resident in Central London since no help can be given with accommodation. M.p.w. 4 weeks. Applications at any time of year to Clare Perham at the above address.

Children

ACTION HOLIDAYS LTD: 'Windrush', Bexton Lane, Knutsford, Cheshire WA16 9BP (tel 0565-654775). Runs a multi-activity holiday centre in Surrey, for children aged 3-15 years.
STAFF required to look after children in all departments of the holiday camp: instructors, supervisory and general support staff. For details of work see entry in the Nationwide chapter.

CAMP CLAREMONT: Freetime Leisure, 149-151 Goldsworth Road, Woking, Surrey GU21 1LS (tel 0483-740242). Multi-activity children's camp.
COUNSELLORS (15). £50 p.w.
INSTRUCTORS (35). £70-100 p.w. Governing body qualifications preferred.
CAMP NURSE. £85 p.w. SRN/SEN.
Hours: 9am-5.30pm, Monday-Friday. No accommodation provided, so applicants must live locally. Ages: 18-35 years. M.p.w. 3 weeks during August. Applicants from America and Australia considered. Applications from January to the Personnel Officer, Freetime Leisure.

THE GROVE: Carshalton, Surrey SM5 3AL (tel 081-770 6617). Four playcentres for 5-11 year olds, run by the London Borough of Sutton.
ASSISTANT PLAYLEADERS (20). Up to £4.20 per hour. To work 36 h.p.w., Monday to Friday. Min. age 18. Vitality and enthusiasm essential, relevant experience desirable. Staff required throughout school holidays, approx. 20 July to 6 September (also Christmas, Easter and half term holidays). M.p.w. full school holiday period of playcentre operation. No accommodation is available. Applicants must be available for interview. Applications from January (closing date 1 April) to Mr Colin Hooker, Play Developement Officer, Education Department, at the above address. (O)

SUMMER SPORTS EXPERIENCE: 12A Merton Park Parade, Wimbledon SW19 3NT (tel 081-543 4207). Run children's activity centres in London and

other parts of south east England during the Easter and summer holidays. DIRECTORS, ASSISTANT DIRECTORS. Wages according to experience and responsibility.
SPECIALIST COACHES, CAMP NURSES, ADMINISTRATIVE STAFF. £70 p.w.
SPORTS ASSISTANTS. £50 p.w.
Teachers, students, student teachers and nurses are welcome to apply. For further details interested persons should contact Summer Sports Experience at the above address.

SURREY HEATH BOROUGH COUNCIL: Leisure Services, Surrey Heath House, Knoll Road, Camberley, Surrey GU15 3HD (tel 0276-686252 ext 397).
SITE LEADERS. £4.95 per hour. Min. age 17. Must hold teaching qualification or have had training for similar types of work, and have experience of working with children.
ASSISTANT SITE LEADERS. £4.18 per hour. Must have experience of working with children.
PLAYLEADERS. £2.75 per hour. Must have experience of working with children.
SPORTS COACHES. £4-5 per hour. Must have coaching certificates.
Period of work 27 July to 14 August. First Aid certificates would be an advantage. Applications to Mr Derek Truman at the above address.

Holiday Centres and Amusements

CHESSINGTON WORLD OF ADVENTURES: Leatherhead Road, Chessington, Surrey KT9 2NE (tel 0372-729560).
RIDE OPERATORS (100) to assist visitors on and off rides. Must be extrovert.
BAR/CATERING STAFF (200). For general duties in the cafeteria, ice cream and hot dog kiosks, bars, etc. The work involves simple food preparation, porter duties, helping in the kitchen and handling cash.
SHOP ASSISTANTS (100). To work in shops, guide book outlets and ticket desks.
GROUND STAFF (20). To help with the maintenance of the grounds, weeding, picking up litter, etc.
CAR PARK ATTENDANTS (15). Needed for bank holidays and during the summer holiday season.
CASHIERS (5). Must be numerate.
AMUSEMENT ARCADE ASSISTANTS (40). To work with coin-operated electronic machines and Western side shows.
Rates of pay according to the age of applicants and the type of job taken. Working hours vary but generally involve 40 hours plus p.w. Min. age 16. No experience

or qualifications necessary for any position and training will be given. Applicants should have a smart appearance and pleasant personality. Limited accommodation available. M.p.w. 4 weeks, between Easter and October. Applications from February onwards, to the Personnel Department, at the above address. (O)

WINDSOR SAFARI PARK: Winkfield Road, Windsor, Berkshire SL4 4AY (tel 0753-830886).
FOOD, BEVERAGE, BAR and KITCHEN STAFF, RETAIL ASSISTANTS, RIDES, AMUSEMENTS and GAMES STAFF, HOUSE and GROUNDSTAFF, TRANSPORT STAFF. Wages dependent on age. Min. age 16. Accommodation not available and must be arranged independently. Staff required all year round, but extra help is needed from March to September plus all school/college and bank holidays. Applications to the Personnel Department, at the above address.

Hotels and Catering

ANGEL INTERNATIONAL RECRUITMENT: 50 Fleet Street (Head Office),

CHESSINGTON WORLD OF ADVENTURES, CHESSINGTON, SURREY KT9 2NE

BRITAIN'S MAJOR THEME PARK AND ZOO

500 STAFF to work in . . . catering, accounts, car park, shops, site clearance, rides etc.
— FROM MARCH TO OCTOBER —

Limited accommodation available.

Application forms from the Personnel Department, at the above address

London EC4 (tel 071-583 1555). Also at 70-71 New Bond Street, London W1Y 9DE (tel 071-409 2884).
Work may be arranged for catering staff. Appointments and arrangements for work can only be made after arrival in London. It is not necessary to write in beforehand, but if you do, enclose an s.a.e. Help cannot be given to aliens without a work permit. Recruitment takes place all year round. (O)

BASIL STREET HOTEL: Basil Street, Knightsbridge, London SW3 1AH (tel 071-581 3311).
DISHWASHERS (2). £135-160 p.w. plus meals. Hours: 8am-4pm, 5-6 days p.w. Duties include washing of crockery and cutlery, as well as keeping the work area clean and tidy.
STILLROOM ASSISTANTS (2). Wages as above. Hours: 7am-3pm, 6 days p.w. Duties consist of dispensing tea, coffee and other hot drinks. Some light washing-up and sandwich-making.
CHAMBER STAFF. £135 p.w. plus meals. Hours: 7am-2pm, 6 days p.w. Duties consist mainly of making-beds, cleaning bedrooms and serving early morning teas.
COMMIS WAITERS/WAITRESSES (2). £135-160 p.w. plus meals. Hours: 7am-3pm, 5-5½ days p.w. To assist the waiters with the service of restaurant meals. Also some light cleaning and banquet portering.
No accommodation available. Applicants must be able to attend interviews. Other unskilled work may also be available. Period of work 10-12 weeks, July-September. Applications to Mr P. Adrados, Personnel, Basil Street Hotel.

THE BERKSHIRE: 350 Oxford Street, London W1N 0BY (tel 071-629 7474).
CHAMBER STAFF. £115 p.w. To work 40 h.p.w. 5 days in a 7-day rota. Min. age 18. No experience necessary.
HOUSE PORTER. £115 p.w. Hours and age as above. Experience not necessary.
BREAKFAST WAITER/WAITRESS. £66 p.w. 24 h.p.w. over 6 days. Hours: 7-11am. Experience in waiting preferred. No accommodation available but meals at work and uniform provided. M.p.w. 2 months. Applications at any time to Mr Philip Mahoney, Personnel Manager, The Berkshire. (O)

BRITANNIA INTER-CONTINENTAL HOTEL: Grosvenor Square, London W1A 3AN (tel 071-629 9400).
CHAMBER STAFF (5). Wages £151 p.w. No experience necessary.
WAITERS/WAITRESSES (4). Wages £148 p.w. Applicants with previous waiting experience preferred. To work 40 h.p.w., 5 days p.w. on a rota basis. Accommodation is not provided. Applications to the Personnel Manager, at the above address. (O)

CADOGAN HOTEL: 75 Sloane Street, Knightsbridge, London SW1X 9SG (tel 071-235 7141).
CHAMBER STAFF, RESTAURANT STAFF. £140 p.w.
RECEPTIONISTS/CASHIERS. £145 p.w.
To work 39 h.p.w. on a rota basis. Min. age 21 years. Some previous hotel experience necessary. M.p.w. 3 months between April and December. Applications from March to the Personnel Manager, Cadogan Hotel. (O)

THE CONNAUGHT HOTEL: Carlos Place, London W1 (tel 071-499 7070).
SUMMER RELIEF CHAMBER STAFF (3). £95 p.w. plus tips and accommodation.
SUMMER RELIEF LUGGAGE PORTERS/VALETS (2) to carry luggage, press guests' clothing, etc. £120 p.w. plus tips.
Period of work June to September. Min. age 20. Applications to the Personnel Manager, at the above address.

CUMBERLAND HOTEL: 1 St. John's Road, Harrow, Middlesex HA1 2EF.
ROOM ATTENDANT (1), KITCHEN CLEANER (1), WAITER/WAITRESS (1). Various vacancies during the year, as well as the summer. Room attendants required July to September. No accommodation available. Wages from £3.70 per hour. Experience is usually required. Applications to the Personnel Manager, at the above address.

FORTE RESTAURANTS, WELCOME BREAK: Scratchwood Service Area, M1 Motorway, Mill Hill, London NW7 3HB (tel 081-906 0611).
WAITER/WAITRESS, CATERING ASSISTANTS, SHOP ASSISTANTS, CLEANERS. Wages £3.44 per hour. To work $37\frac{1}{2}$ h.p.w. 5 days p.w. Accommodation provided free. Period of work between June and October. Applications to the Personnel Officer, Scratchwood Service Area. (O)

THE HOUSE ON THE BRIDGE: Windsor Bridge, Eton, Windsor, Berks SL4 6AA (tel 0753-858430).
WAITING STAFF (6/8). £110 gross plus tips. To work split shifts 10am-3pm and 6-11pm. Experience required.
KITCHEN PORTERS (4). £100 gross. Split shifts or full day, hours as for waiting staff.
Wages according to ability and experience. Min. age 18. B. & L. provided free of charge. Staff required all year. Applications to the Manager at the above address.

THE KENILWORTH and MARLBOROUGH HOTELS: 97 Great Russell

Street, London WC1B 3LB (tel 071-637 3477).
CONFERENCE/BANQUETING WAITING STAFF (2). Wages £3 per hour plus o/t at time and a half. No accommodation available. Should be aged 18-30 and have Silver Service experience.
CHAMBER STAFF (3). £125 p.w. including attendance bonus. No accommodation available.
COMMIS CHEFS (2), CHEFS DE PARTIE (2) to prepare and serve fresh food to 4 star hotel standard. £135-200 p.w. Temporary accommodation available. Should have at least 706/1 & 2 qualifications or equivalent, plus experience of 3-5 star hotel work, and be aged 17-40.
NIGHT PORTER. £119 p.w. for 5 nights p.w. Min. age 18. Should have good references and a pleasant personality.
M.p.w. 4 months around the year. Applications to the Personnel Manager at the above address. (O)

KENSINGTON PALACE HOTEL: De Vere Gardens, London W8 5AF (tel 071-937 8121).
WAITING STAFF (4). Wages and period of work by arrangement. To work 39 h.p.w. 5 days p.w. Applicants must be aged at least 18 and be available for work for at least 4 months. Previous experience preferred. Applications to the Personnel Manager at the above address. (O)

LEITHS IN THE PARK: Divisional Office, New Serpentine Restaurant, Hyde Park, London W2 2UH (tel 071-724 1082).
KITCHEN ASSISTANTS (20), MOBILE ASSISTANTS (20), GENERAL ASSISTANTS (20). Wages £3.75 per hour.
WAITERS/WAITRESSES (10). Wages £2.80 per hour plus tips. Some restaurant experience is essential.
All positions to work 8/10 hours per day, 5/6 days p.w. Min. age 18. Period of work April to September. M.p.w. 2 months. No accommodation available. Foreign applicants must be eligible to work in the UK. Applications from mid-March to the General Manager, at the above address. (O)

LONDON HILTON: 22 Park Lane, London W1A 2HH (tel 071-409 2778).
CHAMBER STAFF (10). £620 per month, plus a £72 per month bonus on completion of contract.
To work a 40-hour, 5-day week on a rota basis. B. & L. available for approx. £40 p.w. M.p.w. 4 months between May and October. Applicants should be aged 18 or over: those with 6 months' previous experience are preferred. Applications to the Personnel Department at the above address as soon as possible.

LONDON HOSTELS ASSOCIATION LTD: 54 Eccleston Square, London SW1V 1PG (tel 071-834 1545). Recruit residential staff for 10 London hostels run for young employed people and full time bona-fide students.
GENERAL DOMESTIC STAFF to do housework and work in kitchens. Wages £36-48 for 6 days p.w. Ave. 30 h.p.w. in morning and evenings, leaving free time for study. Free B. & L. Min. age 18 years. Common sense and willingness to tackle variety of jobs required. M.p.w. 3 months throughout the year. EC nationals welcome to apply. Applications should be sent 2 months before date of availability to Mr T. Perkins, Personnel Manager, London Hostels Association. (O)

LONDON KENSINGTON HILTON: 179-199 Holland Park Road, London W11 4UL (tel 071-603 3355).
TELEPHONISTS (2). £3 per hour. Min. age 24; must speak fluent English and have telephone experience.
CONCIERGES/LUGGAGE PORTERS/DOORMEN (3). £498 per month. Min. age 22.
CHAMBER STAFF (6). £3 per hour. Must speak fluent English; previous experience an advantage.
WAITING ASSISTANT. £460 per month gross plus tips and service charge. Must speak fluent English: previous experience essential. Period of work May to September. Applications to the Personnel Manager at the above address.

LONDON OLYMPIA HILTON: 380 Kensington High Street, London W14 8NL (tel 071-603 3333). A 4-star hotel.
CHAMBER STAFF/LINEN ATTENDANTS. £103 p.w. gross. Min. age 18. Some experience preferable.
BAR/WAITING STAFF. £105 p.w. Experience preferable. Min. age 19, ideal for hotel and catering students.
All staff to work $37\frac{1}{2}$ h.p.w. over 5 days on a 7-day rota. Accommodation in shared quarters offered (subject to availability). M.p.w. 3 months. Foreign applicants with the relevant work permit are welcome to apply. Applications to the Personnel and Training Manager, London Olympia Hilton, at the above address. (O)

THE LOWNDES HOTEL: 21 Lowndes Street, London SW 9ES (tel 071-235 6020). A 78-bedroom hotel Knightsbridge, owned by Hyatt International.
WAITING STAFF. Wages £4 per hour plus tips. To work 40 hours per 5 day week. Hours: 7am-3pm or 3-11pm. Meals provided, and uniform where possible. Simple menu with plate service. Waiting experience preferred but not necessary. No live-in accommodation available. M.p.w. mid-April to end of October.

Applications in writing, enclosing a photograph, to the General Manager, The Lowndes Hotel.

THE MANSION HOUSE: Old Redding, Harrow Weald, Middlesex HA3 6HS (tel 081-945 4227).
WAITING STAFF (2), BAR ASSISTANT (1). Wages £90 p.w. plus o/t. Free B. & L. provided. To work split shifts 5 days p.w. Min. age 18 years old. Applicants with some experience preferred. Period of work by arrangement, at any time of year. Applications to the above address. (O)

MAYDAY STAFF SERVICES LTD: 2 Shoreditch High Street, London E1 6PG (tel 071-377 1352). Office also in the West End: 27 Noel Street, London W1 3RD (tel 081-439 2056) and West London: 35 Goldhawk Road, London W12 8QQ (tel 071-749 3139).
GENERAL CATERING ASSISTANTS & KITCHEN PORTERS. £3.10 per hour. No experience needed, just common sense.
CHEFS. From £4.50 per hour. City & Guilds 706/1 & 706/2 and relevant experience needed.
SILVER SERVICE WAITING STAFF. From £4.40 per hour. Relevant experience (e.g. Directors Dining) needed.
BAR STAFF. From £3.70 per hour. Experience essential. Temporary work approx. 8am-4.30pm Monday to Friday. Occasional evening and weekend work. Work available anytime. No B. & L. Applications to Fiona Saffin (City) or Suzanne Cartlidge (West End) or Elizabeth Evans (West London), Mayday Staff Services Ltd. (O)

MORNINGTON HOTEL: 12 Lancaster Gate, London W2 3LG (tel 071-262 7361).
ASSISTANTS (2) to perform various tasks in the housekeeping department to relieve full time staff who are taking holidays: this will involve working as chamber staff and/or breakfast room assistants. £145 p.w. 40 hours p.w. working either 7am-3pm or 8am-4pm, with days off on a rota. No B. & L. available. M.p.w. 3 months between May/June and September/October. Applicants should be willing workers and of smart appearance. Applications before the end of May to the Services Manager, Ms Edeltraud Ernst, Mornington Hotel.

NEW BARBICAN HOTEL: Central Street, Clerkenwell, London EC1V 8DS (tel 071-251 1565).
SILVER SERVICE WAITING STAFF (5). £136 p.w.
WAITING STAFF. £114.27 p.w.
To work 39 h.p.w. No split shifts. O/t available at time and a half. Min. age

17 years. No accommodation available. Period of work May to October. Applications to the Personnel Manager, at the above address.

OLD JORDANS (Quaker House and Conference Centre): Jordans Lane, Jordans, Beaconsfield, Bucks HP9 2SW (tel 02407-4586).
GENERAL ASSISTANTS (2). £2.80 per hour. To work 40 h.p.w. 5 days p.w. Duties include chamber work, waiting on tables, washing up and kitchen porter work. Free B. & L. provided in own room with use of facilities. Min. age 17. Overseas applicants should speak reasonable English. Applicants must be available for work in June. M.p.w. 2 months. Applications from 1 April to the Warden, at the above address. (O)

RAMADA INN WEST LONDON: 47 Lillie Road, London W6 1UQ (tel 071-385 1255).
WAITING STAFF (2), BAR STAFF (2). Wages £152-167 p.w. plus tips; no accommodation. To work 40 h.p.w. on rota basis. Period of work by arrangement. Applicants should be aged 20-35 and have previous experience. Applications to the Manager at the above address. (O)

ROYAL LANCASTER HOTEL: Rank Hotels Ltd, Lancaster Terrace, London W2 (tel 071-262 6737).
HOUSEKEEPERES/GENERAL ASSISTANTS. £129 p.w. No accommodation available. To work from 8am-4pm, 5 days p.w. Period of work from July-September. Applicants must be physically fit, speak fluent English and be aged under 25. Applications to the Recruitment Officer, Personnel Department, at the above address.

SHERATON HEATHROW HOTEL: Colnbrook by Pass, West Drayton, Middlesex (tel 081-759 2424).
ROOM STAFF (3). To clean room. Wages up to £133.90 p.w.
HOUSE STAFF (2). To assist room staff. Wages up to £133.90 p.w.
WAITING STAFF (3). To serve in bedrooms, the coffee shop and banqueting room. Wages up to £122.36 p.w.
To work 40 h.p.w. 10% shift allowance for the late shift. Meals supplied while on duty and a uniform is provided. Accommodation available. Period of work by arrangement. Applicants should be aged at least 18, of good appearance, well-spoken and outgoing. Applications to the Personnel Manager at the above address. (O)

SMOLLENSKY'S BALLOON BAR AND RESTAURANT: 1 Dover Street, London W1 (tel 071-491 1199). Also: SMOLLENSKY'S ON THE STRAND:

105 The Strand, London WC2R 0AA (tel 071-497 2101). Both restaurants have similar vacancies, as follows:
BUSBOY/GIRL (5). Approx. £7,000 per annum. Duties: helping waiting staff, cleaning tables and general cleaning.
RECEPTIONISTS (2). Approx. £7,500 per annum. Duties: greeting and seating customers.
KITCHEN PORTERS (3). £6,000-7,000 per annum. General cleaning and dishwashing.
M.p.w. 2 months. Dates unspecified. No accommodation available. Applications to the above addresses.

SWALLOW INTERNATIONAL HOTEL: 147c Cromwell Road, London SW5 0TH (tel 071-370 4200).
CHAMBER STAFF, ROOM SERVICE STAFF, BRASSERIE STAFF. Wages approx. £150 p.w. To work 39 h.p.w. over 5 days. No qualifications needed but some experience preferable. Staff required all year round. M.p.w. 4 months. B. & L. available at £25-35 p.w. Applications from March to Miss Sarah Hough, Personnel Department, Swallow International Hotel. (O)

THE SWAN HOTEL: The Hythe, Staines, Middlesex TW8 3JB (tel 0784-452494/454471).
WAITING STAFF (1). £110 p.w. plus tips. Min. age 16.
BAR STAFF (2). £117 p.w. Couple preferred. Min. age 18.
SNACK BAR ASSISTANT (1) £105 p.w. Some experience or basic training is required.
KITCHEN PORTER((1). £98 p.w. Min. age 16.
COMMIS CHEF (1). £125 p.w. Some experience or basic training is required.
GENERAL ASSISTANTS (2). £117 p.w. Couple preferred. Must be able to do a variety of jobs e.g. bar, restaurant or snack bar work.
To work 5½ days p.w. on split shits. No o/t. Accommodation is available free of charge. Wages quoted above will vary according to age, experience and qualifications. No experience is necessary unless otherwise stated. M.p.w. 6 weeks (commitment of 6 months preferred) from Easter to the end of September. Applications (with photograph) to Mr & Mrs Kothe, at the above address. (O)

THE TOWER THISTLE HOTEL: St. Katherine's Way, London E1 9LD (tel 071-481 3745).
CHAMBER STAFF. £148.20 p.w. Hours: 7.30am-3.30pm over 5 days including weekends.
KITCHEN PORTERS. £134.55 p.w. Hours: 7am-3.15pm or 2.45-11.00pm. Shift work on a 5-day rota.

WAITING STAFF. Approx. £140 p.w. depending on restaurant. Early and late shifts. To work 39 h.p.w. on a 5 day rota.
Uniform and free meals on duty provided, plus staff discounts. Applicants must have some previous experience. Min. age 18. M.p.w. 3 months. No accommodation provided. Applications from late May to Sarah Caselton, Personnel Assistant, at the above address.

VINCENT HOUSE: Pembridge Square, London W2 4EG (tel 071-229 1133). Residential club for business people.
GENERAL ASSISTANTS required to help with housekeeping and restaurant. £62-£75 p.w. dependent on age, plus free B. & L. To work 38 h.p.w. Ages: 18-25 years. Work available all year round. Applications to the Personnel Manager, Vincent House. (O)

WORTHY HOTELS LTD: 152-156 North Gower Street, London NW1 2ND (tel 071-388 0099).
HOUSE ASSISTANTS, RECEPTIONISTS, ASSISTANT FRONT OFFICE MANAGER, KITCHEN PORTERS (2), WAITING STAFF (2). Wages by arrangement. Period of work June to September. Applications to the above address.

Medical

CURI DOMI-CARE AT HOME: 54 Chertsey Street, Guildford, Surrey GU1 4HD (tel 0483-302275).
CARERS (residential and non-residential) to care for elderly and disabled people in their own homes. Positions are either residential (nationwide) or non-residential (local to Surrey). Wages vary according to the position being offered but are typically £150-195 p.w. plus accommodation and travel expenses, as relevant. Period of work by arrangement. Applicants are given an interview and training session. Applications to the above address.

Outdoor

C.F. BARKER AND SONS (MARQUEES) LTD: 47 Osbourne Road, Thornton Heath, Surrey CR7 8DD (tel 081-653 1988). Operates in South East England.
MARQUEE AND TENT ERECTORS (30-40). Approx. £2.95-3.05 per hour. To work Monday-Friday 8am-6pm, Saturday 8am-noon. O/t paid after 5pm on weekdays and afternoon on Saturdays. Finishing time often 8.30pm or later in mid-summer. No accommodation available so must make own arrangements in Croydon area. Min. age 18 years. No previous experience required. General duties in connection with the erection and dismantling of marquees including

loading and unloading vehicles. Expected to work in all weathers. Period of work June to September. Applications, enclosing s.a.e. from March to Mr A. C. Barker, Director, C. F. Barker and Sons (Marquees) Ltd.

BEAR FARM: Binfield, Bracknell, Berkshire RG12 5QE (tel 0734-343286). TRACTOR DRIVERS (1-2) to assist contractor/farmer with haymaking and harvest work. Wages to be arranged. Must have some experience of baling or foreloading. Possible period of work July to September. Applications to Mr John Skidmore, Bear Farm.

HIGHFIELDS KENNELS & CATTERY: Hare Street Village, nr Buntingford, Hertfordshire. Twelve miles from Cambridge.
KENNEL/CATTERY HELP. Wages by arrangement. Hours 8.15am-6pm. General kennel duties/cat and dog housekeeping. Some experience preferred. Self-catering accommodation for female only. Min. age 17 years. Driver preferred. M.p.w. June to September/October. Applications to Mrs Justice, Highfields Kennels & Cattery.

LOLMAX KENNELS LTD: Cooks Hole Road, Enfield, Middlesex (tel 081-363 4921/4667).
KENNEL STAFF. £80 p.w. Hours: 7.30am-5.30pm, 6 days p.w. Would suit veterinary student or keen animal lover. Accommodation provided. Kennels are located in the middle of a recreation park with facilities for riding, swimming, etc. Applications to Mr T. M. Nicholls at the above address.

THRALES END: Harpenden, Hertfordshire (tel 0582-712464).
FARM HANDS (2-3). Wages at the agricultural rate. To work 40 h.p.w. plus o/t. Most farm work connected with harvest, some work with livestock (sheep). Previous experience helpful, driving licence essential. Min. age 18. Staff needed from June until August. During August it is possible to work 30-40 hours o/t p.w.
CASUAL HANDS (2-4). Wages £2.25 per hour. Employed on a daily basis to work on a 'pick your own' unit, picking or working cash tills. Must be able to communicate well with the public. Min. age 17. Staff needed from July until September.
M.p.w. 4 weeks. Accommodation not available. Interview sometimes necessary. Applications from May onwards to J. W. Pigott, at the above address. (O)

Sport

MAGNET LEISURE CENTRE: Holmanleaze, Maidenhead, Berkshire SL6 8AW (tel 0628-33899). Also WINDSOR LEISURE POOL: Clewer Mead, Stovell Road, Windsor (tel 0753-850004).

SEASONAL RECREATION ASSISTANTS (10). Work includes lifeguard and general poolside duties, setting up and dismantling sports equipment, involvement in children's summer holiday activity programme, cleaning and other duties as required. Wages depend on age and qualifications. For those aged 16 or over wages are £2.40-3.00 per hour. Period of work from July to September. The work can involve some shift, evening and weekend work. Applicants should be aged over 16. The following qualifications are desirable: RLSS Bronze Medallion, RLSS Pool Bronze Medallion, First Aid Certificate and coaching qualifications. Applications to the Duty Manager at one of the above addresses.

ROYAL BOROUGH OF KINGSTON-ON-THAMES: Leisure Services, The Guildhall, Kingston, Surrey KT1 1EU (tel 081-399 9684).
SPORTS LEADERS to assist or lead sports courses in the parks, etc. Wages £4-7 per hour. Should be aged 20 or over and have previous experience.
PLAYLEADERS to assist with or lead playchemes. Wages £100-150 p.w.
LEADERS and ASSISTANTS for art courses. Competitive rates of pay. Should be aged 19 or over and have experience. Applications should be sent for the attention of Janet Russell at the above address. (O)

Language Schools

ANGLO-EUROPEAN STUDY TOURS LTD: 8 Celbridge Mews, London W2 6EU (tel 071-229 4435).
TEACHERS OF ENGLISH as a foreign language (200+). £160-200 p.w. Usually 3 week courses of 5 mornings and 2 afternoons p.w. No accommodation available. Min. qualifications a degree plus TEFL certificate. Some teaching experience preferred. Teaching English to small groups of foreign students in the morning and various additional classes on 2 afternoons. Some sport and cultural visits. M.p.w. mid-June to the end of August. Candidates must be fluent English speakers. Applications to the Director of Studies, Anglo-European Study Tours Ltd.

ANGLO WORLD LONDON: 8 Queens's Road, Hendon, London NW4 2TH (tel 081-202 4351).
EFL TEACHERS for general and executive courses, teaching English to adults. Hours: full or part-time (30 or 15 hours per week). Ave. 9.30am-4.30pm, Monday to Friday. No extra-curricular activities required. Min. age 23 years. TEFL qualifications and 2 years experience essential. Teachers required throughout July and August. Applications to the Director of Studies, Anglo World London.

CREST SCHOOLS OF ENGLISH: 29 Hillcrest Avenue, Edgware, Middlesex HA8 8NZ (tel 081-958 8539).
TEFL TEACHERS (6). Wages by arrangement. To work Monday to Friday, mornings and/or afternoons. No accommodation available. Min. age 21 years. Must have TEFL qualification and experience. Period or work April to August or part thereof. Applications to the Crest Schools of English.

EF LANGUAGE TRAVEL: EF House, 1-3 Farman Street, Hove, Sussex BN3 1AL (tel 0273-723651).
COURSE LEADERS. Wage from £105 p.w. Time off by arrangement with foreign leaders. Teaching experience desirable. To organize leisure activities as well as teach. M.p.w. 3/4 weeks in July/August.
ACTIVITIES ORGANIZER. Wages by arrangement. To work 6 days p.w. Should be sports-orientated person with organizational experience to co-ordinate group activities. M.p.w. 8 weeks from end of June. Free B. & L. Min. age 21 years. Applications a.s.a.p. to the Residential Courses Manager, EF Language Travel.

THE ELIZABETH JOHNSON ORGANISATION: Education Department, West House, 19/21 West Street, Haslemere, Surrey GU27 2AE (tel 0428-52751).
ENGLISH TEACHERS/SUPERVISORS. Native speakers of English required for English language holiday courses for young people from abroad during the Easter and summer vacations. M.p.w. 3 or 4 weeks or longer. Involvement in excursion and activity programme as well as tuition, is expected. Some special vacancies for those qualified to coach tennis. Flexibility and enthusiasm essential. Previous TEFL experience desirable. Further information from the Education Department, The Elizabeth Johnson Organisation.

INTERNATIONAL COMMUNTIY SCHOOL: 4 York Terrace East, Regent's Park, London NW1 4PT (tel 071-935 1206/2613).
TEACHERS OF ENGLISH as a foreign language. Wages and hours by arrangement. Accommodation not available. TEFL qualification essential. M.p.w. 3 weeks between 1 June and 1 September. Applications from 1 April to the Summer School Director, International Community School.

INTERNATIONAL COLLEGE: 9 Palace Gate, London, W8 5LS (tel 071-581 9485). Schools in Central London.
TEACHERS of English as a foreign language. Normal working hours: 3 hours per morning and 2-3 hours per afternoon, Mondays to Saturdays. Minimum period of work 3 weeks between mid-June and the end of August. Applicants must be graduates aged at least 21, holding a Royal Society of Arts Preparatory

Certificate, and have had 2 years experience of teaching in summer schools. Applications to the Director of Studies, at the above address.

INTERNATIONAL LANGUAGE ACADEMY LONDON: 4 Russell Gardens, Holland Road, Kensington, London W14 8EY (tel 071-371 1344).
TEFL TEACHERS (14). £200+ p.w. Min. qualifications a degree plus RSA Certificate, B.Ed with TEFL or PGCE. Must have 6 months min. teaching experience. M.p.w. 6 weeks during July and August. Applications from May onwards to the Principal, at the above address.

KING'S SCHOOL OF ENGLISH (LONDON): 25 Beckenham Road, Beckenham, Kent BR3 4PR (tel 081-650 5891).
TRAVEL MANAGER to organize excursions, social evenings, airport transfers, etc. Wages from £240 p.w. Hours approx. 9.30am-6.30pm, 5 days p.w. Should be outgoing, helpful, and should preferably have some knowledge of Italian and/or Spanish. Must know London and its entertainments. B. & L. not available, although help may be given in finding accommodation. Period of work 10 June to the end of August. Applications from Easter to the Principal, King's School of English, at the above address.

PADWORTH COLLEGE: nr Reading, Berkshire RG7 4NR (tel 0734-832644/5).
TUTORS OF ENGLISH as a foreign language. £190 p.w. live in. 25 h.p.w. teaching; also considerable involvement in social/pastoral duties. Min. age 21 years. Must have experience and TEFL training. Social organisers also needed. Free B. & L. in own bed-sitting room. Applications from January to Dr Sheila Villazon, Principal, Padworth College.

PARKLAND LANGUAGE SCHOOL: Leighton Park, Reading RG2 7DF (tel 0734-313214/874853).
EFL TUTORS (8). Min. £180 p.w. To teach European students aged 11-17. Period of work 3 weeks in July. To do 18 hours teaching plus one excursion per week and some help with activities. 1 day off p.w. Applicants should be graduates with TEFL qualifications and/or experience. Min. age 21. Some free accommodation is provided for staff. Applications to the Director at the above address.

REGENT SCHOOL: 19-23 Oxford Street, London W1R 1RF (tel 071-734 7455).
EFL TEACHERS (up to 5). Wages £10.55 per hour. To work either full-time (5 hours per day between 8.45am and 4pm) or part-time (approx. 3 hours per day). Period of work begins in July: teachers are wanted for a minimum of 4 weeks. Applicants must hold at least the RSA TEFL certificate, and have

2 years TEFL experience. Applications to Madeleine du Vivier, Principal, at the above address.

SELS SCHOOL OF ENGLISH: 64 Long Acre, Covent Garden, London WC2E 9JH (tel 071-240 2581).
ASSISTANT to work in the tea room and clean premises. Wages £3.50 per hour. To work 8-10 hours per day, Monday to Friday and alternate weekends. Period of work by arrangement. Ages: 18-48 years. Knowledge of Italian useful.
CLERKS/SECRETARIES. £4-£5 per hour. Approx. 40 h.p.w. Must have typing and word processing experience. Long periods of employment preferred. Applications to Mr Y. Raiss, Sels School of English, at the above address.

TASIS ENGLAND AMERICAN SCHOOL: Coldharbour Lane, Thorpe, Surrey TW20 8TE. Runs summer programme for American and international students.
COUNSELLORS. To supervise sports and activities, such as visits and trips all over England, and act as teaching aides. Wages according to relevant experience. Driving licence necessary. B. & L. provided. Applications, including c.v., by 15 March to Mr David West, Director of Summer Programmes, Tasis England American School, at the above address.

VICTORIA SCHOOL OF ENGLISH: 28 Graham Terrace, Sloane Square, London SW1 (tel 071-730 1333).
ENGLISH TEACHERS for overseas students. From £170 p.w. Part-time only. Hours: 9.45am-2pm Monday to Friday. No accommodation provided. Min. age 22 years. TEFL qualification required and English mother tongue essential. M.p.w. 4 weeks between 1 June and 30 September (with possibility of long-term posts). Applications from 1 May to Mr Robert Baldwin, Principal, Victoria School of English.

WEST COUNTRY

Avon
Cornwall
Devon
Dorset
Gloucestershire
Somerset
Wiltshire

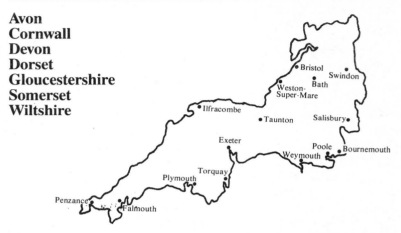

Virtually every region in the South West has a demand for hotel and catering staff, especially along the coasts of Dorset, Devon and Cornwall, which are lined with hotels. Local residents are hard pushed to fill all the seasonal vacancies. However, more and more employers are unable to provide accommodation and it is difficult to find temporary lodgings at a reasonable price. Another drawback, which seems to be on the icrease, is that in some towns, such as Weymouth and Bridport, the work on offer is only part-time and would not be enough to live on if you were new to the area and keen to save money.

The Jobcentre in Penzance recruits for local holiday camps during both Easter and summer, as well as for employers on the Scilly Isles; however, recruitment there is in January for a start in February for their peculiarly long season. The Jobcentre in Bournemouth (185-187 Old Christchurch Road) deals with the West Dorset area and usually has large numbers of hotel and catering vacancies all year round; but few of the positions are live in. Bournemouth Jobcentre also has a varied selection of summer jobs including shop assistants, gardeners and beach workers.

For those wishing to work in a city, Swindon or Bristol could be good places to start looking. Swindon is full of employment agencies and opportunities should be plentiful. Bristol is possibly the only area away from the coast where there is an extensive demand by retailers for more staff over the summer.

Business and Industry

BARNARD AND GOODING: Keward Farm, Pawlett, Bridgewater, Somerset (tel 0278-684664).
ICE CREAM SALES STAFF (5) to sell ice creams from tricycles at agricultural shows and in towns in Somerset. Wages £2.30 per hour plus commission. Accommodation not provided. Min. age 17. To work over the summer, from July to September. Applications to the above address.

Children

ROCKLEY POINT SAILING SCHOOL: Hamworthy, Poole, Dorset BH15 4LZ (tel 0202-677272).
MATRONS (4). £55 p.w. Shift work. Free B. & L. Min. age 20 years. Some experience of looking after children is needed as staff must take responsibility for groups of children attending residential sailing courses, and be able to cook good plain food for them. M.p.w. 6 weeks between March and September. Applicants must be available for interview. Applications from January to Peter or Barbara Gordon, Rockley Point Sailing School. (O)

Holiday Centres and Amusements

ALSTON FARM CARAVAN SITE: Malborough, Kingsbridge, South Devon TQ7 3BJ (tel 0548-561260).
GENERAL ASSISTANT (1). Wages by arrangement according to age and experience. To work 5-6 hours per day, 7 days p.w. Free B. & L. for women only. Duties will be toilet cleaning, collecting tent fees, helping generally on the camp and farm, and cooking a mid-day meal for two people. Needed anytime between mid-May and mid-September. Min. age 18 years. Applications from April to mid-July, to Mr A. Shepherd, Alston Farm Camping and Caravan Site. (O)

ATLANTIC LEISURE PARK: Sandmouth Bay, Bude, Cornwall (tel 0288-2563).
COOK/CHEF (1). Must be aged 23 or over.
BAR STAFF (3). Must be aged 18 or over.
Wages by arrangement. Work available from Spring Bank Holdiay (end of May) to early September. Applications to the Manager at the above address. (O)

BREAN LEISURE PARK: Coast Road, Brean Sands, Somerset TA8 2RF (tel 0278-751595).
BAR STAFF (4). To work evenings 7.30pm-12.30am. Min. age 18 years.

CHEFS/COOKS (2). Hours: 9am-3pm or 6-11pm.
POOL ATTENDANTS (2). Hours: 9am-3pm or 3-9pm. Must have Bronze Medallion lifesaving qualification.
CAR PARK ATTENDANTS (2). 10am-4pm.
GENERAL ASSISTANTS (2). Litter clearing, painting, glass washing, etc.
AMUSEMENT ARCADE ASSISTANTS (2). To work 9am-3pm or 3-10pm.
RECEPTIONISTS (2). To welcome incoming holidaymakers to the caravan and camping park.
WAITING STAFF (4). To work 11am-4pm or 4-11pm.
CHILDREN'S ENTERTAINERS (2). For children aged 4-12.
From £3 per hour. No B. & L. available so vacancies therefore more suitable for local applicants. Period of work mid-July to early September. Interviews held in March and June. Application forms available from March onwards from the Administration Manager, Brean Leisure Park.

COURTLANDS WATER SPORT AND FIELD STUDY CENTRE: Kingsbridge, South Devon TQ7 4BN (tel 0548-550227).
OUTDOOR PURSUITS INSTRUCTORS (6). £40-75 per week. Age under 30 years. Qualifications and experience in canoeing (BCU), sailing (RYE), climbing, caving, orienteering, water-skiing, archery and general outdoor pursuits required.
GENERAL ASSISTANTS (2) for kitchen, bar and domestic duties. £50 per week. Would suit two friends. Age under 30 years. All positions live in. 6 days p.w. Period of work February to November. All applicants must be available for interview. Applications a.s.a.p. to Mr A. Garland, Courtlands Centre.

FRESHWATER CARAVAN PARK: Burton Bradstock, nr Bridport, Dorset DT6 4PT (tel 0308-897317).
BAR, OFFICE, SUPERMARKET, RESTAURANT STAFF and SWIMMING POOL ATTENDANTS. Wages by arrangement. Accommodation available. M.p.w. 6 weeks June to September. Applications from January to the Manager, Freshwater Caravan Park.

HYDE HOUSE LEISURE CENTRE & ACTIVITY HOLIDAYS CENTRE (DORSET): London Office: 6 Kew Green, Richmond, Surrey (tel 081-940 7782). Children's activity centre near Wareham, Dorset.
SPORTS INSTRUCTORS (25) including water-skiing, windsurfing, sailing, canoeing, climbing, orienteering, etc. To work 6 hours per day plus 1 duty evening p.w. Those with special qualifications in any sports given preference, but any young, fit, competent sportsmen/women who have a genuine interest in teaching sport to young people aged 8-18 will be considered. Teaching in

a 1:10 ratio. In-house training courses given, with the emphasis on safety. Period of work for full-time instructors March to October, for part-time July to September.

COOKS (4). To work 7 hours per day in shifts to cover breakfast and evening meal. Preference given to those with qualifications but experience taken into account.

CLEANERS (4). To work 7 hours per day, sometimes in shifts. Should have enthusiasm for work, self-motivation and good standards. £45 p.w. 6 day week. Free B. & L. Min. age 17 years. M.p.w. 2 months between March and October. Applications with s.a.e. to Mr C. McCarthy. Operations Manager at the London office. (O)

LYNCOMBE LODGE: Churchill, nr Bristol, Avon BS19 5PG (tel 0934-852335). Outdoor activity centre with riding school, farm, dry ski slope and hotel.

GROOMS(2). Must be able to ride well. Riding school open 8am-5.30pm.

GENERAL HOTEL STAFF (2). Must be quick, responsible and willing to work odd hours occasionally. Hours: 8am-2pm, and 6.30-10.30pm. Wages approx. £40 p.w. plus free B. & L. 5 days p.w. Flexible hours on a shift basis. Work available during all vacations. M.p.w. 2 months. Applications anytime to John or Sally Lee, Lyncombe Lodge. (O)

ROCKLEY PARK: Napier Road, Hamworthy, Poole, Dorset BH15 4LZ (tel 0202-679393).

BAR STAFF, CATERING STAFF, GENERAL ASSISTANTS, KIOSK & ICECREAM PARLOUR STAFF, GRILL COOKS, FAST FOOD COOKS, WAITING STAFF, SWIMMING POOL ATTENDANTS to work on holiday estate. Wages and hours to be arranged, including some evening and weekend work. Accommodation available. Foreign applicants with fluent English are welcome to apply. M.p.w. from 5 May to 12 September. Applications to J. McConnell, Rockley Park. (O)

SLIMBRIDGE YOUTH HOSTEL: Shepherd's Patch, Slimbridge, Glos GL2 7BP (tel 0453-890275).

SEASONAL ASSISTANT WARDEN (1-2). £69 p.w. plus free B. & L. To work approx. 40 h.p.w. per 5 day week, including split shifts, weekend work and working until 11.30pm, 2 nights p.w. Duties are varied: domestic, gardening, catering, reception work, etc. M.p.w. 7 months betweeen 1 March and 31 October. Min. age 18. No experience necessary but some catering experience is useful. Those interested must be available for interview, including those applying from overseas. Interview expenses payable for travel within England only. Applications from January to Jim Parsons, at the above address. (O)

SOMERWEST WORLD: Minehead, Somerset (tel 0643-704011). ACCOMMODATION STAFF, BAR STAFF, WAITING STAFF, KITCHEN STAFF, SHOP ASSISTANTS, QUALIFIED LIFEGUARDS, NURSES (RGN), NURSERY NURSES (NNEB), CLEANERS, SECURITY STAFF, EXPERIENCED COOKS, SUPERVISORS, CLERICAL STAFF, SUPERVISORS, PORTERS, MAINTENANCE STAFF and many more (around 1,000) to work in a Holiday Centre. Wages £60-70 p.w. plus B. & L. To work a 39-hour week. Applicants should be aged over 18 and of smart appearance. Training will be given. M.p.w. 6 weeks between March and October. Applications from January to the Personnel Mangager at the above address.

TWITCHEN CARAVAN PARK: Twitchen House, Mortehoe, Woolacombe, North Devon EX34 7ES (tel 0271-870476). CATERING STAFF (6), BAR STAFF (8), SWIMMING POOL ATTENDANTS (4), CLEANERS (6), WASHING UP STAFF (4), GENERAL ASSISTANTS (4). Wages approx. £2.80 per hour. To work 39 h.p.w. 6 days p.w. O/t available during busy periods. Limited free B. & L. Catering and bar staff must have previous experience. Pool attendants must have Bronze Life Saving Award. M.p.w. 3 months between May and mid-September. Applications a.s.a.p. to the Personnel Department, Twitchen Caravan Park, at the above address. (O)

WESTERMILL FARM: Exford, nr Minehead, Somerset TA24 7NJ (tel 064 383-238). Camp site, six log cottages and flat on 500-acre farm, by a river in the middle of Exmoor. FARM TOURISM ASSISTANTS (2). Wages specified on application. Long hours, with 1 day off p.w. B. & L. provided with family. Min. age 18 years. Duties include signing people in and out, checking self-catering units, working in shop, cleaning showers and toilets, grass-cutting, log cottage painting and some cooking. Must be conscientious, intelligent and a hard worker with a practical nature. One assistant needed from mid-May, the other from the beginning of July. Both to work until early September or October. Applications and further details with s.a.e. from January to Mrs J. Edwards, Westermill Farm. (O)

WOODSIDE ADVENTURE CENTRE: First Raleigh, Bideford, North Devon (tel 02374-74496).

COOK. To work 7 hours per day in shifts to cover breakfast and evening meal. Preference given to those with qualifications, but experience taken into account.
CLEANER. To work 7 hours per day, sometimes in shifts. Should have enthusiasm for work, self motivation and good standards. Wages £45 p.w. To work 6 days p.w. Free B. & L. Min. age 18 years. M.p.w. 2 months between March and October. Applications with s.a.e. to Mr C. McCarthy, Operations Manager, Woodside Adventure Centre (London Office), 6 Kew Green, Richmond, Surrey (tel 081-940 7782). (O)

Hotels and Catering

THE ANCHOR HOTEL AND SHIP INN: Porlock Weir, Somerset TA24 8PB (tel 0643-862636/862753).
BAR STAFF. £110 p.w. To work 5 days p.w. Split shifts including weekends. Min. age 18. Experience preferred.
KITCHEN ASSISTANTS, SILVER SERVICE WAITER/WAITRESS. £100 p.w. To work 5 days p.w. Split shifts including weekends. Min. age 17.
B. & L. available at approx. £17 p.w. M.p.w. July to September for bar staff, and June to November for kitchen and restaurant staff. Applications from January, in writing, to the Personnel Department, The Anchor Hotel and Ship Inn.

ATLANTIC HOTEL: Sunnyside Road, Woolacombe, North Devon EX34 7DG (tel 0271-870469). Friendly, 2-star family-run hotel overlooking the bay at Woolacombe.
RESTAURANT STAFF, CHAMBER STAFF, KITCHEN STAFF and GENERAL ASSISTANTS (5). Wages by arrangement plus bonus and tips. To work 40 h.p.w. with 1 day off p.w. Min. age 18. Experience preferred but not essential. Must be adaptable and of good appearance. Non-smokers only. Free B. & L. All uniforms provided. M.p.w. 12 weeks between Easter and late September/October. Applications, including details of work experience and current photograph, to Mrs Pugh, Proprietor, Atlantic Hotel.

THE BOURNEMOUTH MOAT HOUSE HOTEL: Knyveton Road, Bournemouth, Dorset BH1 3QQ (tel 0202-293311).
SILVER SERVICE WAITING STAFF. Min. £126 p.w. To work 39 h.p.w. over 5 days, split shifts. Previous silver service experience necessary.
CHAMBER PERSONS. £110 p.w. Previous experience is helpful.
B. & L. subject to availability. M.p.w. 12 weeks at any time of year. Candidates must be of neat appearance, and also available for interview. EC applicants holding relevant work permits considered. Applications a.s.a.p. to Miss Elizabeth Lovely, Personnel Manager, at the above address. (O)

BOVEY HOUSE HOTEL. Beer, Seaton, East Devon EX12 3AD (tel 029 780-241).
GENERAL ASSISTANT for chamber and reception work, and waiting. £3.10 per hour live-in. To work approx. 40 h.p.w. over $5\frac{1}{2}$ days. Period of work from mid-May to mid-September. Only those who can work the full season will be considered. Applicants should be 18 or over. Previous experience not essential but should have a sense of humour. Applications to Mrs J Gosden or Mrs Cole, at the above address. (O)

BUDOCK VEAN HOTEL: Mawnan Smith, Falmouth, Cornwall TR11 5LG (tel 0326-250288).
WAITING STAFF (6). Wages £75 p.w. plus bonus depending on experience. Hours by arrangement but usually 40 p.w., live-in. **Do not** apply if you cannot work for a minimum period of at least 3 months. Experience preferred. Applications with s.a.e. to the Manager, Budock Vean Hotel.

BURCOTT MILL: Burcott, Wells, Somerset BA5 1NJ (tel 0749-73118).
ASSISTANT to clean and make beds in bed and breakfast rooms, and serve in tea rooms. Wages and hours by arrangement; Period of work from 1 July to 30 September approx. Experience an advantage but not essential. Applications to Mrs A. Grimstead at the above address.

CLIFFSIDE HOTEL: East Overcliff Drive, Bournemouth (tel 0202-25724).
WAITING STAFF. Wages negotiable. Hours 7.30-10.30am, and 6-9pm. To work 5 days p.w. No accommodation available. Meals provided on duty. Previous experience preferred although training will be given. References required. M.p.w. June to August and/or August to October. Applications to the Manager, Cliffside Hotel. (O)

DEVON BEACH HOTEL: The Esplanade, Woolacombe, Devon EX34 7DJ (tel 0271-870449).
RESTAURANT, CHAMBER and KITCHEN STAFF, PORTERS (12). From £80 p.w. plus free B. & L. To work 40-48 h.p.w. Some experience preferred but not essential. M.p.w. 12 weeks between May and October. Applications from March to Mrs W. Morrall, Managing Director, Devon Beach House. (O)

DURRANT HOUSE HOTEL: Heywood Road, Northam, Bideford, North Devon EX39 3BQ (tel 0237-472361).
WAITING STAFF (2), KITCHEN ASSISTANTS (2) BAR PERSON. £65 p.w. plus tips. Approx. 45 h.p.w. Free B. & L. Min. age 18 years. Experience necessary. Silver service experience preferred for waiting staff. M.p.w. 2 months

between 1 May and 30 September. Applications from 1 March to Mrs Maria Borg, Proprietor, Durrant House Hotel. (O)

EXETER COURT HOTEL: Kennford, nr Exeter, Devon EX6 7UX (tel 0392-832121).
GENERAL CATERING STAFF (12). £2.50 per hour. Shared accommodation and meals provided free. To work 5 days p.w. Applicants should be at least 18, of smart appearance and good workers who are able to mix easily with people. Write a.s.a.p. to the Personnel Manager at the above address for an application form.

FAIRHAVEN SEA FRONT HOTEL AND RESTAURANT: 40 The Esplanade, Weymouth, Dorset DT4 8DH (tel 0305-760200).
WAITING STAFF (5), CHEFS AND GRILL COOKS (3), KITCHEN ASSISTANTS (2). Wages by arrangement plus tips. To work 6 days p.w. Meals provided and accommodation may be available. All staff must be available from the end of May to September. Some jobs are suitable for foreign students wishing to perfect their English. Applications, with photograph, from March onwards, to the Manager, Fairhaven Hotel. (O)

GARA ROCK HOTEL: East Portlemouth, nr Salcombe, South Devon TQ8 8PH (tel 054884-2342).
RESTAURANT STAFF (5), KITCHEN ASSISTANTS (3), KITCHEN PORTERS (2), CHAMBER STAFF (4), BAR STAFF (2), RECEPTIONISTS (3), GENERAL ASSISTANT. Wage details on application, dependent on age and experience. All positions offer free B. & L. and amenities. To work 6 days p.w. M.p.w. 6 months between April and end of October. Applications from January to the Manager, Gara Rock Hotel. (O)

Gara Rock Hotel East Portlemouth, Nr. Salcombe, South Devon TQ8 8PH Tel: (054 884) 2342

Are you cheerful, bright, polite and hardworking young person, but under 25 years? If so, you are what we are looking for to help run this unique privately-run hotel in South Devon.
The positions we have available for 1992 are:
OFFICE/RECEPTIONISTS: Computer and good public relation skills required.
ENTERTAINMENT ASSISTANT: To run Hotel Mini club and assist Managing Director with other evening entertainments — 20 years or over, experience working with children necessary.
BAR STAFF: Smart and good customer skills required.
2nd CHEF: Good kitchen experience necessary.
KITCHEN ASSISTANTS: Some culinary knowledge required.
RESTAURANT STAFF: Good customer skills required.
GENERAL ASSISTANTS: Good customer skills required.
CHAMBER STAFF and KITCHEN PORTERS.
Weekly wage details on request, includes full board and lodging, use of hotel facilities i.e. Pool Tennis & Games Room. Use of Gym and Sauna for senior positions. Beaches etc. plus contractual bonus. Good training given. A unique hotel in which to gain catering experience.
Apply January onwards for work between Easter and end of October to the Manager, Gara Rock Hotel.

THE GLOBE INN: Frogmore, Kingsbridge, South Devon TQ7 2NR. KITCHEN HELP, WAITING ASSISTANT, BAR STAFF. £2.80 per hour plus tips. Accommodation is available, terms to be negotiated. To work 30-40 h.p.w. — mornings, lunchtime and evening work, with one full day a week off. Period of work July and August. Min. age 18. Applications before 1 March to Mr and Mrs Brian Corby, at the above address. (O)

GORDONS HOTEL: Cliff Street, Cheddar, Somerset BS27 3PT (tel 0934-742497). Family-run hotel. GENERAL ASSISTANTS (2). £45-50 p.w. To work 5½ days p.w. Free B. & L. Min. age 18 years. No experience necessary. Work includes waiting, reception, bar and chamber work. M.p.w. 8 weeks between Easter and October. Applications not later than 1 April to Mrs Barker, Proprietor, Gordons Hotel. (O)

GREAT WESTERN HOTEL: Cliff Road, Newquay, Cornwall YR7 2PT (tel 0637-872010). WAITING STAFF (5), BAR STAFF (4), KITCHEN STAFF (2-3), CHAMBER STAFF (5). Wages as per Catering and Wages Act plus tips. Experience preferred. Free B. & L. provided. Hours by arrangement. Min. age 18 years. Staff required from April to October. Applications with s.a.e. from January to Mr Fitter, Great Western Hotel. (O)

HEADLAND HOTEL: Headland Road, Newquay, Cornwall (tel 0637-872211). SILVER SERVICE WAITING STAFF. £2.75+ per hour plus tips. Must have silver service experience. CHAMBER STAFF. £2.65+ per hour plus tips. To work a 33-hour, 5/6-day week. Previous experience an advantage. BAR STAFF. £3 per hour plus tips. To work a 40-hour, 6-day week. Previous experience an advantage. Period of work from May/June to October/November. Applications to Mr M. Sanders at the address. (O)

HUNTSHAM COURT: Huntsham Valley, nr Tiverton, Devon EX16 7NA (tel 03986-365). WAITERS/WAITRESSES (2-4). CHAMBER STAFF (2-4), CHEFS/COOKS (3), GARDENERS (2), MAINTENANCE STAFF (2). Wages range from £50 to £130 p.w. No qualifications or experience necessary since training is given, but must have team spirit. The work is both varied and interesting. Free B. & L. provided. M.p.w. 12 weeks, staff required all year round. Qualified cooks from abroad are welcome to apply. Applications to Andrea Bolwig, Director, Huntsham Court. (O)

HUXTABLE FARM: West Buckland, Barnstable, N. Devon EX32 0SR (tel 05986-254). Small farm guest house offering gourmet cooking for up to 12 guests, plus children.
GENERAL ASSISTANTS (1/2). £60 p.w. $5\frac{1}{2}$ days p.w. including weekends. To live as one of the family, loft sharing. M.p.w. 6 weeks between March and October. Applications should have waiting experience and be able to cook and serve breakfast and occasional dinners on their own. Must be willing to help on the farm if not busy in the house. Car-drivers preferred (a car can possibly be lent if petrol used is paid for). Applications to Mrs J. Payne a.s.a.p. at the above address. (O)

K'S EATING HOUSE: 2 Station Road, Swanage, Dorset BH19 1AE (tel 0929-422396).
COUNTER ASSISTANTS, GENERAL CAFE WORKERS AND KITCHEN ASSISTANTS.
Excellent wages and good working conditions. Basic 39 hours per 6-day week. O/t available. Accommodation can be arranged, subject to availability. Neat and tidy appearance essential. Work available between May and September. Applications with photograph and s.a.e. to the Manager, K's Eating House.

KNOLL HOUSE HOTEL: Studland, near Swanage, Dorset BH19 3AH (tel 092 944-251 or 379 for Chefs only). A reknowned country house family holiday hotel in National Trust Reserve overlooking Studland Bay.
WAITING STAFF (10) for dining room including wine service. £85 p.w.
HOUSEKEEPING STAFF (10). £85 p.w.
CHEFS (4). £95-120 p.w.
To work 39 h.p.w. 5 days p.w. Free B. & L. available for all staff; excellent staff rooms with all facilities e.g. sitting rooms, colour TV, etc. Min. age 19 years. Good educational background needed. M.p.w. the whole season from March to October. Only applicants able to work for at least 3 months considered. Applicants from EC countries are welcome. Apply a.s.a.p. (enclosing s.a.e. or IRC) to the Staff Controller, Knoll House Hotel, or telephone during the season. (O)

LANGTRY MANOR HOTEL: Derby Road, Bournemouth, Dorset BH1 3QB (tel 0202-553887).
GENERAL ASSISTANT for restaurant and bar.
WAITING STAFF (2) for the restaurant.
£90 p.w. To work 40 h.p.w. per 5 day week, split shifts. Accommodation provided. Period of work from June/July to September/October. Applications

to B. Thompson, General Manager, at the above address. (O)

LIVERMEAD CLIFF HOTEL: Torquay, Devon TQ2 6RQ (tel 0803-299666).
ROOM ATTENDANT. Wages £3 per hour. To work $32\frac{1}{2}$ h.p.w.
WAITING STAFF (2). Wages £100 p.w. To work 39 h.p.w.
Accommodation not provided. To work the full summer season. Applicants
should be aged over 18. Previous experience an advantage. Applications to Mr
J. F. Poat at the above address.

MR & MRS I. S. MACDONALD: The Flat, 1 Barton Road, Woolacombe,
North Devon (tel 0271-870752). Fish and chip takeaway in a popular resort,
3 minutes' walk from the sea.
COUNTER ASSISTANTS (3). £122-140 p.w. on an hourly basis. Serving
takeaway food, some general cleaning when preparing food and shutting shop.
Need little training but lots of sympathy.
ASSISTANT FRYER. Training given. £134-140 p.w. on an hourly basis.
To work 48 hours per 6-day week. Free B. & L. in comfortable flat with
excellent facilities. M.p.w. 6 weeks between May and September. Must have
pleasant appearance and sense of humour. Excellent English essential.
Applications enclosing s.a.e. and photograph from March to Mr & Mrs I. S.
MacDonald at the above address.

NARRACOTT GRAND HOTEL: Beach Road, Woolacombe, Devon EX34 7BS
(tel 0271-870418). Situated near a surfing beach.
WAITING STAFF, PORTERS, KITCHENS STAFF, ROOM STAFF. Wages
specified on application. M.p.w. between March and November. Longer periods
possible. Applications, including details of work experience and photo, to Mr
C. D. Tree, Narracott Grand Hotel.

THE NATIONAL TRUST: Castle Drogo, Drewsteignton, Devon (tel 064
73-2629).
WAITING STAFF, KITCHEN ASSISTANT. Min. £2.95 per hour if aged 21
or over. Hours part-time. Some previous experience an advantage. Period of
work March to October. Applications to the Property Catering Manager, The
National Trust.

'PENKERRIS': Penwinnick Road, St. Agnes, Cornwall TR5 0PA (tel
087255-2262).
GUEST HOUSE ASSISTANT on an au pair basis. Accommodation provided
in exchange for domestic help. Wages according to duties and season. The guest
house is open throughout the winter. The job is suitable for foreign students

wishing to perfect their English. M.p.w. 3 months, longer preferred, although 3 weeks acceptable over Christmas and Easter. Applications a.s.a.p. to Mrs Dorothy Gill-Carey at the above address. (O)

PONSMERE HOTEL: Perranporth, Cornwall (tel 087 257-2225). HOTEL STAFF for all departments. Wages according to experience. Free B. & L. Period of work between Easter and October. Applications with s.a.e from March to Mr W. Batchelor, Ponsmere Hotel. (O)

RADFORDS COUNTRY HOTEL: Lower Dawlish Water, Dawlish, South Devon EX7 0QN (tel 0626-863322). Small country hotel. WAITER/WAITRESS/GENERAL HELP (2). From £100 p.w. plus tips, 1 free day p.w. Free B. & L. M.p.w. 3 months from 1 June to 15 September. Candidates who are not available from the beginning of June cannot be considered. Applications from March to Mr and Mrs T. Crump, Radfords Hotel. (O)

RISING SUN HOTEL: Harbourside, Lynmouth, North Devon EX35 6EQ (tel 0598-53223). A 14th-century thatched inn on the harbourside. WAITING STAFF (4). Should be flexible and have a friendly personality. BAR ASSISTANT. Should be honest. Applicants with some experience preferred. Wages £100 approx. p.w. plus good tips, accommodation and all food provided while on duty. To work 40 h.p.w. on split shifts plus o/t, with $2\frac{1}{2}$ days off per week. There is a very friendly working atmosphere. Applicants should be aged 18 or over. Period of work all year round (except January). Applications to the Manager at the above address. (O)

RIVER YEALM HOTEL: Newton Ferrers, nr Plymouth, South Devon. Popular dinghy, sailing and windsurfing centre. STUDENT STAFF required for all departments in the hotel. Very good wages and conditions. Applications not considered unless able to stay until season ends in October. Applications from Easter onwards to Mr D. G. Wilson, River Yealm Hotel. (O)

RIVIERA HOTEL: Burnaby Road, Alum Chine, Bournemouth, Dorset BH4 8JF (tel 0202-763653). WAITER/WAITRESS (2). £110 p.w. plus tips. To work 36 h.p.w. 6 days p.w. Experience required. Min. age 19. CHAMBER STAFF (2). £95 p.w. To work 36 h.p.w. 6 mornings p.w. Experience preferred. Wages may be increased depending on experience. B. & L. available for approx. £30 p.w. M.p.w. 3 months between March and November.

Applications in February to Mr R. M. Lipscombe, Riviera Hotel. (O)

ROSKARNON HOUSE HOTEL: Rock, Wadebridge, Cornwall PL27 6LD (tel 020 886-2785/2329).
GENERAL ASSISTANT (1/2). Min. £70 p.w. for 45 h.p.w. basic, plus o/t. To work 6 days per week. Any catering or housekeeping knowledge useful. ASSISTANT COOK, KITCHEN PORTER. Wages and hours negotiable. Free B. & L. M.p.w. 6 weeks from 25 May to 12 October. Work also available for 2-4 weeks at Easter. Applications in late March to Mr Veall, Roskarnon House Hotel. (O)

THE ROYAL YORK AND FAULKNER HOTEL: The Esplanade, Sidmouth, South Devon EX10 8AZ (tel 0395-513043/513184).
WAITING STAFF (8). £100.50 p.w. plus tips. To work 42 hours over 5½ days.
BEDROOM CLEANERS, DINING ROOM RELIEF (6). £100.50 p.w. plus tips. To work 42 hours over 5½ days. Some o/t available.
PORTER/BAR STAFF (3). £137.50 p.w. plus tips. To work 45 hours over 5½ days.
KICHEN ASSISTANTS (3). £116.50 p.w. To work 45 hours over 5½ days.
HOUSEKEEPER. £143 p.w. To work 40 hours over 5 days. Some previous hotel experience essential.
Front of house applicants must have white shirt/blouse, black trousers/skirt, black leather shoes and socks or medium tights. All staff should have common sense, a pleasant manner, smart appearance, a sense of humour and be willing, conscientious, adaptable and trustworthy. All rates quoted are live-in, with all meals provided. For live-out rates add £25 p.w.; meals on duty provided. Staff needed at Christmas and in the summer season, from mid-March to the end of October. M.p.w. 4 months. Applications preferably in January/February, with photograph, c.v. and two references, to Mr Peter Hook, Managing Director, The Royal York and Faulkner Hotel.

ROYAL BATH HOTEL: Bath Road, Bournemouth, Dorset (tel 0202-555555).
CHAMBER STAFF (2). £119 p.w. To work 39 hours on straight shifts over 5 days p.w. Min. age 17. Qualifications not necessary.
WAITING STAFF (2). £113 p.w. plus tips. To work 39 h.p.w. over 5 days p.w. on split shifts; some o/t available. Silver Service experience an advantage, but training will be given. Staff receive meals while on duty. Work available around the year. Applications to the Personnel Manager at the above address. (O)

ROYAL BEACON HOTEL: The Beacon, Exmouth, Devon EX8 2AF (tel 0395-264886/265269).

CHAMBER STAFF (2), RECEPTIONISTS (2), BAR STAFF (2), KITCHEN ASSISTANTS (2), PORTER (1). Pay according to the Wages and Catering Act. To work 38 hours per 5-day week. Deductions made for B. & L. M.p.w. 4 months between 1 April and 31 October. Also vacancies at Christmas, lasting 3-4 weeks. Applications to Mr D. J. Larke, Royal Beacon Hotel. (O)

SAUNTON SANDS HOTEL: nr Braunton, North Devon EX33 1LQ (tel 0271-890212).
WAITING STAFF (5). To work split shifts in a $5\frac{1}{2}$-day week. Should have experience of silver service.
BAR STAFF (2) to work split and some straight shifts in a 5-day week. Cocktail experience required.
Wages by arrangement plus tips. Accommodation available. Period of work from late June to September. A high standard of service is expected of applicants. Applications to the Manager at the above address.

SOUTH ALLINGTON HOUSE: Chivelstone, Kingsbridge, South Devon (tel 054 851-272).
GENERAL ASSISTANT for a country bed and breakfast establishment. Duties include general cleaning and helping with cream teas and snacks. £65 p.w. plus accommodation in own room. To work approx. 7 hours per day, 6 days p.w. Period of work from mid-July to end of August. Applicants must be non-smokers, of smart appearance, experienced in this kind of work, and lovers of the countryside. Applications to Mrs B. J. Baker, at the above address.

SUNNYDENE HOTEL: 11 Spencer Road, Knyveton Gardens, Bournemouth, Dorset BH1 3TE (tel 0202-22281).
GENERAL ASSISTANTS (4). £40 p.w. 6 days p.w. Split shifts: 8am-1pm and 4.30-8pm. Free B. & L. Must like children and dogs, and have a very even temper and lots of patience, as well as a lively sense of humour. Assistants must be prepared to help with any aspect of hotel work including cooking, cleaning, waiting on tables, bedroom and bar work. M.p.w 10 weeks between the end of May and early October. Must be prepared to stay until 11 September. Applications from March enclosing a recent photograph and s.a.e., to Mrs M. A. Jackson, Proprietor, Sunnydene Hotel. (O)

TARR STEPS HOTEL: Hawkridge, Dulverton, Somerset (tel 064 385-293).
BEDROOM and WAITING STAFF (3). Wages by arrangement. $1\frac{1}{2}$ days off p.w., all afternoons free. Free B. & L. in staff cottage. Min. age 18 years. Experience not essential, but adaptability important. Staff required for the whole season, March until end of December. Applications with s.a.e. and recent

photograph from January to D. H. Keane, Tarr Steps Hotel. (O)

THE THREE HORSESHOES: Branscombe, nr Seaton, Devon (tel 0297-80251).
KITCHEN ASSISTANT AND WAITING/GENERAL ASSISTANT. £90 p.w.
To work 40 h.p.w. in a family-run country pub near the coast. Accommodation
is provided. Period of work from June to October. Applicants should be of
smart appearance and have a friendly manner. Applications in April to Mr J.
Moore, at the above address. (O)

TORCROSS APARTMENT HOTEL: Torcross, Kingsbridge, South Devon TQ7
2TQ (tel 0548-580206). Hotel in a remote part of Devon, 8 miles from
Dartmouth.
GENERAL ASSISTANTS (4). Approx. £75 p.w. To work 36 h.p.w. over 5
days. Duties include cleaning apartments, bar work, kitchen work, etc. Free
B. & L. available in staff flat in hotel. Applicants should have common sense.
Students preferred. Period of work Easter to September, m.p.w. 1 month.
Interview not necessary. Applications (full letter and photograph) from March
to Sandro or Frankie Signora, Torcross Apartment Hotel, at the above address.
(O)

TORS HOTEL: Lynmouth, North Devon (tel 0598-53236).
SILVER SERVICE WAITER/WAITRESS. £105 p.w. Experience, or the ability
to learn, required.
CHAMBER PERSON, PORTERS, KITCHEN PORTERS. £95 p.w. To work
39 h.p.w. No experience needed.
RECEPTIONIST. £110 p.w. 39-hour week. Trained manual tab; computer
experience an advantage.
All staff work 6 days p.w. Free B. & L. Bonus and holiday pay at end of season
(not before). All staff must work for duration of season from end of March
to end of December. Applications with details of previous experience and
photograph a.s.a.p. to the Manager, The Tors Hotels. (O)

TREGENNA CASTLE HOTEL: Golf Club, St. Ives, Cornwall TR26 2DE
(tel 0736-795254).
SILVER SERVICE WAITER/WAITRESSES (6), BAR STAFF (1), CHEFS (2).
Approx. £105 p.w. live out; live in £90. To work 39 h.p.w. 5 days p.w. in split
shifts. Applicants for waiting positons must have experience of silver service.
Min. age 18. M.p.w. 3 months between April and September. Applications by
April to the General Manager, Tregenna Castle Hotel. (O)

TREGURRIAN HOTEL: Watergate Bay, Newquay, Cornwall TR8 4AB (tel

0637-860280). A 28-bedroom hotel, 100 yards from the sea. WAITING STAFF/CHAMBER STAFF (4). £66 p.w. plus end of season bonus. To work a 39-hour, 6-day week. Serving breakfast and dinner only. Free B. & L. for girls only, in shared accommodation. Experience preferred but not essential as training can be given. M.p.w. mid-May to late September. Applications, enclosing s.a.e. and photograph, from 1 March to Mrs M. C. Molloy, Tregurrian Hotel. (O)

UNICORN CREST HOTEL: Sheep Street, Stow-on-the-Wold, Cheltenham, Gloucesterhsire GL54 1HQ (tel 0451-30257). WAITING STAFF (approx. 3), KITCHEN PORTERS (approx. 2). Wages and hours by arrangement. Split shifts. O/t paid after 39 h.p.w. Possibility of live-in accommodation. Meals provided. M.p.w. June to 30 September. Applications anytime to the General Manager, Unicorn Crest Hotel. (O)

WHITSAND BAY HOTEL, GOLF AND COUNTRY CLUB: Portwrinkle, Torpoint, Cornwall PL11 3BU. HOTEL STAFF (all grades). Live in or out. No experience necessary. M.p.w. mid-March to end of October. Written applications only, with s.a.e. and photograph, a.s.a.p. to the Manager, Whitsand Bay Hotel. (O)

WOODLANDS HOTEL: Cotman Cross, Sidmouth, Devon EX10 8HG (tel 0395-513120). WAITER/WAITRESS (2), KITCHEN PORTER (1). £99 p.w. live in. To work 39 h.p.w. Training may be given. Free B. & L. M.p.w. 14 weeks, between March and November. Applications from March onwards to Mr Robert Bastyan, Woodlands Hotel. (O)

WOOLACOMBE BAY HOTEL: Woolacombe, Devon EX34 7BN (tel 0271-870388). WAITING STAFF (6), ROOM STAFF (6), KITCHEN STAFF (6), BAR STAFF (6), PORTERS (6). To work 44 h.p.w. B. & L. provided. Min. age 18 years. M.p.w. 4 months between Easter and October. Staff are also required over Christmas and New Year (22 December to 2 January approx). Foreign applicants are welcome to apply. Applications from March to the Manager, Woolacombe Bay Hotel. (O)

YEOLDEN COUNTRY HOUSE HOTEL: Durrant Lane, Northam, Bideford, Devon EX39 2RL (tel 0237-474400). WAITING STAFF (2). Wages approx. £109 p.w. GENERAL ASSISTANT (1). Wages approx. £119 p.w.

All staff work 40 h.p.w. No qualifications or experience needed, but applicants should have common sense. B. & L. available at £40 p.w. Period of work 1 July to 30 August. Applications a.s.a.p. to the Manager, at the above address. (O)

Outdoor

DITTISHAM FRUIT FARM: Capton, nr Dartmouth, Devon TQ6 0JE (tel 080 421-452).
FRUIT PICKERS (8). Pce. wk. rates of 15-20p per pound of fruit picked. 6/7 days p.w. Min. 6 hours per day. No accommodation available; tents may be pitched at Little Cotton Caravan Site, near Dartmouth. Bicycle an advantage. Period of work approx. 20 June-21 July. Applicants should telephone Mr Kain in May to reserve a job. (O)

ELWELL FRUIT FARM: Netherbury, Bridport, Dorset DT6 5LF (tel 030 888-283).
FRUIT PICKERS (6). Wages at standard agricultural rates. To pick apples and pears 40 h.p.w. 5 days p.w. No accommodation available. Min. age 18. Staff needed from September to mid October. Applications, either by phone or by letter (enclosing an s.a.e.) from May onwards, to Mr and Mrs P. H. Jackson, Elwell Fruit Farm. (O)

FORDE ABBEY FRUIT GARDENS: Forde Abbey, nr Chard, Somerset TA20 4LU.
HELPERS required in soft fruit and pick-your-own business for picking and administrative work. Wages at standard agricultural rate and/or pce. wk. rates, according to job. Must be hard workers prepared to work early shifts and some Sunday mornings. Job most suited to student applicants. Some accommodation and camping facilities available. Period of work mid-June until the end of July. Early applications recommended. Apply in writing (with s.a.e.) to A. R. Davies, Prossers Cottage, Tatworth, Chard, Somerset TA20 2SG.

KEENE & CLIVE LTD: The Moat, Newent, Gloucestershire GL18 1JX (tel 0531-820363).
APPLE PICKERS (6). Pce. wk. rates. Careful hand-picking. Pickers needed from 30 September. Hours of work are by arrangement according to the quantity and speed of ripening of the fruit, but usually from 7am to 2.30pm. A campsite with showers and toilets is available for those bringing their own tents. Min. commitment 4 days p.w. Applications from May onwards to Mr Michael Keene, at the above address. (O)

NEWTOWN FARM: Newent, Gloucestershire Gl18 1JX (tel 0531-820240).

ASSISTANTS (20+) to plant and cut lettuce, and maintain and harvest runner beans. Wages at Agricultural Wages Board rates or pce. wk. Early start (often 6am). To work 5-6 days p.w., plus o/t where necessary. Accommodation provided on a campsite with shower and toilets, some self-catering accommodation also available at a charge. Period of work May to September; preference given to those who can start in May. All applicants must be over 18 and physically fit. Applications, enclosing s.a.e., to Mr J. Davison at Ploddy House, Newent, Glos. (O)

NYNEHEAD FRUIT FARM: East Nynehead, Wellington, Somerset TA21 0DA (tel 0823-461349).
STRAWBERRY PICKERS (60). Payment at pce. wk. rates.
STRAWBERRY PACKHOUSE WORKERS (10). Wages at Agricultural Wages Board rates.
HARVEST SUPERVISORS (3). Wages by arrangement, depending on experience. The above to work for approx. 6 weeks from early June.
APPLE PICKERS/PACKERS (6). Wages at Agricultural Board rates. Period of work from August to September. Limited accommodation available. Applications to Mrs J. E. Butterley, Partner, at the above address. (O)

PERCIVAL GROWERS LTD: Brangay Farm, Brangay Lane, Rodney Stoke, Cheddar, Somerset BS27 3LU (tel 0749-870530).
PICKERS (10-5) to work on a market garden, harvesting, washing and packing strawberries, salad onions, lettuces, etc. Also some weeding, hoeing and irrigation work. Wages at the current agricultural rate, according to age: a bonus system is operated on the amount harvested per day. To work from 20-50 hours per week. Working hours may be any time between 7am and 9pm, depending upon orders; some weekend work, including Sunday harvesting. Period of work from May to September. Minimum period of work 8 weeks; must be prepared to face strenuous work. Applications enclosing s.a.e. for reply to Mr T. A. Percival Growers Ltd.

YEO BROS. PAULL LTD: North Street, Martock, Somerset TA12 6DJ (tel 0935-824391); also at Southampton (tel 0703-788878). A marquee hire company operating throughout the UK.
MARQUEE ERECTORS (80), £2.44 per hour with o/t and night out allowance paid. Standard 39-hour week, working 8am-5pm over 6 days p.w. Ample o/t available — up to 20 h.p.w. Must be 18+, fit and able to stay away on site. Accommodation is not provided, except on site. M.p.w. 4 weeks between April/May and September/October. Applications from April to Mr A. Drummond, Operations Manager, at the above address. (O)

Sport

ADVENTURE INTERNATIONAL ENTERPRISES LTD: Belle Vue, Bude, Cornwall EX23 8JP (tel 0288-55551).
OUTDOOR ACTIVITY INSTRUCTORS (approx. 20) to instruct in a variety of water and land based activites. Training available. Min. age 18. Free B. & L. is provided. Applications to Mr C. Wilson, Centre Manager, at the above address. (O)

HIGHWORTH RECREATION CENTRE: The Elms, Highworth, Wiltshire SN6 7DD (tel 0793-762602).
LIFEGUARDS (6). £3.38 per hour. To work 30 h.p.w. approx., Monday to Saturday. Should have Pool Lifeguard Bronze Medallion. Required May to September.
HOLIDAY ACTIVITY ASSISTANTS (5). £3.50 per hour. To work 30 h.p.w. Monday to Friday. Experience of teaching children/sports necessary. Required July to August. Accommodation is not available. M.p.w. 5 weeks. Applications to Mr Steve Wood, Manager, Highworth Recreation Centre. (O)

POOLE WINDSURFER CENTRE: 111 Commercial Road, Lower Parkstone, Poole, Dorset (tel 0202-741744).
WINDSURFING INSTRUCTORS (2). £15-20 per day depending on experience, etc. Hours 8.30am-6.30pm. To work 1-5 days p.w. Help given with finding local accommodation. Must have RYA qualification or equivalent for teaching, supervising staff and maintaining school on Poole Park Lake. Perks include use of latest windsurfing and mountain bike equipment, and working in a friendly atmosphere. M.p.w. 1 month during college holidays. Applications with s.a.e., a.s.a.p. to James Ellis, Partner, Poole Windsurfer Centre.

ROCKLEY POINT SAILING SCHOOL: Hamworthy, Poole, Dorset BH15 4LZ (tel 0202-677272).
SAILING INSTRUCTORS (40). £40-50 p.w. To work 6 days p.w. Free B. & L. Min. age 18 years. Should have RYA level 5 min. qualification and thorough knowledge of sailing. M.p.w. 6 weeks between March and September. Applicants should be available for interview. Applications from January to Peter or Barbara Gordon, Rockley Point Sailing School. (O)

SEASCOPE SAILIING SCHOOL: 162 Lake Road, Hamworthy, Poole, Dorset BH15 4LW (tel 0202-672442). RYA-approved Sailing School.
SAILING INSTRUCTORS (2/3). Basic wage approx. £15 per day of attendance: min. 5 days p.w. Must be thoroughly experienced in sailing and seamanship,

dinghies and cruisers, with at least 2 years' practical experience, or hold RYA Instructors Certificate and be over 21 years. Full-time for whole season or m.p.w. 2 months from April to October.
PART TIME SAILING INSTRUCTORS. Pay and qualifications as above. To teach practical sailing and seamanship. No board provided, therefore suitable for persons living or staying locally. Send applications a.s.a.p. to Mr J. Chapman, Principal, Seascope Sailing School. (O)

SKERN LODGE OUTDOOR CENTRE: Appledore, Bideford, Devon EX39 ING (tel 0237-475992).
INSTRUCTORS OF OUTDOOR ACTIVITIES (10). £45-80 p.w. 5 days p.w. including evenings. Full B. & L.provided. Min. age 21. Must have clean driving licence (more than a year old). First Aid qualifications (St. John's Certificate) and Life Saving qualifications (RLSS Bronze Medallion) are necessary. Applicants should also have at least one of the following qualifications: MLC, BSWF, RYA or BCU SI. Staff required from February to November. M.p.w. 8 weeks. An interview is always necessary. Applications to Mr Mike Bennet, Operations Manager, at Skern Lodge Outdoor Centre.

WEST-ANSTEY FARM: Waddicombe, Dulverton, Somerset (tel 039 84-354). RIDING ASSISTANTS (2). Hours vary depending on schedule of activities. Min. age 16 years. Must be fairly light, a good rider and have had experience of conducting treks and caring for ponies, horses and people. Sense of fun, helpfulness and a cheerful disposition essential.
GENERAL ASSISTANT also required to help with accommodation and meals. May also join one ride a day. Must be able to get on with both adults and children. Pocket money plus B. & L. provided. Non-smokers only. Work available all year round. M.p.w. 10 weeks. Applications a.s.a.p. enclosing s.a.e.and a photograph to the Proprietor, West-Anstey Farm. (O)

WOODSIDE ADVENTURE CENTRE: First Raleigh, Bideford, North Devon (tel 023 74-74496).
OUTDOOR PURSUITS INSTRUCTORS (20). Full time and part time. £45 p.w. plus free B. & L. Min. age 18 years. Teaching groups of children various sporting activities such as water-skiing, sailing, surfing and canoeing. Approx. 36 h.p.w. 6 days p.w. Period of work for full-time instructors March to October; for part-time instructors July to September. M.p.w. 1 month. Applications wih s.a.e to Mr C. McCarthy, Operations Manager, Woodside Adventure Centre (London Office), 6 Kew Green, Richmond, Surrey (tel 081-940 7782). (O)

Language Schools

ANGLO-CONTINENTAL EDUCATIONAL GROUP: 33 Winborne Road, Bournemouth BH2 6NA (tel 0202-557414).
TEACHERS OF ENGLISH (100) for adult and junior courses in Bournemouth. To teach 20, 25 or 30 lessons p.w. RSA Cert/Dip. TEFL or equivalent qualifications required, with experience of teaching English as a Foreign Language.
TEACHERS OF ENGLISH AND SPORT (30).
HOUSE STAFF (12) for residential junior centre. To work 6 days p.w. with some evening duties. Experience with children needed.
SPORTS STAFF (12). Hours as above. Cert.Ed/PGCE preferable; experience with children essential.
In 1991, salaries ranged from £140-225 p.w. according to qualifications and experience. No accommodation, except on some residential junior courses. Min. age 23 years. Period of work between 1 June and 30 August. Applications from the beginning of March to Mr F. E. Herring, Director, Anglo-Continental Educational Group.

INTERLINK SCHOOL OF ENGLISH: 126 Richmond Park Road, Bournemouth, Dorset BH8 8TH (tel 0202-290983).
TEACHERS OF ENGLISH (20 +). £136-£177 p.w. according to qualifications and experience. To teach between 25 and 30 lessons p.w. No accommodation. Experience in teaching English as a foreign language required. M.p.w. 3/4 weeks between 15 June and 28 August. Applications from February for Easter session and from 1 May for summer session, to Mr James Milson, Director of Studies, Interlink School of English. (O)

MIDLAND SCHOOL OF ENGLISH STUDIES LTD: 62 Littledown Avenue, Queens Park, Bournemouth, Dorset BH7 7AS (tel 0202-303265).
TEACHERS (up to 16). Wages £150-220 p.w. Hours approx. 9am-4.30pm Monday to Friday, plus one excursion day p.w. (9am-6pm) and one extra-curricular evening. Most weekends off. No B. & L. Free lunches usually available. Final year students from teacher training colleges or PGCE students studying English preferred. Ability to speak French an advantage. Should be keen and able to discipline large groups. Must be capable of team work. M.p.w. 3 weeks between 7 July and 21 August. Applications between January and early June to Miss A. Burton, Director, Midland School of English Studies Ltd.

MILLFIELD SCHOOL 'VILLAGE OF EDUCATION': Street, Somerset BA16 0YD (tel 0458-45823).

TEACHERS (approx. 30) of specialist activities, including sports, creative arts, English for foreign students. Rates of pay depend on qualifications and experience but not less than £94 p.w. Normally 5-hour day but some evening and weekend work expected. To work 6 days p.w. B. & L. available in exchange for evening/weekend duties. Preferably young teachers or final year college students, PE specialists especially welcome. Governing bodies' coaching qualifications (for sport) essential. M.p.w. 1 week between 29 July and 23 August. Applications a.s.a.p. to Mr John Davies, Director of Holiday Courses or Mrs Carolyn Steer, Millfield School. (O)

RICHARD LANGUAGE COLLEGE: 43-45 Wimborne Road, Bournemouth, Dorset BH3 7AB (tel 0202-555932).
TEACHERS of EFL (20). £190-220 p.w. depending on qualifications and experience. Hours 9am-5pm Monday-Friday (six or seven 45-minute lessons per day). Help can be given in finding accommodation. Must have first degree in foreign languages/English literature and RSA Preparatory Certificate in TEFL. To teach at all levels adults of mixed nationality in classes of about 10 students. M.p.w. 2 weeks between 1 June and 30 August. Applicants from America, Canada or Australia will be considered. Applications from 31 March to the Director of Studies, Richard Language College. (O)

SIDMOUTH INTERNATIONAL SCHOOL: May Cottage, Sidmouth, Devon EX10 8EN (tel 0395-516754/512643).
EFL TEACHERS (8). £190 p.w. depending on qualifications. Hours 9am-5pm. Accommodation can be arranged. To teach all levels and mixed nationalities from 14 years upwards. Period of work mid-June to end of August. Applications from 1 March to the Director of Studies.
COURSE LEADERS (6). £140+ p.w. To work 40 h.p.w. with 1½ days off. B. & L. is included. Work involves organizing sport and outdoor activities, and applicants should have experience of working with teenagers and juniors as well as an interest in sport. Min. 6-week contract from 24 June to 29 August. Applications from 1 March to Mrs M. S. Michelmore, at the above address.

SUL HOLIDAYS LTD: Little Penquite, Golant, Fowey, Cornwall PL23 1LA (tel 0726-833761). Holiday language centres in Truro, St. Austell, Bodmin, Redruth, Falmouth, Torpoint, Saltash, Wadebridge, Liskeard, Plymouth, Tavistock, Launceston and Bideford.
EFL TEACHERS. Approx. £250 for 12 weekday mornings, 2½ hours per morning. Own accommodation must be arranged. Applicants must have a degree in English or a modern language, or have TEFL qualification, and be a native English-speaker. Period of work Easter and July/August. Applications to Mr C. M. Retallack, Director, Sul Holidays Ltd. (O).

SOUTH COAST

Channel Islands
Hampshire
Isle of Wight

Kent
East Sussex
West Sussex

As well as work connected with the holiday industry, southern England is a good area for agricultural work. Despite increased mechanization in the hop harvest, it is possible to find work in the hop fields during the month of September. Land work and fruit picking jobs will often be advertized in Local Jobcentres.

Hotel and catering jobs should not be hard to come by along the southern coast. In Hastings, for example, many hotels open just for the holiday season and vacancies are generally for unskilled workers. Early inquiries are advisable in view of the likely difficulties in finding accommodation. Holiday camps in the area, such as the Coombe Haven Holiday Park or Camber Sands Leisure Park, will always be in need of seasonal summer staff.

The South Coast is one of the principal centres for English language schools which often require teachers, youth leaders and supervisors. The majority of schools can be found at coastal resorts: Hastings, Bexhill, Eastbourne, Brighton, Hove and Bognor Regis, and in Tunbridge Wells and Canterbury.

The Dover Harbour Board has a limited number of seasonal opportunities within the Port, involving manual duties on a shift basis between April and September.

Sporting activities such as golf tournaments generate a short-term requirement for staff to help with catering and car parking. The Farnborough Air Show (Hampshire) in September and the Sandown Races (Isle of Wight) may both offer short-term work. In Southampton, exhibiting companies employ canvassers during the weeks running up to the Boat Show at Olympia in London. Vacancies also exist for taxi and van drivers, warehousemen and construction workers.

Business and Industry

ALDERSHOT ICECREAMS: 12 St. Michaels Road, Aldershot, Hampshire GU12 4JC (tel 0252-23041).
ICE CREAM SALES STAFF (3) to drive ice-cream vans. To work on a self-employed basis, earning wages as well as commission on sales. Tax, insurance and vehicle expenses are covered by Aldershot Icecreams. Working hours can be arranged to suit, and work may be available at any time of year. Min. age 19. Applicants should be local, or from the surrounding area, and have a clean driving licence. It is essential that candidates should know the area well. Applications to Mr A. Vella, at the above address.

BILLINGSHURST COACHES LTD: High Street, Billingshurst, Sussex RH14 9QV (tel 0403-783555).
COACH DRIVER. £160 p.w. plus tips, and o/t at £4 per hour available. To work 40 h.p.w between May and July. Min. age 21 and must hold a PSV licence. Applications to Mr G. R. Perrott at the above address. (O)

CHILSTONE GARDEN ORNAMENTS: Sprivers, Horsmonden, Kent TN12 8DR (tel 089 272-3266).
WORKSHOP HELPERS (2) to help with the mixing, etc. Must be strong and energetic.
OFFICE ASSISTANT to help with general office duties. Typing would be an advantage. Wages and hours by arrangement. Applicants must find own accommodation. To work over the summer vacation. Applications to the Manager. (O)

Children

ACTION HOLIDAYS LTD: 'Windrush', Bexton Lane, Knutsford, Cheshire WA16 9BP (tel 0565-654775). Runs a multi-activity holiday centre in Hampshire, for children aged 3-15 years.
STAFF required to look after children in all departments of the holiday camp: instructors, supervisory and general support staff. For details of work see entry in the Nationwide chapter.

SUMMER SPORTS EXPERIENCE: 12A Merton Park Parade, Wimbledon, London SW19 3NT (tel 081-543 4207).

DIRECTORS, ASSISTANT DIRECTORS, SPECIALIST COACHES, NURSES, MONITORS, etc. required to work in children's activity centres in parts of South East England. See London chapter for details.

SUPERCHOICE ADVENTURE LTD: Southdowns, Bracklesham Bay, nr Chichester, West Sussex PO20 8JE (tel 0234-671000).
MANAGERS and MULTI-ACTIVITY INSTRUCTORS (80) to organize and supervise an outdoor activities programme for children and teenagers at holiday camps throughout the UK. Wages from £40 p.w. Free B. & L. provided. To work 6 days p.w. plus some evenings. Min. age 18 years, 20+ preferred. Period of work from April to September; m.p.w. 4 weeks. Experience/qualifications in sports and outdoor pursuits, and working with children, an advantage but not essential as training is available. Activities include rifle-shooting, archery, abseiling, canoeing and trampolining. Applications to the Personnel Department at the above address.

Holiday Centres and Amusements

ATHERFIELD BAY HOLIDAY CAMP: Chale, Ventnor, Isle of Wight PO38 2JD. Medium-sized holiday camp, 8 miles from Ventnor, situated on own foreshore.
WAITING STAFF (8). Basic wage of £72 for approx. 40 h.p.w. Plus tips.
KITCHEN PORTERS (8). Basic wage £76. Hours as above.
BAR STAFF (2). Basic wage £80. Hours as above plus o/t.
SNACK BAR ASSISTANTS (4), STILLROOM ASSISTANTS (2). Basic wage and hours as above.
Free B. & L. Experience not essential but must have friendly personality. Use of camp facilities when off duty. Min. age girls 16, boys 17. Training given. Employment from 5 May to 20 September. M.p.w. 16 weeks. Applications, **enclosing s.a.e.** for quick reply, **from 15 March** to Mrs M. Williamson, Atherfield Bay Holiday Camp. (O)

BRIGHTSTONE HOLIDAY CENTRE: Brightstone, Isle of Wight PO30 4DB (tel 0983- 740537).
WAITING STAFF (12), SERVICE ROOM ASSISTANTS (8), KITCHEN ASSISTANS (4), SNACK BAR ASSISTANTS (4). £2.56 per hour at age 18. To work 39 hours per 6-day week. No experience required as full training given. Min. age 16. B. & L. available at £26 p.w. Staff needed from February to the Manager, at the above address.

CALSHOT ACTIVITIES CENTRE: Calshot, Spit, Fawley, Hampshire SO4 1BR (tel 0703-92077).

WATERSPORTS INSTRUCTORS (10). Wages £140 p.w. To work 9am-6pm, 6 days p.w., plus two evenings. Two weeks paid holiday. Age: 20-30 years. Must have experience and qualifications in dinghy sailing, canoeing, windsurfing, etc. Experience in skiing or climbing an advantage.
VOLUNTARY ASSISTANT INSTRUCTORS (2-4). Hours as above. To help with young persons outdoor activities in return for help towards relevant qualifications, e.g. RYA, BCU, etc. Age: 20-30. Must have relevant outdoor experience in sailing, canoeing, etc.
Period of work 2-4 weeks. Free B. & L. available for all positions. Work available from June to August. M.p.w. 1-2 weeks. Applicants may be asked to attend an interview. Applications to Calshot Activities Centre, at the above address. (O)

NEW FOREST COUNTRY HOLIDAYS: Godshill, Fordingbridge, Hants SP6 2JZ (tel 0425-653042).
BAR STAFF (2) to serve drinks and clear tables. £2.85 per hour. Experience is essential.
CATERING STAFF (2) to cook in a take-away and serve customers. £2.85 per hour.
SHOP ASSISTANTS (2) to stack shelves and serve customers. £2.85 per hour.
CARAVAN CLEANERS (2) to prepare caravans for letting. £3.30 per hour.
All staff work 40 h.p.w. on a rota, including weekends. O/t is available. Period of work June to September. Accommodation can be arranged and training is given to reliable applicants. Applications to Mr John Cotterill at the above address. (O)

NEW FOREST DISTRICT COUNCIL: Leisure Department, Appletree Court, Lyndhurst, Hants SO47 7PA.
KITCHEN ASSISTANTS (4/5) to work in staff restaurant and at functions as necessary. Duties include washing-up, preparing food, etc. Silver Service experience an advantage.
LEISURE ATTENDANTS for 5 recreation centres in the New Forest area. Duties include acting as lifeguards, putting out sports equipment, cleaning changing rooms, etc. Applicants over 18 preferred; training in lifesaving will be given. Wages approx. £3 per hour. To work throughout the summer. Applications to the Leisure Department, at the above address. (O)

PGL YOUNG ADVENTURE LTD: Alton Court, Penyard Lane (874), Ross-on-Wye, Herefordshire HR9 7AH (tel 0989-764211). Over 2,500 staff needed to assist in the running of activity centres in the Isle of Wight, Hertfordshire and Guernsey.

INSTRUCTORS in canoeing, sailing, windsurfing, pony trekking, hill walking, fencing, archery, judo, rifle shooting, fishing, motorsports, arts and crafts, drama, English language and many other activities. Min. age 18 years.
GROUP LEADERS to take responsibility for small groups of children and ensure that they get the most out of their holiday. Min. age 20 years. From £30 p.w. pocket money and full B. & L. provided. Previous experience of working with children necessary. Vacancies available for short or long periods between February and October. Requests for application forms to the Personnel Department, PGL. (O)

SMARTS AMUSEMENT PARK LTD: Seafront, Littlehampton, West Sussex BN17 5LL (tel 0903-721200).
CASHIERS (30). £2.50 per hour. To work 5/6 days p.w. This may include Saturdays and Sundays. Applicants should be aged 18 or over and preferably have experience of handling cash.
RIDE ATTENDANTS. Min. £2 per hour, plus o/t. if working after 6pm. Min. age 16 years.
RIDE OPERATORS. £20+ per day. Min. age 18 years. Some accommodation available. Period of work 30 March to end of September. M.p.w. 1-31 August. Applications to the General Manager at the above address. (O)

SOUTHCOAST WORLD: (Butlins Ltd), Bognor Regis, West Sussex PO21 1JJT (tel 0243-841190).
CATERING STAFF, WAITERS/WAITRESSES, CLEANERS, SHOP AND BAR STAFF, LIFEGUARDS, AMUSEMENT PARK ATTENDANTS, CLERICAL STAFF (around 900) to work in a holiday centre. £110 for a 39-hour, 6-day week. A small deduction is taken for B. & L. Applicants must be over 18 and of smart appearance. Training will be given. Season runs from early February to late October. Work is also available at Christmas and New Year. Applications for January to the Personnel Department at the above address.

SUSSEX BEACH HOLIDAY VILLAGE: Earnley, nr Chichester, West Sussex PO20 7JP (tel 0243-671213).
BAR STAFF (12). To work split shifts. Min. age 18 years. Must be trustworthy with money.
WAITING STAFF (6). To work split shifts. Must have good manners and presentable appearance.
RETAIL FOOD PERSON. To handle cash, with some cleaning work also.
CHEFS and KITCHEN STAFF also required, preferably with experience.
All staff receive £72.15 p.w. (plus tips as for bar and waiting staff). Free B. & L. provided. Must be adaptable and trustworthy. M.p.w. 6 weeks between

Easter and the end of September. Experience an advantage, but full training will be given. Applications to Mr Andy Barnsdale, Operations Manager, Sussex Beach Holiday Village.

Hotels and Catering

THE ALBION HOTEL: Freshwater Bay, Isle of Wight PO40 9RA (tel 0983-753631).
DINING ROOM WAITERS/WAITRESSES (6). To work $5\frac{1}{2}$ days p.w., with split shifts for breakfast, lunch and dinner. Age: 18-25 years. Some experience desirable.
CHEFS (3). Wages vary according to position, age and experience. To work $5\frac{1}{2}$ days p.w., with split shifts for all meals. Age: 18-35 years. Must be college trained and have good hotel experience. Wages by arrangement. B. & L.provided free. Applicants must be available for the whole season, from Easter until the end of October. Applications from February to the Managers, The Albion Hotel. (O)

THE ANCHOR INN: Barcombe, nr Lewes, Sussex BN8 5BS (tel 0273-400414). A small inn situated in a riverside setting providing a high standard of cuisine and pleasant service.
GENERAL ASSISTANTS (2). £45 p.w. plus tips. 1 day off p.w. Free B. & L. Must be 16-20 years of age, a hard worker and with a pleasant manner. Elementary knowledge of cooking an asset. M.p.w. $2\frac{1}{4}$ months from 1 July to mid-September. Applications in May/June to C. D. Bovet-White, The Anchor Inn. (O)

BOTLEIGH GRANGE HOTEL: Hedge End, Southampton SO3 2GA (tel 0489-787700).
WAITING STAFF (2), KITCHEN ASSISTANT (1). Wages by arrangement plus tips. To work 45 h.p.w. over 5 days. Period of work June to September. Accommodation is available. Applicants should be presentable with pleasant personalities. Foreign applicants must be able to speak fluent English. Applications to the Manager at the above address. (O)

CASTLEMAINE HOP FARM: Horsmorden, Tonbridge, Kent TN12 8HG (tel 089 272-2213).
COOK/CATERER. Wages £200+ p.w. To cook at least one hot meal per day, plus other meals, for up to 20 farm helpers. Car owner essential. Must be able to cook economically and get on well with people. Period of work approx.

$3\frac{1}{2}$ weeks between 30 August and 30 September. Applications enclosing s.a.e. in March to the above address. Selection will be made in May.

HOTELS OF THE CINQUE PORTS LTD: Mermaid House, Rye, Sussex (tel 0797- 223065). Eight hotels in Rye, Hastings, Deal, Canterbury, Uckfield and Alfriston.
BAR, FOOD and PORTERAGE STAFF (4). Approx. £80-90 gross p.w. for a 5-day week. Some accommodation available, but preference given to local applicants. Age: 17/18 years. Period of work May to September. Staff should be able to work whole summer period. Applications to Hotels of the Cinque Ports Ltd.

CONGRESS HOTEL: 31-41 Carlisle Road, Eastbourne, Sussex BN21 4JR (tel 0323-32118).
GENERAL ASSISTANTS. Approx. £100 p.w. plus tips. free B. & L. To work $37\frac{1}{2}$ h.p.w. Period of work March to November. No experience or qualifications needed. Applications to the Congress Hotel, at the above address. (O)

COPTHORNE HOTEL: Copthorne, West Sussex RH10 3PG (tel 0342-714971).
HOUSEKEEPING, FOOD and BEVERAGE STAFF required for a variety of operational positions. Wages vary depending on position. All shifts are based on a 40-hour, 5-day week. Accommodation is available. Uniforms, meals and use of a TV room are provided. Applicants should be over 18 years of age and ideally have some hotel or catering experience, although training can be given. A positive attitude, smart appearance and a commitment to work hard are important. Applicants must be available for a period of at least 3-6 months between April and November. Applications to Helen Neave, Personnel and Training Manager, Copthorne Hotel.

DUKE OF NORMANDIE HOTEL: Lefebvre Street, St. Peter Port, Guernsey, Channel Islands (tel 0481-21431).
CHAMBER/WAITING STAFF (7). £125 p.w. Must have some experience.
KITCHEN PORTER. £120 p.w. Must have some experience. Hotel is open throughout the year, some staff also required starting September. Applications anytime to the Manager, Duke of Normandie Hotel.

ELVEY FARM COUNTRY HOTEL: Pluckley, nr Ashford, Kent (tel 023 348-442).
DOMESTIC ASSISTANTS (1 or 2) to work in a farm hotel: duties to include waiting at table, cleaning, ironing, washing-up, some cooking, answering phone, and generally helping with the family. Wages to be arranged. Shifts approx.

8am-4pm or 3-11pm, including weekends. Staff required all year round. Applicants should have a pleasant manner, be hard working and like working with children. Some catering experience an advantage. Applications to Mrs Harris at the above address. (O)

FARRINGFORD HOTEL: Freshwater Bay, Isle of Wight PO40 9PE (tel 0983-752500).
WAITING STAFF (4). £90 p.w. Split shifts, 5 days p.w. Experience preferred.
BAR PERSON. £110 p.w. Split shifts, 5 days p.w. Experience essential.
RECEPTIONIST. £100 p.w. Straight shifts. Experience essential for use of OMRON billing machine.
Free B. & L. Min. age 18 years. M.p.w. 12 weeks July, August and September. Staff required throughout the year. Applications to Mr & Mrs Cerise, Managers, Farringford Hotel. (O)

GEORGE HOTEL: High Street, Rye, East Sussex TN31 7JP (tel 0797-222114). WAITING STAFF (2) for general restaurant duties, but may be required to work elsewhere in the hotel if necessary. Training is given but experience is an advantage. Should have an open, friendly personality and enjoy working with people.
BAR ASSISTANT for general bar work, including bar duties at functions. Basic knowledge of bar work necessary. Friendly personality needed and ability to fit in with the local trade.
Wages £2.25-2.50 per hour, 40 h.p.w. plus o/t. To work 5 days p.w. on a rota basis. Limited accommodation is available in the hotel, or help is given finding a room locally. Uniforms and meals provided. Period of work from May onwards. Min. age 18. Applications to Mr G. M. Scott, at the above address. (O)

GRAND HOTEL: Grand Parade, St. Leonard's-on-Sea, Hastings, East Sussex TN38 0DD (tel 0424-428510).
GENERAL HOTEL WORKERS (2) to clean bedrooms and work in the laundry and kitchen. £2 per hour. Accommodation available for one person only. Period of work July and August. Applications to Mr Peter Mann, at the above address. (O)

THE HAMPTON INN: 72 Western Esplanade, Herne Bay, Kent CT6 8DL (tel 0227-374576).
BAR/KITCHEN STAFF (1/2). £2.75 per hour. Variable working hours including weekends. M.p.w. 4 weeks between July and 7 September. No B. & L. available. Applicants should be aged over 18 and able to cook, serve food, calculate the

cost of rounds, etc. Applications a.s.a.p. to V. Gardiner at the above address.

HOSPITALITY INN: South Parade, Southsea, Portsmouth, Hants PO4 0RN (tel 0705-731281).
SILVER SERVICE STAFF. To wait on customers from table d'hote and à la carte menus, and serve at functions and banquets. Wages vary according to age and experience, plus tips. To work 5 days out of 7; shifts are 6.30am-noon, 10am-2.30pm or 6.30-10.30pm. Accommodation available.
Applications to the Manager at the above address.

HYDRO HOTEL: Mount Road, Eastbourne, East Sussex BN20 7HZ (tel 0323-20643).
ROOM ASSISTANTS (4). £2.65 per hour if living in, £3 per hour if living out. To work $27\frac{1}{2}$ hours over a 5-day week. Accommodation available in shared room.
WAITING STAFF (4). Wages £104 p.w. if living in, £124 p.w. if living out. To work 39 hours over a 5 or 6-day week. Experience preferred but not essential. Full training given. Min. age 16.
Applications to the Personnel Manager, at the above address.

KINGSWAY HOTEL: Marine Parade, Worthing, West Sussex BN11 3QQ (tel 0903-237542).
GENERAL ASSISTANTS. Min. £100 p.w. Min. 39 h.p.w. Free B. & L. Duties include restaurant, bar and stillroom work. Min. age 18 years. M.p.w. 8 weeks between June and mid-September. Foreign applicants with good English are welcome. Applications, enclosing s.a.e., to Mr B. M. Howlett, Proprietor, Kingsway Hotel. (O)

LAKE HOTEL: Shore Road, Lower Bonchurch, Ventnor, Isle of Wight PO38 1RF (tel 0983-852613).
CHAMBER STAFF (2). To work 39 h.p.w. Shifts 7.30am-12.30pm, and 6.30-10pm, 6 days p.w. Some experience required. Should be tidy and a fast worker.
WAITING STAFF (2). 43 h.p.w. To work 6 days p.w., hours as above. Some experience required. Should be polite and a fast worker.
All staff receive £85 p.w. Free B. & L. Should have a sense of humour and be able to work under pressure. M.p.w. $3\frac{1}{2}$ months between Whitsun and end of October. Applications from January to Mr Wyatt, Lake Hotel. (O)

LITTLE HODGEHAM: Bull Lane, Bethesden, Kent (tel 0233-850323).
GENERAL ASSISTANTS (1/2) to work in an upmarket guest house. To wait

on tables, clean rooms, mow grass, clean the pool, etc. £50 p.w. Free B. & L. provided. Bicycle may be borrowed (guest house not near shops). M.p.w. 6 months from Easter to September. Applicants must be honest and clean with good manners and speech. Gardening and/or catering experience an advantage. Applicants from the USA, Canada and Eastern Europe are welcome. Applications a.s.a.p. to Miss Erica Wallace at the above address. (O)

THE LONSDALE COURT HOTEL: 51/61 Norfolk Road, Cliftonville, Margate, Kent CT9 2HX. Tel Margate (0843) 221053.
WAITING STAFF (4), ROOM ATTENDANTS (2) and BAR STAFF (1). Details of wages and hours given on application. Free B. & L. is provided. Applicants must be over 16 and over 18 if applying for the bar job. M.p.w. 3 months between May and October. Applications from 1 March to Bob Smith, Partner, at the above address. (O)

LUCCOMBE HOTELS LTD: Luccombe Hall Hotel, Shanklin, Isle of Wight PO37 6RL (tel 0983-862719).
WAITING STAFF (7). £85 p.w. Split shift, breakfast and dinner, finishing 9pm. approx. Silver service experience needed.
KITCHEN STAFF (6). £95 p.w. Shifts as above.
CLEANING STAFF (4). £85 p.w. Hours 7.45am-1pm. Accommodation available. Period of work March to October. Applications from March to Mr Drewery, Luccombe Hotels Ltd. (O)

OLD PARK HOTEL: St. Lawrence, Ventnor, Isle of Wight (tel 0983-852583). STAFF required for BEDROOMS, DINING ROOM, KITCHEN and CAFE. Wages by arrangement. Approx. 38 h.p.w. Free B. & L. Min. age 19 years. Previous experience preferred. M.p.w. 6 weeks between May and October. Applications in April and May to Mr & Mrs R. Thornton, Old Park Hotel.

THE PORTELET HOTEL: St Brelade, Jersey, Channel Islands (tel 0534-41204). A family hotel on the coast catering for 160 guests.
HALL PORTERS (2), COMMIS BARMAN (1), COMMIS WINE WAITER (1). From £110 p.w. To work 42 h.p.w. 6 days p.w. Min. age 18. Full-board accommodation is available at £25 p.w. Period of work May to October. M.p.w. 3 months. Applicants from the EC with a good knowledge of English may apply. Applications from February onwards to Mr Richard Heron, Manager, at the Portelet Hotel.

POST HOUSE HOTEL: Northney Road, Hayling Island, Hampshire PO11 0NQ (tel 0705-465011).

SILVER SERVICE WAITERS/WAITRESSES (6) to work in the Commodore restaurant. Wages approx. £3 per hour. Min. age 17. Accommodation available. WINE WAITING STAFF (2) to recommend, sell and serve wine. Wages £3.25 per hour. Min. age 18. Accommodation may be available. ROOM ASSISTANTS (6) to service guests' bedrooms. Wages approx. £3 per hour. Min. age 16. No accommodation available. Period of work June-September. Applications to the Personnel Manager, at the above address. (O)

PRIORY HOTEL: Priory Road, Seaview, Isle of Wight (tel 0983-613146). WAITING STAFF (6), KITCHEN PORTER, COMMIS CHEF and CHAMBER STAFF. Wages depend on age and the level of previous experience. B. & L. provided. Min. age 16 years. Period of work from 20 May to October or November. Applications to D. Battle, Manager, at the above address.

RANK MOTORWAY SERVICES LTD: Farthing Corner, M2, Rainham, Kent ME8 8PQ (tel 0634-377812). CATERING ASSISTANTS (10) to prepare and serve food and drink, clear and clean 3 self-service restaurants. Should have knowledge of food hygiene controls. RETAIL ASSISTANTS (3) to sell, price and stock shelves in the shop. Should have experience of handling money. CLEANERS 2-4 to clean all public areas. Wages for all positions £2.25 per hour if under 18, £2.45 for 18-21 year olds, and £2.58 per hour if aged 21+. Accommodation is not available. To work either full-time (5 days p.w.) or part-time (weekends). Shift work on a rota basis. Min. age 16, but 18+ preferred. Period of work June/July to September. Applicants should have a smart appearance and a pleasant personality in order to work effectively with a large number of customers. Applications to the above address. (O)

ROSE & CROWN HOTEL: Lyndhurst Road (A337), Brockenhurst, Hampshire (tel 0590-22225). Small, busy old-world country inn situated in the heart of the New Forest, with three bars and a restaurant. GENERAL STAFF required for waiting, catering, bar and general duties. Min. age 18 years. M.p.w. May to September. Bar staff should be smart and attractive. Applications with s.a.e. to B.T. Parkin, Proprietor, Rose & Crown.

THE ROYAL ESPLANADE HOTEL: Ryde, Isle of Wight, PO33 2ED (tel 0983-62549). WAITING STAFF (6), KITCHEN PORTERS (6), CHAMBER STAFF (6), BAR STAFF (2). From £60-72.50 p.w. plus £10 weekly bonus and tips. To work 39 hours per 6-day week. Max. age 28 years.

TRAINEE BAR MANAGER. From £72.50 p.w. plus £10 weekly bonus. To work 6 days p.w.
Free B. & L. No experience needed. Period of work end of March to beginning of October. Applications enclosing photograph to Mr P. Almeida, General Manager, The Royal Esplanade Hotel.

SHANKLIN HOTEL: Clarendon Road, Shanklin, Isle of Wight (tel 0983-862286).
WAITING ASSISTANT. £92 p.w. plus tips. To work from 8.30-11am and from 6-8.30pm, 6 days p.w.
BEDROOM CLEANERS. £80 p.w. To work from 8.30am-12.30pm. 6 days p.w.
KITCHEN ASSISTANTS. £110 p.w. To work from 8am-noon and from 6-8.30pm. To work 6 days p.w.
BAR STAFF. £3 per hour. To work from 6.30-9pm: days by arrangement.
No accommodation available. Applicants must be mature, responsible, and of clean and tidy appearance. There is also the possibility of employment at the Trouville Hotel, Seafront, Sandown (tel 0983-420141). Applications to Miss J. M. Moorman at the above address.

SPINDLEWOOD COUNTRY HOUSE HOTEL AND RESTAURANT: Wallcrouch, Wadhurst, East Sussex TN5 7JG (tel 0580-200430).
WAITING/GENERAL ASSISTANTS (1/2) required for waiting duties in the restaurant and some light housework in the country house hotel. £130 p.w. (plus tips) for 5 days work p.w., usually in split shifts including weekends. M.p.w. 2 months between June and September. Accommodation is available in single rooms. Applicants should be neat and tidy, of cheerful disposition and must enjoy working with the public and living in the country. Applications with photograph attached to Mr R. V. Fitzsimmons, at the above address. (O)

STOCKS HOTEL: Sark, via Guernsey, Channel Islands (tel 0481 83-2001).
SILVER SERVICE WAITRESS for general waiting duties in two restaurants, including cleaning. Must be capable of Silver Service work.
KITCHEN PORTER for general kitchen cleaning duties, including some vegetable preparation in two kitchens with prize-winning chef. Must be able to work cleanly, efficiently and quickly.
To work on the isolated and unspoilt island of Sark. Wages £95 p.w. tax fre with no deductions. B. & L. provided. Maximum 60 h.p.w., 6 days p.w. Period of work from April to October. Applicants should preferably be aged 20-35 approx. and able to adapt to the unique working environment. For further details contact Paul Armogie, Stocks Hotel. (O)

WARNER CLUB HOTEL: Bembridge, Isle of Wight (tel 0983-873931).
WAITING STAFF. Wages, hours and dates of work to be arranged. To work
39 h.p.w. over 6 days p.w. Accommodation provided. Min. age 18. Applications
to Jenny Juby, Warner Club Hotel.

Outdoor

ADRIAN SCRIPPS LTD: Moat Farm, Five Oak Green, Paddock Wood,
Tonbridge, Kent TN12 6RR (tel 089 283-2406).
HOP PICKERS. Approx. £140 p.w. Work involves mechanical picking of hops
for a period of 4-5 weeks from 1 September.
PIECEWORK FRUIT PICKERS to pick apples and pears growing on small
trees for 4-5 weeks from early September. Self-catering accommodation and
camping facilities provided. Min. age 18. For more details write to Adrian
Scripps Ltd, at the above address. (O)

APPLE PIE FARM LTD: Cranbrook Road, Cranbrook, Kent TN17 4EU (tel
081-948 8132).
APPLE PICKERS (30). Wages in line with the current rate for casual work.
During the height of the season (September to October) applicants may work
as many hours as required by the employer or crop. Free, simple accommodation
is provided. No qualifications necessary. Staff required from August to October.
Applications to Mr J. Pollitzer at the above address. (O)

ASHMERE FARM: Meopham, Gravesend, Kent (tel 0474-814397 or
0227-87468).
FARM WORKERS to help with hay and grain harvest. Wages at agricultural
rate. Possibility of tent or caravan on site. Some farming experience preferred,
along with knowledge of English and experience of tractor driving. Agricultural
students with some practical experience of general farm work welcome. Driving
licence essential; car owner preferred. Period of work 1 July to 30 October.
Applications to Mr J. R. French, Ashmere Farm. (O)

BEECHIN WOOD FARM: St. Mary's Platt, Borough Green, nr Sevenoaks,
Kent TN15 8QN (tel 0732-882037). Located 1 mile from shops.
FRUIT PICKERS (30). Locally fixed piece rates for strawberry, raspberry,
blackcurrant, redcurrant and plum picking. Hours usually 8am-4pm and may
include weekends. No B. & L. provided, but space for caravans and tents. Min.
age 16 years. No experience needed. Period of work June to September.
Applications enclosing s.a.e. from May to W. Chaplin Ltd. at the above
address. (O)

S. C. AND J. H. BERRY LTD: Gushmere Court Farm, Selling, Faversham, Kent (tel 0227-752205/752838).
HOP PICKERS/DRIVERS/OAST CREW (20). Wages at standard Agricultural Wages Board Rates. There may also be employment for an additional 4 workers to be paid pce. wk. rates. To work a standard 39 hours p.w. plus at least 16 hours o/t. Longest hours are expected of the oast crew. Work cannot be guaranteed during wet weather. B. & L. available for approx. £10 p.w. in caravan accommodation (self-catering): blankets, pillows and separate kitchen, lounge and shower facilities are provided, but applicants should bring their own sleeping bags, towels, etc. as well as wellington boots and waterproof clothing. Workers are needed for the entire period between 24 August and 20 September. Applicants should be students over 18 years old: possession of a driving lience would be an advantage. Overseas applicants with EC passports considered. Applications should be sent from 1 May (with IRC if needed) to Mr J. P. S. Berry at the above address.

ROBERT BOUCHER & SON: Newlands Farm, Teynham, Sittingbourne, Kent ME9 9JQ (tel 0795 521-347).
PICKERS (20) to pick high-quality strawberries, cherries and gooseberries to be sold to supermarkets. Pce. wk. rates. To work 6 hours per day. Min. age 16. Campsite with facilities provided free of charge (no dogs or camper vans allowed). Work available June to September. Applications from March onwards to Mr R. C. Boucher at the above address.

BRAMSHOT HOUSE: Fleet, Hampshire GU13 8RT (tel 0252-617304). About 45 minutes by train from London.
GARDENERS/PAINTERS/CARPENTERS (1-2). £20 p.w. Flexible working arrangement, averaging 3-5 hours per day, 15-25 p.w. Plenty of free time for sightseeing. Self-contained fully furnished flat provided, also produce from the garden when available, and use of bicycle, tennis court and swimming pool. Skills in painting, gardening or carpentry essential. Applications to Mrs P. A. Duckworth, at the above address. (O)

CASTLEMAINE HOP FARM: Horsmonden, Tonbridge, Kent TN12 8HG (tel 089 272-2213).
HOP PICKERS (17). Good hourly rate plus bonus. To work 53-60 h.p.w. Monday to Saturday. Hostel B. & L. at approx. £15-20 p.w. Work includes tractor driving, bine cutting and loading, bine separation, sorting etc. Ability to drive an advantage. Approx. $3\frac{1}{2}$ weeks in September.
LORRY DRIVER for hop harvest. High wages. 60 h.p.w. Monday to Saturday. B. & L. as above. Current driving licence essential. Must be physically strong.

HOP DRYERS' MATES (2). Good wages and long hours. Accommodation suitable for males only in bunkhouse in oast. Work involves loading and unloading hops into kiln, and operating mechanical press. Must be physically fit and have stamina. Period of work as above.
SUPERVISOR to assist with the harvest of 50 acres of top fruit. Must be responsible and hard working. Hours include o/t and weekends as required. Car owner preferred. Period of work July to October. Telephone 0892-723905 for further information.
FARM ASSISTANTS also needed for 3-4 weeks during late April/May for work mainly with hops. Normal hourly rate. Hostel accommodation with own catering is available.
Applications for all positions, **enclosing an s.a.e.**, to Castlemaine Farms Ltd, should be sent **after** 1 March. EC applicants welcome. Selection is made in May.

CERTFORD LIMITED: Brompton Farm, Brompton Farm Road, Strood, Rochester, Kent ME2 3QZ (tel 0634-717390).
FRUIT & VEGETABLE PICKERS & PACKERS. Wage at pce. wk. rates. Up to 60 h.p.w. Min. age strictly 18 years. Site for tents available, with showers and toilets. Bring own cooking equipment, waterproofs and wellies. Period of work 1 June to 30 September. Students from EC member countries only, are welcome. Applications from 1-30 April (those received prior to this date will not be answered until April) to the Farm Secretary, Certford Limited.

ELPHICKS FARM: Hunton, Maidstone, Kent (tel 06272-758).
HOP HARVESTERS, APPLE PICKERS (6). Wages at agricultural rate. To work 8-9 hours per day. Accommodation in caravan. Driving licence an advantage but not essential. Min. age 19 years. Period of work end of August to end of September. Applications enclosing s.a.e. no earlier than 1 April and no later than 31 May to Mr R. L. Day, Elphicks Farm.

GADDENS CLOSE FARM: Ringwood, Hampshire (tel 042 54-6832).
ESTATE WORKERS in New Forest area. Short working holidays in summer or winter. Free B. & L. Students only. UK driving licence essential. Applications to the Proprietor, Gaddens Close Farm.

GREAT HOLLANDEN FARM: Mill Lane, Hildenborough, nr Sevenoaks, Kent TN15 0SG (tel 0732-832276).
PICKERS (40), PACKERS (10). Pce. wk. rates. To work from 6am-1pm. Camp site provided, but workers must bring their own tents and cooking equipment.
GAUGERS (5), QUALITY CONTROLLERS (2). £3 per hour. Hours as above, plus some evening work available for gaugers. Accommodation available.

Staff needed from 20 May to mid-September. M.p.w. 2 weeks. Min. age 18. Applicants must be available for interview. Applications to the above address.

HIGH BEECHES GARDENS CONSERVATION TRUST: The High Beeches, Handcross, West Sussex RH17 6HQ (tel 0444-400589).
ASSISTANT GARDENER to mow grass and generally help in a large heritage garden near Haywards Heath and Crawley that is open to the public. Wages at Agricultural Wages Board rate. Hours 8am-5pm, 5 days p.w. Part-time arrangement considered. No accommodation or public transport available. Period of work 1-3 months over the summer. Applicants should be careful and conscientious and good with garden machinery. Applications to Mrs Anne Boscawen, at the above address. (O)

HILL FARM ORCHARDS: Droxford Road, Swanmore, Hampshire SO3 2PY (tel 0489-878616).
APPLE PICKERS (up to 500), SOFT FRUIT PICKERS (up tp 30), GENERAL FARM HELP (up to 10). Pay as set by Agricultural Wages Board and pce. wk. rates at the height of the seasons. To work from 8.30am-3.30pm Monday-Friday. Campsite available. Staff needed from June to November. M.p.w. 1 week. Applications a.s.a.p. to Mr Paul Roberts, Farm Manager, at the above address. (O)

KETTLETHORNS: Adlam's Lane, Sway, Hampshire SO41 6EG (tel 0590-682567).
FARM ASSISTANTS for New Forest family farm. Outdoor farm duties including experience in haymaking, building, animal and land management, repairs or help in the house including housework, painting and gardening in exchange for holiday activities: swimming, riding, country shows, simulated clay pigeon shooting, beach, etc. There is also one place for a light, experienced horse person to help break and school young horses and then carry on in exchange for holiday activities. Winter hunting can be arranged with sufficient notice, when work schedule permits. Free B. & L. Period of work 3/4 weeks or longer. Agricultural students welcome for several months up to 1 year, pre-college, etc. References given for all students. Students taken all year round, summer and winter. Applications to Mrs C. M. Nicholson-Pike, Kettlethorns.

H. B. LOWE: Baron Place, Mereworth, Maidstone, Kent ME18 5NF (tel 0622-812229). Farm set in a rural location, growing quality strawberries, raspberries and redcurrants for local markets and supermarkets.
SOFT FRUIT PICKERS (50), FRUIT PACKERS (5-10). Pce. wk. rates. Approx. 6 hours per day. Min. age 16. Campsite and bunkhouse with new

facilities provided. Pleasant working conditions. Work available from early June to September. Applications to H. B. Lowe at the above address. (O)

MARE HILL FRUIT FARM: West Mare Lane, Mare Hill, Pulborough, West Sussex RH20 2EA (tel 079 882-432).
STRAWBERRY PICKERS. From early June to mid-July.
GOOSEBERRY PICKERS. June.
RASPBERRY PICKERS. Late June to mid-July.
BLACKCURRANT PICKERS. Late July.
All payment by quantity of fruit picked in a saleable condition. Emphasis on working holidays (i.e. short working day), 5 hours per day approx. Free camping site; pickers must have own tents, stoves and cooking equipment. Elsan toilets provided, and cold showers. Communal hut with sink and mains water, television, radio, etc. available out of fruit picking hours or wet days. Ages: 18-24 years. EC students welcome. No full-time employment available (camp closes mid-August). Early season arrivals particularly welcome. Bookings with s.a.e. from 1 March only. Enquiries with s.a.e. (otherwise cannot guarantee reply) anytime to Mare Hill Fruit Farm. (O)

MENGEHAM HOUSE: Hayling Island, Hampshire PO11 9JX (tel 0705-463833).
ESTATE MAINTENANCE STAFF (2). Max. £10 p.w. 6 hours per day. Weekends off. Free B. & L. Work includes re-building, painting and repair work, log splitting, hedge cutting, lawn mowing and odd jobs. Must be strong. Tennis court, canoes and windsurfer available and yachting in 33 ft. ketch. Period of work mid-June to mid-September. Foreign applicants wishing to improve their English especially welcome. Applications to Mr and Mrs R. W. Selby, Mengeham House. (O)

MURDOCH & ALLFREY LTD: Clock House Farm, Coxeath, Maidstone, Kent ME17 4PG (tel 0622-734173).
SOFT FRUIT PICKERS/PACKERS (25). £20-30 per day: pce. wk. rates for picking; packing takes place in late afternoon at an hourly rate of £2.70. No qualifications required. Must bring own tent but showers, etc. provided. M.p.w. 2 weeks between 1 June and 31 September. Applications from 1 January to Mr R. K. Pascall, Director, at the above address. (O)

PARIS FARM: Rocks Road, East Malling, Kent ME19 6AX (tel 0732-842042). FRUIT AND VEGETABLE PICKERS (15). Hours: 8am-3pm. No B. & L. available. Min. age 18 years. Period of work 1 July to end of September. Applications from the last week in June to W. Chaplin, Paris Farm. (O)

POLDHURST & CHINA FARMS: Upper Harbledown, Canterbury, Kent CT2 9AR (tel 0227-464911).
HOP PICKING MACHINE OPERATORS. Accommodation available with cooking facilities and hot water showers. Work includes cutting and transporting hop bines, tractor driving and operation of picking machines. Period of work late August through September. Applications after 1 May to the Farm Manager, T. G. Redsell Ltd, at the above address. (O)

SPELMONDEN ESTATE CO LTD: Spelmonden Farm, Goudhurst, Kent TN17 1HE (tel 0580-211400).
HOP, APPLE and PEAR PICKERS. Hop harvesting approx. £150 per $50\frac{1}{2}$-hour week, involving mechanical picking of hops. Apple and pear picking is mainly pce. wk. rates per bin, for a limited number of persons. Self-catering accommodation free. Min. age 18 years. Period of work 5 weeks from approx. 1 September. Applications enclosing s.a.e. to The Director, Spelmonden Estate Co. Ltd.

SWIGS HOLE FARM: Horsmonden, nr Tonbridge, Kent TN12 8DE (tel 089272-2651).
FRUIT PICKERS (15). Wages at standard agricultural rate plus o/t and bonus. To work approx. 8 hours per day, 5 days per week. Free bunkhouse accommodation with showers and cooking facilities. Previous experience of fruit picking not necessary. M.p.w. 3 weeks between early August and mid-October. Applications showing your address and telephone number clearly, from 1 June to R. O. March and Partners, Swigs Hole Farm. (O)

WAKELEY BROTHERS (RAINHAM, KENT) LTD: Otterham Buildings, Rainham, Gillingham, Kent ME8 7XB (tel 0634-32121).

HOP PICKERS for the harvest, to drive tractors and work in the hop garden and machine shed. Basic wage £2.69 per hour, £4.03 per hour at o/t rates. To work from 7.30am-6pm, 5 days p.w., including 1 hour lunch break and 1 hour o/t, plus 4 hours on Saturdays from 8am-noon at o/t rates. Period of work approx. 1-30 September. Applicants should have a full driving licence and be hard working.
FRUIT PICKERS. Pce. wk. rates. To work from 8am-5pm, 5-7 days p.w. as necessary. Period of work September-October. Accommodation with hot showers, etc., and a canteen serving hot meals available. Applications to Mrs J. Newell, Wakeley Brothers.

WOODEND: West Stoke, Chichester, Sussex PO18 9BP (tel 0243-575268). Country manor house in quiet rural setting.
GENERAL ASSISTANT for household duties, cooking, gardening and helping with hay harvest in season. £20-30 p.w. according to ability. Free B. & L. Should like animals. Experience unnecessary if adaptable and willing to work. Applications to Miss E. M. Broad, Woodend. (O)

Sport

BOSHAM SAILING: Bosham Lane, Bosham, West Sussex PO18 8HN (tel 0243-572555).
SAILING INSTRUCTORS (12). Approx. £105 p.w. for 5 day week. Approx. £47 for extra 2 days. B. & L. available at £16 p.w. Min. age 17 years. RYA Instructors Certificate required. M.p.w. 1 weekend between May and September. Applications a.s.a.p. to Mrs P. Hillsdon, Principal, Bosham Sailing.

HAMBLE DINGHY SAILING SCHOOL: Mercury Marina, Satchwell Lane, Hamble, Southampton SO3 5HQ (tel 0703-73003).
SAILING INSTRUCTORS (20). £60-150 p.w. depending on age and experience. Must have RYA instructor's certificate. To work 9am-5pm. 5-7 days p.w. depending on length of stay.
CAMP MANAGER (1-2). £100-150 p.w. depending on age and experience. To work 24 hours with time off during the day, 5 days p.w. Post suitable for a teacher or PE instructor. Min. age 25.
CAMP CATERER (1-2). £100 p.w. Catering experience necessary. To work 5 days p.w.
B. & L. available free or at a modest charge, depending on duties. Staff needed from June to September. M.p.w. 1 week, but preference given to those able to work 4 weeks or longer. Applicants must be available for interview. Foreign applicants must speak fluent English. Applications from January to J. C. Whitelock, at the above address. (O)

MID SUSSEX DISTRICT COUNCIL; 'Oaklands', Oaklands Road, Haywards Heath, West Sussex RH16 1SS (tel 0444-458166 ext 2276).
RECREATION ASSISTANTS. To work in the leisure centres at Haywards Heath, Burgess Hill or East Grinstead in any of the vacation periods. Wage rates given on application. Applicants must have a keen interest in a variety of sports and hold the RLSS Pool Bronze Medallion Life Saving qualification. Applicants must already live within easy travelling distance of the Leisure Centres and must be available to work weekdays, evenings and weekends on a shift basis. Applications a.s.a.p. to the Personnel Officer including dates when available for work.

WALNUTS LEISURE CENTRE: Lynchgate Road, Orpington, Kent BR6 0TJ (tel 0689 70533).
SPORTS CENTRE ASSISTANTS (4). Approx. £4 per hour. To work 36 h.p.w. with some weekend work. Min. age 18. Must have RLS bronze medal. Any other coaching qualifications and First Aid certificates an advantage. Work includes general lifeguard duties, erecting and dismantling sports equipment, cleaning and preparation of sports and changing areas and patrolling building. M.p.w. 4-6 weeks, between third week in July and mid-September. No accommodation is available. US and Canadian applicants are welcome. Applications, as early as possible, to Miss Jane Allen, Assistant Manager, Walnuts Leisure Centre.

YMCA NATIONAL CENTRE: Fairthorne Manor, Curdridge, Southampton, Hampshire SO3 2GH (tel 0489-785228).
ACTIVITY INSTRUCTORS. Wages on application. B. & L. provided. To work 5 days p.w. includng evenings. Required to teach canoeing, climbing, archery and sailing. Recognised qualifications preferred i.e BCUTI/Prof, GNAS, MLC(S) or RYA Sea II, or international equivalents. However, a comprehensive training programme suitable for all activites is arranged at Easter, and lasts one week. Applications to the Personnel Manager, by February 1992, to the above address. (O)

Language Schools

CICERO LANGUAGES INTERNATIONAL: 42 Upper Grosvenor Road, Tunbridge Wells, Kent TN1 2ET (tel 0892-547077).
TEACHERS to teach English as a foreign language to students of many nationalities (average age 25). £7 per hour. 2-5 hours per day, 5 days p.w. Opportunities for taking students to films, concerts, theatre, etc. Period of work June to September. Applicants must have EFL qualifications. Experience also

important. Punctuality and a professional attitude are essential. Applications to the Director of Studies, Cicero Languages International.

EAST DENE CENTRE: Bonchurch Village Road, Ventnor, Isle of Wight (tel 0983-857374). An Allnatt Centre for schools and youth groups.
EFL TEACHERS to provide lessons in conversational English during the mornings and to assist leaders with running pre-set afternoon leisure activities. £90 p.w. plus full B. & L. Flexible hours. Needed Easter, July and August. Kitchen and catering assistants sometimes also required. Send a full c.v. with s.a.e. to the East Dene Centre, at the above address.

EAST SUSSEX SCHOOL OF ENGLISH: 19 Reynolds Road, Hove, Sussex BN3 5RJ (tel 0273-777784).
EFL TEACHERS (3). Wages for 1991 were £133 p.w. for 14 h.p.w., or £226 p.w. for 28 h.p.w. Period of work July and August. M.p.w. 1 month, i.e. either July or August. Self-catering accommodation is available if required. Applicants must have PGCE in TEFL or TESOL, or RSA Certificate/Diploma in TEFL; experience is also required. Applicants with PGCE in modern languages or English plus at least one year's experience in TEFL abroad are also acceptable. Applications to Elaine Evans at the above address.

EMBASSY STUDY TOURS LTD: 44 Cromwell Road, Hove, East Sussex BN3 3ER (tel 0273-707481). Runs a variety of centres throughout England, principally in the South.
EFL TEACHERS (100+) for junior and adult vacation courses from mid-June to end of August. Should have qualifications and experience, preferably with summer school experience. Salary from £120 p.w. including full B. & L. in return for residential support and help with activities and excursions.
ACTIVITY HELPERS/ORGANIZERS (50+). Wages from £75 p.w. including free B. & L. on campus. To supervise and implement social and sports programme, and accompany students on excursions, etc. Must be hard-working, motivated and self-disciplined. Should also have experience or knowledge of various sports.
Period of work mid-June and mid-August. Applications to the Recruitment Officer at the above address.

THE ENGLISH LANGUAGE CENTRE: Friars Gate Farm, Marden Hill, Crowborough, Sussex TN6 1XH (tel 0892-661195). A British Council-recognised school.
ENGLISH TUTORS(3). £93 p.w. plus free B. & L. Time off by arrangement. To teach English from set syllabus to small groups of overseas students aged

12-19 years. Lessons for 3 hours, 5 mornings p.w. plus supervision of excursions, sports and social activities. Must have genuine interest in country life and young people. Applicants must be well-dressed, with a sense of responsiblity and authority. Non-smokers only. Age: 20-50 years. M.p.w. 3-4 weeks from 21 March to 8 April, and 18 June to 1 September.
COURSE MANAGER (1). £93 p.w. plus free B. & L. and 1 day off per week. To organize student activities and excursions, transport and community work, with several office responsibilities. Other conditions as above. M.p.w. 17 June to 25 August.
Applications in writing to Mr D. R. C. Forsyth, Manager, The English Language Centre.

GEOS. ENGLISH ACADEMY: 55-61 Portland Road, Hove, Sussex BN3 5DQ (tel 0723-735975).
TEACHING STAFF (25) to teach multi-national groups of up to 12 in a fully equipped school with extensive materials. Wages up to £10.20 per teaching hour: to work 15-25 hours per week. Help given in finding accommodation. Period of work 2 July-24 August. Min. qualification necessary is a RSA certificate in TEFL or equivalent. Applications to Julie Stewart at the above address.

HASTINGS ENGLISH LANGUAGE CENTRE (HELC): St. Helens Park Road, Hastings, East Sussex TN34 2JW (tel 0424-437048/441549).
EFL TEACHERS (7) £240 p.w. for 30 hours, £200 for 25 hours or £120 or 15 hours per week. Applicants must have RSA Preparatory Certificate and TEFL experience. Period of work 15 June to late August. Applications to Hastings English Language Centre.

INTERNATIONAL HOSPITALITY LTD: 177 Middlebridge Street, Romsey, Hampshire SO51 8HH (tel 0794-512470/514558).
ENGLISH TEACHERS (up to 25). Approx. £75-150 p.w. To work 12-21 h.p.w. Min. age 22 years. TEFL qualification preferred. No B. & L. provided. Periods of work mid-March to the end of April and 8 June-26 September. Applications from 1 February to the Course Director, International Hospitality Ltd.

INTERNATIONAL STUDENT SERVICES: 58 Chapel Road, Worthing, West Sussex BN11 1B9 (tel 0903-211060/31216).
TEFL TEACHERS (28) for work in Brighton, Bognor and Worthing. £5.50-8.50 per hour: to work 12, 15 or 24 hours per week. Period of work mid-June to mid-August. Min. qualification necessary a related degree: TEFL qualifications or experience preferred. Foreign applicants may be taken on as social leaders/organizers in some instances. Applications to Susan Maghrabi. (O)

INTERNATIONAL STUDY TOURS (IST): 12 Eversfield Road, Eastbourne, East Sussex BN21 2AS (tel 0323-644830). Study holiday courses for German groups at centres throughout Southern England.
ENGLISH TEACHERS (38-40). £115-210 p.w. Additional payment made if involved with afternoon activities or Saturday excursions. No B. & L. Preference given to qualified teachers. Period of work March to April, and June, July and August. Apply in first instance to Mr R. Lewis.

KENT LANGUAGE AND ACTIVITY COURSES (KLAC): Aldergate, Aldington Road, Lympne, Hythe, Kent CT21 4 PD (tel 0303-67284/261133). SUMMER STUDY COURSE TEACHERS to teach EFL, sports, etc. Approx. £220-260 p.w. plus B. & L. Duties include teaching foreign children aged 12-18 in public schools for 3/4 week courses in South East England. Ages: 25-32 years. Preferably graduates in English or Modern Languages, with EFL qualifications, e.g. RSA, etc., or teachers currently working in primary or secondary schools. Period of work 3-4 weeks from early July. Applications to J. M. N. Horwood, MA (Cantab), KLAC.

KENT SCHOOL OF ENGLISH: 3, 10, 12 Granville Road, Broadstairs Kent CT10 1QD (tel 0843-68207).
VACATION ENGLISH LANGUAGE TEACHERS (5-10). £200 p.w. min. Hours 9am-12.15pm plus 3 afternoons and 3 evenings p.w. Additional 2 out of 3 Saturdays to accompany excursions. B. & L. available at £25 p.w. Min. age 22 years. Must have a degree or teaching diploma and English teaching experience. Specialist qualification in English preferable. Teachers must also help run activities, excursions and leisure pursuits. M.p.w. 3 weeks between end of June and end of August. Applications from late April to the Principal, Kent School of English. Please attach a recent photograph.

LIVING LANGUAGE CENTRE: Highcliffe House, Clifton Gardens, Folkestone, Kent CT20 2EF (tel 0303-58536; fax 0303-851455).
EFL TEACHERS (50) for centres in Oxford, Gravesend, Rochester and Folkestone. £150 p.w. depending on qualifications. Free accommodation available. Duties include teaching in the morning and organizing sports and activities in the afternoon. Some evening activities also. Period of work 6 July to 28 August. All teachers must be graduates with EFL qualifications. Applications to Mr Mackenzie-Bowie, Living Language Centre.

PILGRIMS LANGUAGE COURSES LTD: 8 Vernon Place, Canterbury, Kent CT1 3HG (tel 0227-762111).
SPORTS/EFL TEACHERS (25) to work in Canterbury and other towns. Wages

from £135 p.w. Full board provided, and accommodation may be available if necessary. To work a 30-hour, 5-day week, not necessarily Monday-Friday. Courses of 3 weeks between July and August. Applicants must be qualified in either EFL teaching or sports coaching. Applications from January to Mrs Liz Harrison, Director of Children's Courses, Pilgrims Language Courses.

SWANDEAN SCHOOL OF ENGLISH: 7 Oxford Road, Worthing, Sussex BW11 1XO (tel 0903-31330).
EFL TEACHERS (10). To work $13\frac{1}{2}$ h.p.w., or 23 h.p.w., plus opportunities for working on the social programme. Should possess RSA Prep. Certificate or Diploma.
SOCIAL PROGRAMME LEADERS (4) to accompany students on excursions and other social/sporting activities. Must be extroverts aged 18-25 with an interest in sports. Period of work July-August. Wages on application. Please apply to Helen Scarlett at the above address. (O)

Y.E.S. EDUCATIONAL CENTRES: 12 Eversfield Road, Eastbourne, East Sussex B21 2AS (tel 0323-644830). Holiday language courses for European student groups at several centres in South of England.
ENGLISH TEACHERS (36-40). £115-270 p.w. for 3-6 hours daily, Monday-Friday. Some activity supervision also available for which additional rates pro rata payments will be made. No B. & L. Must have TEFL experience; qualified teachers given preference. M.p.w. 3 weeks between 6 and 24 April (Easter) or 15 June and 31 August (Summer). Please apply to Mr J. Blackwood, Director of Studies, Y.E.S. Educational Centres.

EAST ANGLIA

Cambridgeshire
Essex
Norfolk
Suffolk

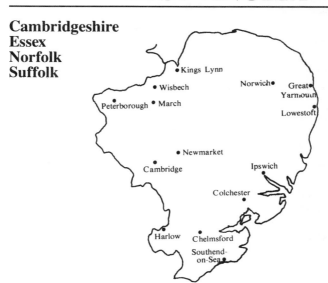

The Fenlands of Norfolk and Cambridgeshire are among the principal agricultural areas of Britain: subsequently, fruit picking, packing and processing jobs are not difficult to find if you are at the right place at the right time. Norwich and King's Lynn are the major centres, and production line workers will be required, especially in canning factories.

Temporary workers for amusement arcades, caravan parks and hotels are required in Great Yarmouth which, after Blackpool, is Britain's premier entertainment resort. Although vacancies in King's Lynn seem to have declined, Hunstanton, along the coast, often has difficulty in recruiting seasonal staff for hotel and catering vacancies. In general, however, temporary accommodation is almost as hard to find as in the south, especially at short notice.

As a major tourist and language school centre, a number of associated jobs can be found in Cambridge. The town's Jobcentre also has occasional vacancies for college cleaners and 'bedders' (room cleaners) for summer conferences and people to work in boathouses. They have a 'Temporary Desk' which has information on jobs lasting from one day to six months, with the average employer wanting an eight-week commitment. There is also agricultural work available in the area, picking cherries, strawberries, and later in the year harvesting potatoes. The Doblers pub in Stirton Street is a pick-up point around 7.30am for those wanting a day's work.

The Royal Norfolk, The Suffolk and The East Country Show also create a demand for car park attendants, ticket sellers, catering and waiting staff, stand minders and canvassers. These jobs last only for a few days. Phone the local tourist information offices for dates.

Business and Industry

ANGLIA CANNERS: Estuary Road, King's Lynn, Norfolk PE30 2HT (tel 0553- 766299). Part of Associated British Foods, canning both seasonal and non-seasonal products.
PROCESS WORKERS (200). £3.24 per hour plus shift premium. Shifts: 6.30am-2.15pm, 2.15-10pm and 10pm-6.30am, Monday to Friday. Overtime is available. Applicants should be physically fit and healthy, with a positive attitude. B. & L. is not provided. Staff required from May to October. M.p.w. depends on the availability of soft fruit and fresh vegetables. Applications from February to Mr Ringard, Anglia Canners.

ANGLIAN PROCESSORS LTD: Merton, nr Watton, Thetford, Norfolk IP25 6QL (tel 0953-882907/882930).
FACTORY ASSISTANTS (20) to work in a vegetable processing plant. The nature of the work prevents any specialiazation: the job may involve anything from making up containers for vegetables to maintaining the factory's hygiene. Waterproof footwear must be worn, and protective clothing is supplied. Wages are approx. £2.50 per hour in daytime, or £3 per hour for evening work. To work 84 hours over 7 days per week: the plant operates 24 hours per day, 7 days p.w. during the bean and pea picking season. No accommodation is available. M.p.w. between the middle of July and the end of August: exact dates depend on the progress of the harvest. Applicants must have common sense. Applications to J. Seaman or Mrs M. Smith, Anglian Processors Ltd.

BRITISH & BRAZILIAN PRODUCE COMPANY (SALES) LTD: Church Farm, Earl Stonham, Stowmarket, Suffolk IP14 5EE (tel 0449-711681).
FRUIT PACKERS (approx. 24). £100 p.w. Hours 8.30am-4.30pm Monday to Friday with half an hour lunch break. Some evenings and weekend o/t available. **No accommodation is available therefore only local applicants with own transport need apply.** No experience needed. M.p.w. 1 month between June and September. Applications in writing from mid-June to Personnel Director, Mrs P. A. Hicks, British & Brazilian Produce Co.

EASTERN STAFF SERVICES: 8 Northgate Street, Ipswich, Suffolk IP1 3BZ. Other branches at: 49 Abbeygate Street, Bury St. Edmunds IP33 1LB; 62 Sidney Street, Cambridge CB2 3JW; 1 Bank Passage, Colchester CO1 1HZ; 157 Hamilton Road, Felixstowe IP11 7DR; 3B St. Andrews Hill, Norwich NR2 1AD. OFFICE, TECHNICAL and INDUSTRIAL STAFF for range of temporary assignments. Wages and hours by arrangement. No B. & L. Applicants must have good standard of typing and/or shorthand and/or audio and/or word processing, plus a high standard of written English. M.p.w. one day between June and September. Applications to the Temporary Staff Consultant, Eastern Staff Services. (O)

GRAND UK HOLIDAYS: Aldwych House, Bethel Street, Norwich NR2 1NR (tel 0603-619933).
COURIERS (25). £90 nett p.w. plus tips. To work on eight-day coach tours. Applicants must be friendly, have an outgoing personality and ability to relate to those over fifty-five. Accommodation provided. Staff needed from May to September. Applications to the above address.

JENNINGS THE BOOKMAKERS: 72 The Stow, Harlow, Essex CM20 3AH (tel 0279-439661).
BETTING SHOP CASHIERS (2 in Hemel Hempstead area, 2 in Harlow area and 2 in Stevenage area). Approx. £3.40 per hour. 5 hours per day, Monday to Friday afternoons; $7\frac{1}{2}$ hours on Saturday. Min. age 18 years. Should be accurate with figures and money, and have a pleasant disposition towards the public. Required from June to September on an occasional basis. Applications to Mr Arbuckle, at the above address.

Holiday Centres and Amusements

THE THURSFORD COLLECTION: Thursford Green, Thursford, nr Fakenham, Norfolk NR21 0AS (tel 0328-878477). Tourist attraction comprising steam engine museum, narrow gauge railway, old fairground organs, a gondola ride and live concerts.
SHOP STAFF, CAFE STAFF, RIDE ATTENDANTS (25). Wage according to age and experience. To work on shifts to cover 7 days p.w., 10.30am-5.30pm, and noon-5.30pm. Experience of working with tills preferred. Must be honest and have a bright and cheerful personality to work with the public. Min. age 14, but school leaving age preferred. No accommodation provided. Staff needed from Easter until end of August, and also at Christmas. Applicants must be available for interview. Applications to Linda Palmer, at the above address, up to 6 weeks before date when available for work. (O)

Hotels and Catering

THE FELIX: Undercliff Road, Felixstowe, Suffolk IP11 8AD (tel 0394-283942). CATERING STAFF. Wages depend on previous experience and aptitude. To work 30 hours or more per 5 or 6 day week. M.p.w. 8 or 9 weeks at any time of year. Min. age 18. Previous experience of bar and catering work an advantage but not essential as training will be given. Local applicants preferred as no accommodation is provided. Applications from February/March to The Felix, at the above address.

THE FERRY BOAT INN: 131 Ferry Road, Felixstowe, Suffolk IP11 9RZ (tel 0394-284203). CATERING STAFF. Wages depend on previous experience and aptitude. To work 30 hours or more per 5 or 6 day week. M.p.w. 8 or 9 weeks at any time of year. Min. age 18. Previous experience of bar and catering work an advantage but not essential, as training will be given. Local applicants preferred since no accommodation is provided. Applications from February/March to The Ferry Boat Inn, at the above address.

FIELD STUDIES COUNCIL: Flatford Mill Field Centre, East Bergholt, Colchester, Essex CO7 6UL (tel 0206-298283). A residential field centre running courses in environment and art and craft subjects. DOMESTIC ASSISTANTS (up to 4). £55-60 p.w. plus free B. & L. Duties include laying tables, waiting, washing up, and general household work. To work split shifts 7.30am-12.30pm and 5.30-8.30pm with 1½ days off p.w. Should be aged 20-30 years. Driving licence and some interest in enviromental education helpful. Opportunities to join in with centre activities during free time. Staff needed from February to December. M.p.w. 4 weeks. Telephone the Centre Secretary (do not write) from January to check the availability of posts. (O)

RAVENSCOURT GUEST HOUSE: 138 Lynn Road, Wisbech, Cambridgeshire PE13 3DP (tel 0945-585052). GENERAL ASSISTANT (1). £35 pw. To work 6 mornings, 8am-noon and 2/3 evenings p.w. on a rota basis. Should be aged between 18 and 24, speak good English and be smartly dressed. No experience is necessary. Free B. & L. provided. Duties include receiving guests, cleaning, bed-making, etc. M.p.w. 6 weeks between 1 February and mid-October. Applicants, from EC countries welcome. Applications, enclosing a photograph, from January onwards to Mr J. P. Parish, Proprietor, Ravenscroft Guest House.

SWAN HOTEL: High Street, Lavenham, Suffolk CO10 9QA (tel 0787-247477). WAITING STAFF (3). Wages and hours to be arranged. To work 5 days p.w. Uniform and meals provided free while on duty. Applicants should be aged 20-35 and have silver service waiting experience. No accommodation available therefore local applicants only need apply.

Medical

THE NORFOLK CARE SEARCH AGENCY: 19 London Road, Downham Market, Norfolk PE38 9BJ (tel 0366-384448).
CARE of the ELDERLY (20). £140-175 pw. Live-in positions to supervise semi-disabled or elderly persons day and night. Full B. & L. Ages: 22-70 years (19 if in nursing training). Must be trained, experienced (e.g. in nursing home) or mature enough to take charge of household. M.p.w. 2 weeks at any time. Applications to Mrs V. A. Parker, Proprietor, The Norfolk Care Search Agency. (O)

Outdoor

ANGLIA ALPINES: Needingworth Road, Bluntisham, Huntingdon, Cambridgeshire PE17 3RJ (tel 0487-840103).
NURSERY WORKERS (8). Wages from approx £3.32 per hour dependent upon age. Flexible hours but min. of 30 hours p.w. Preference given to those with horticultural experience. M.p.w. 2 months between June and October. Applications to the General Office, Anglia Alpines. (O)

BOXFORD SUFFOLK FARMS LTD: Hill Farm, Boxford, Colchester, Essex CO6 5NY (tel 0787-210348).
FARM WORKERS/FRUIT PICKERS. Up to 20 people needed at height of season. Wages at agricultural or pce. wk. rates; some o/t available. Work involves apple-picking and harvesting of vegetables; careful handling of produce essential. Staff needed from August throughout the summer. No minimum period of work. Some caravan space available at £15 p.w. Tent space with toilet and washing facilities provided at a small charge. Applications from February onwards to Mrs Peake or Marion Hibben, at the above address. (O)

FIVEWAYS FRUIT FARM: Fiveways, Stanway, Colchester, Essex CO3 5LR (tel 0206-330244).
FRUIT PICKERS (20). To pick soft fruit and apples. Wages at pce. wk. rates, approx. £80-130 per 5-7 day week. Hourly work also available. Period of work May to October. Hours flexible. Meadow available for camping. Supermarket, post office, off-licence and launderette within a short walk. Residential caravan

for relaxation with hot/cold water, microwave, cooker, television, shower room and toilet facilities. Applications a.s.a.p. to Fiveways Fruit Farm. (O)

FRIDAYBRIDGE INTERNATIONAL CAMP LTD: Wisbech, Cambridgeshire (tel 0945-860255).
GENERAL AGRICULTURAL WORKERS to pick strawberries and apples, cut broccoli and celery, and help with many other jobs. 5-6 days p.w. Bed, breakfast, packed lunch and evening meal provided at a reasonable weekly charge. Min age 17 years, max. 30. Must be fit. Club, disco, swimming pool, tennis court, plus many other facilities. Vacancies available from end of May to end of October. M.p.w. 3 weeks. Send stamp for brochure (applications on official forms only) to Dept. VW, Fridaybridge International Camp Ltd.

GREENS OF DEREHAM: Norwich Road, Dereham, Norfolk (tel 0362-692014).
STRAWBERRY PICKERS. Workers are paid in cash daily, at normal pce. wk. rates. Min. age 17. Working day may last until 4pm. Camping area provided. Workers needed throughout July. UK residents only need apply. Applications to Greens of Dereham, at the above address.

HATCHMAN'S FARM: Woodham Walter, nr Maldon, Essex CM9 6RB (tel 024 541-2020).
AGRICULTUAL SEASONAL WORKERS (4-5) to pick and grade apples and pears. Wages at standard agricultural rate. To work about 5 hours per day, 4 days p.w. No accommodation is provided but there is a campsite nearby. Would suit fit and enthusiastic students. UK residents only need apply. Period of work end of August to October. Applications to Mrs R. J. Lindsay, Hatchman's Farm.

HUDSONS FARMS: Badliss Hall, Ardleigh, Colchester, Essex (tel 0206-230306).
WORKERS (20-30). To pick and plant fruit and vegetables outside and in a glasshouse. Payment at pce. wk. rates. Working hours from 7am (weather permitting) until 2pm, or later subject to crop and weather. Campsite, showers, cooking facilities, toilets and sheltered area are provided. Period of work from June to October. Applicants with a liking for outside work preferred. Applications to S. Hudson at the above address. (O)

INTERNATIONAL FARM CAMP: Hall Road, Tiptree, Essex CO5 0QS (tel 0621- 815496).
FRUIT PICKERS and GENERAL FARM WORKERS. Pce. wk. rates. Hours 8am-5pm Monday to Friday. Approx. £35 pw for full B. & L. Age: 18-25 years.

M.p.w. 2 weeks between early June and end of September. Few vacancies between mid-July and end of August. Applications as early as possible; s.a.e. (or IRC if writing from abroad) essential for reply, to International Farm Camp. For non-EC applicants places are strictly limited to full-time students who have not completed their studies.

LANGHAM FRUIT FARMS LTD: Malting Farm, Langham, Colchester, Essex CO4 5NW (tel 0206-272559).
FRUIT PICKERS (up to 50). Wages at standard rate based on age. Hours 9am-3.30pm. Applications to Langham Fruit Farms Ltd.

NEWTON FRUIT FARMS: Mudcroft Farm, Newton, Wisbech PE13 5HF (tel 0945-870254).
APPLE PICKERS (30). £25-35 per day. To work 7am-4pm Monday to Friday, with evenings and weekends as necessary. Self-catering accommodation provided in caravans at a charge of £5 p.w. per caravan. Bedding and cooking equipment not provided. Wet-weather clothing essential. Applicants must be fit and healthy and over 20. Nationals from EC countries are welcome to apply. Staff needed from early September to mid-October. M.p.w. 2 weeks. Applications from 1 April onwards. (O)

OAK TREE FARM: Hasketon, Woodbridge, Suffolk (tel 0473-735218).
STRAWBERRY PICKERS. Pce. wk. rates. Usually 6 days p.w. with Saturdays off. Min. 8 hours per day when picking. Campsite and hostel accommodation available. Min. age 18 years. Period of work 4 weeks from approx. 25 June. M.p.w. 3 weeks. Applications before 1 April enclosing s.a.e. to Mrs R. Stephenson, Oak Tree Farm. (O)

R. & J. M. PLACE LTD: Church Farm, Tunstead, Norwich NR12 8RQ.
FRUIT PICKERS (250). Agricultural wages and/or pce. wk. rates; details on
application. To work a 6-day week, excluding Saturday. Accommodation
available in converted farm buildings for approx. £30 p.w. including breakfast.
Must be in good health. No previous experience necessary. Social activities
in camp, as well as canoe club on Norfolk rivers. Open between end of June
and mid-September. Applications with s.a.e. to the Organizer, R. & J. M. Place
Ltd. (O)

RED HOUSE FARM: Dennington, Woodbridge, Suffolk IP13 8EQ (tel 072
875-628).
STRAWBERRY PICKERS (8-10). Pce. wk. rates. To work up to 8 hours per
day, but usually 5-6, 6 days p.w. (weather permitting).
STRAWBERRY PACKERS (3-4). Pce work rates. Similar hours, but possibly
needed to work Saturday and Sunday mornings depending on season and amount
of fruit to pack. Campsite provided with cooking facilities, showers, etc. Min.
age 17. Staff needed from second week in June to 31 July or mid-August.
Applications to Mrs T. Craggs, at the above address. (O)

C. & A. SANDERSON: Bramley House, Cox's Lane, Wisbech, Cambridgeshire
PE13 4TD (tel 0945-583023).
SRAWBERRY PICKERS (8-10). Pce. wk. rates. Monday to Friday and
sometimes Sunday mornings. Early morning start. Free campsite, washroom
with hot and cold water and W.C. Limited caravan accommodation also available
at small charge. Workers must be willing to work hard. Period of work approx.
3-4 weeks, commencing late June. Applications to A. Sanderson, Bramley
House. (O)

WILLIAMSON (FRUIT FARMS) LTD: Park Lane Farm, Park Lane,
Langham, Colchester, Essex CO4 5NL (tel 0206-230233).
RASPBERRY/APPLE/PEAR PICKERS (50). Pce. wk. rates, approx. wage
£100 p.w. To work Monday to Friday 7.30am-4.45pm, with some weekend work.
Accommodation available at £15 p.w. on campsite or in dormitories with kitchen,
mess room, showers, toilets and TV. Ages: 18-23 years. M.p.w. 3 weeks. Staff
needed in July for raspberries and August to October for apples and pears.
Applications from 1 March to Mr B. Havis, at the above address. (O)

Sport

BRADWELL SAILING CENTRE: Bradwell Waterside, Southminster, Essex
CM0 7QY (tel 0621-76256).

SAILING (6), CANOEING (2), and WINDSURFING (2) INSTRUCTORS. Wages negotiable. Approx. 8 hours per day. RYA Certificate desirable but not essential. Free B. & L. available. M.p.w. 3 months between April and October inclusive. Applications in January/March to the Principal, Bradwell Sailing Centre. (O)

BRENTWOOD DISTICT COUNCIL: The Brentwood Centre, Doddinghurst Road, Brentford CM15 9MN (tel 0277-229621).
FOOTBALL REFEREES (3) needed from May-June, and July-August.
TRAMPOLINE COACHES (2), HOLIDAY SCHEME RECREATION ATTENDANTS (3) needed from 23 July-30 August.
JUDO COACH needed July to September.
LIFEGUARDS (3), HEALTH SUITE ATTENDANTS (4), RECREATION ATTENDANTS (4) needed July-October.
Wages and hours by arrangement. Applications to Janette Dean at the above address. (O)

CHELMSFORD BOROUGH COUNCIL: Riverside Ice and Leisure Centre, Victoria Road, Chelmsford, Essex CM1 1FG (tel 0245-269417).
LIFEGUARDS (6) to supervise 3 swimming pools, do some teaching and administer first aid if necessary. £3 per hour, hours by arrangement. Period of work from June to October. Applicants should be at least 18 and possession of RLSS Bronze Medallion an advantage. Applications to K. G. Reed at the above address. (O)

SHENFIELD SPORTS CENTRE: Oliver Road, Shenfield, Brentwood, Essex (tel 0277-226220).
SPORTS COACHES. Wages £4-5 per hour. To work from 9.15am-12.30pm daily.
SPORTS SUPERVISORS. Wages £3.25 per hour. To work from 1.15-4.45pm daily. Staff needed thoughout the school holidays. Applicants should be either qualified sports instructors or students on a PE course. Min. age 18. Applications to K. Coleman, Assistant Manager, at the above address. (O)

Language Schools

BRIAR SCHOOL OF ENGLISH: 8 Gunton Cliff, Lowestoft, Suffolk NR32 4PE (tel 0502-57381).
TEACHERS £5.80 per hour. To work up to 6 hours daily and lead excursions on Saturdays. TEFL qualifications or experience preferable. Applicants must possess either a degree or a teacher's certificate.
COURIER to meet groups at air and sea ports and lead them on excursions

to London, Cambridge, Norwich, etc. Up to £120 p.w. Knowledge of places to be visited an advantage. Min. age 18. Period of work 2 July-31 August. Applications to Mr N. J. Doe, at the above address.

EAST ANGLIAN SCHOOLS OF ENGLISH: Burebank College, Aylsham, Norfolk (tel 0263-733203).
ASSISTANT TUTORS. Based in Norfolk and Yorkshire. From £90 p.w. for a 6-day week. Graduate teaching experience preferred, but enthusiastic person who would assist with social/sport programme acceptable. Period of work from 22 June or 6 July, for 4 or 6 weeks. Free B. & L. Driving licence useful. Applications to the Secretary for Summer Schools, East Anglican Schools of English.

EUROYOUTH LTD: 301 Westborough Road, Westcliffe, Southend-on-Sea, Essex SSO 9PT (tel 0702-341434).
TEACHERS OF ENGLISH. Native English speakers required to teach English as a foreign language to continental students in Southend. Easter and summer courses. Previous experience desirable especially in EFL. Min. age 21 years. Send s.a.e for details of job. Written applications with details of experience, qualifications, availablility dates and wages expected, to Euroyouth Ltd.

STUDIO SCHOOL OF ENGLISH: 6 Salisbury Villas, Station Road, Cambridge CB1 2JF (tel 0223-69701).
TEACHERS OF EFL (10-20). £8-12 per hour. Hours vary between 15 and 30 p.w. No B. & L. Applicants must be graduates, preferably with TEFL qualification and/or experience. M.p.w. 4 weeks between June and September. Applications between January and April to Mr Geoff Brock, Principal, Studio School of English. (O)

MIDLANDS

Bedfordshire
Cheshire
Derbyshire
Hereford & Worcester
Leicestershire
Lincolnshire

Northamptonshire
Nottinghamshire
Oxfordshire
Shropshire
Staffordshire
Warwickshire
W. Midlands

The Midlands region covers a number of large towns — with Birmingham at its centre — so office temping, warehouse or factory work, and retail are all areas likely to provide good opportunities for jobs. The larger local authorities, such as Birmingham and Coventry, take people on temporarily as play leaders and recreation assistants. There are occasional opportunities for market research, and it is worth trying car dealers for driving jobs delivering cars all round the country, particularly in August.

There is also scope for work in the tourist industry, particularly in and around Stratford-upon-Avon. The Royal Show at Stoneleigh always needs catering and waiting staff, which are taken on at the Coventry Jobcentre. The Birmingham Superprix road race in August also offers opportunities of this kind, and in Staffordshire, Alton Towers Leisure Park takes on temporary ride attendants, shop staff, etc.

Some fruit picking and hop picking work is available in the Vale of Evesham and Lincolnshire, but the Midlands is an area where 'pick your own' farms are popular.

Oxford is a popular centre for language schools and there are opportunities for EFL teachers and also sports instructors and social organizers.

Business and Industry

APEX RECRUITMENT SERVICES LTD: 3rd Floor, 33-35 Regent Street, Oxford OX1 2AY (tel 0865-791454).
SECRETARIES (5). Wages approx. £150 p.w. Should have typing to RSA II standard.
CLERICAL ACCOUNT WORKERS (5). Wages approx. £150 p.w. Should have knowledge of purchase or sales ledger.
LABOURERS (5). Wages approx. £120 p.w.
CATERING STAFF (6). Wages approx. £130 p.w.
All the above to work 37½ h.p.w.
ENGINEERS (4). Wages approx. £350 p.w. To work 35 h.p.w. Applicants should have MI Mech E or MIEE qualifications.
ACCOUNTANTS (2). Wages approx. £350 p.w. To work 38 h.p.w. Qualified applicants with ACCA, ACA or CIMA needed.
Period of work from May/June to 30 September. Applications to Apex Recruitment Services, at the above address. (O)

INFO-TEC RECRUITMENT: 9 Park End Street, Oxford OX1 1HH (tel 0865-245899).
SECRETARIAL and CLERICAL POSITIONS, WORD PROCESSING OPERATORS. £4.50 per hour. No accommodation. Must have good typing (40 w.p.m.) and shorthand (80 w.p.m.) skills. Previous office experience preferred. Applications from April.
SECRETARIAL TRAINING. Learn typing and word processing to employment standards within 5 weeks, other courses also available. Course fees and details on request.
Applications and enquiries to Mr Charles Sweeney, Director, Info-Tec.

K. H. TAYLOR LTD: The Freezing Station, Sheffield Road, Blyth, Worksop, Nottingham (tel 0909-591555).
INSPECTION and QUALITY CONTROL PERSONNEL, PACKERS, STACKERS (approx. 50). Wages £3.89 basic, £4.36 o/t. To work 8-12 hours per day, in shifts of 6am-2pm, 2-10pm and 10pm-6am. To work Monday to Friday, with some weekend work available. No experience or qualifications needed. Interview not necessary. Applications from the beginning of June to K. H. Taylor Ltd., at the above address.

Children

ACTION HOLIDAYS LTD: 'Windrush', Bexton Lane, Knutsford, Cheshire WA16 9BP (tel 0565-654775). Multi-activity holiday centres in Greater London,

Hampshire and Cheshire for children aged 3-15 years.
STAFF required to look after children in all departments of the holiday camp in Cheshire: instructors, supervisory and general support staff. For details of work see entry in Nationwide chapter.

BROOMFIELDS RECREATION CETRE: Broomfields Road, Appleton, Warrington, Cheshire WA4 3AE (tel 0925-68768/68729). Summer sports school.
HEAD COACH (1). Wages approx. £115 p.w. Hours 9am-6.30pm, Mondays to Fridays. Duties include co-ordinating the other coaches, providing equipment and keeping class registers.
GENERAL COACHES (5) to organize sports classes. Wages £100 p.w. To work from 9am-4pm Mondys to Fridays.
Period of work from end of July to the end of August. Min. age 18. Applicants must have either a sports qualification or all-round experience in coaching activities. Applications to the personnel Manager at the above address.

CAMPUS CENTRES: Llangarron, Ross-on-Wye, Herefordshire HR9 6PG (tel 0989-84757).
INSTRUCTORS (approx. 20). To teach sailing, canoeing, windsurfing, climbing, abseiling, archery, rifle shooting, etc. Min. age 18, preferred age 21. Also expected to assist with evening entertainments several nights p.w. Applicants must be competent in their chosen sport, and preference is given to those holding relevant qualifications, e.g RYA, BCU, MLTB, etc.
CHEFS (4-6). Must be 706/1, 706/2 qualified, and/or have relevant experience.
KICHEN STAFF, DOMESTIC STAFF and GROUP LEADERS. Approx. 4-6 in each category required.
SITE MAINTENANCE WORKERS/DRIVERS/STORES (6). Drivers must have a clean driving licence and be at least over 21 years of age; applicants over 25 years preferred.
NURSES (2). Must be RGN qualified.
ADMINISTRATORS (2).
Free B. & L. available for all positions. Wages £35-50 p.w. Wages for senior staff negotiable. To work 50-60 hours over a 6-day week. Min. age 18 years, unless specified otherwise. Period of work February to November. Applicants must have a flexible attitude to working hours, and a willingness to muck in with all aspects of centre life where necessary. Applications a.s.a.p. to Julie Smith, Personnel Manger, at the above address. (O)

LEICESTER CHILDREN'S HOLIDAY HOME: Mablethorpe, Quebec Road, Mablethorpe, Lincolnshire LN12 1QX (tel 0507-472444).
CHILD MINDERS (12), KITCHEN STAFF (2). £41 p.w.

DINING ROOM STAFF (2). £41 p.w.
DOMESTICS (2). £2.20 per hour.
COOK. £67 p.w.
To work a 6-day week (extra days paid pro rata). Free B. & L. provided. Work includes looking after children aged $7\frac{1}{2}$-12 years, playing with them and taking them to the beach. Staff needed from beginning of May to end of August. Preference given to applicants able to work entire season. Min. age 18. Applications from March to the Warden, Leicester Children's Holiday Home.

MANSFIELD DISTRICT COUNCIL: Civic Centre, Chesterfield Road, South Mansfield, Notts NG19 7BH (tel 0623-663026).
PLAYSCHEME LEADERS (25) to organize a variety of play and sports facilities for able-bodied and disabled children aged 5-14 years. Wages approx. £3.80 per hour for leaders, £3.24 per hour for assistants. Period of work from 27 July to 21 August. Applicants must have knowledge of arts and crafts, sport, dance, drama or music, etc. For further details contact Beatrix Kirby, Community Play Developement Worker, on the above number before 20 April, for an informal chat. (O)

SOUTH BEDFORDSHIRE DISTRICT COUNCIL: The District Offices, High Street North, Dunstable, Bedfordshire LU6 1LF (tel 0582-474095).
PLAYLEADERS (25) to supervise children aged 5-15 on a summer playscheme, including arts and crafts activities, sports and games. From £3.50 per hour depending on qualifications and experience. **No accommodation available, therefore positions suitable for local applicants only.** Hours vary from 3-25 hours per week. Period of work four weeks only over the summer. Applicants must be aged at least 18 and should enjoy working with children and be dependable, punctual, hardworking, imaginative and responsible. Training is provided. Applications to Maggie Laid at the above address.

WREKIN DISTRICT COUNCIL: Leisure and Community Services Department, PO Box 211, Malinslee House, Telford, Shropshire (tel 0952-202507).
PLAYLEADERS (100+). Pay varies according to age and in 1991 those aged 18 were paid £2.89 per hour, and those aged 21 and over £3.68 per hour. To work 25 or 36 h.p.w. No accommodation is provided. Applicants should be enthusiastic, well-organized and good communicators, as well as having experience of working with, and organizing activities for, groups of young people. Applications to Sue Howe at the above address. (O)

Holiday Centres and Amusements

ACORN VENTURE LTD: 137 Worcester Road, Hagley, Stourbridge DY9 0NW (tel 0562-882151/886569). A multi-activity centre.
INSTRUCTORS (40). £40-80 p.w. To work with school and youth groups. Must have relevant sporting qualification to instruct in outdoor pursuits such as canoeing, windsurfing, climbing, land-yachting, etc.
SITE WORKERS AND CATERERS (12). Wages £35-50 p.w. Work involves maintaining the camp site and preparing meals.
NURSE. Pay negotiable.
CENTRE MANAGERS (2) Wages £140 + p.w. Centre comprised of two sites, each with a capacity of between 50 and 60. The centre manager heads a team of senior staff, instructors, caterers and maintenance staff, and is responsible for ensuring the efficient operation of the centre. Relevant experience and qualifications are a distinct advantage.
Staff needed from April to September. No m.p.w. Free B. & L. available. Interview preferable. Applications a.s.a.p. to Mr Tim Boldry at the above address. (O)

DERBYSHIRE ACTION HOLIDAYS: Kirby House, Main Street, Winster, Matlock, Derbyshire DE4 2DH (tel 062 988-716). Outdoor activity holiday camps for youth groups and adults, run in conjunction with a gift and crafts shop.
OUTDOOR ACTIVITY INSTRUCTORS. £10 per day. Involves specialist activities, such as canoeing, climbing, caving, walking, camping, cycling, etc. as well as cross-country skiing in the winter.
SHOP STAFF (1). £30 p.w.
Staff for these positions are employed on a casual basis, as and when work is available. Hours to be arranged according to requirements. M.p.w. 1 day, with work available all year round. Appropriate experience necessary. School or college students peferred. Free B. & L. provided. Applications from Easter to Mr Geoff Williams, Organizer, Derbyshire Action Holidays. (O)

FUNCOAST WORLD: Skegness, Lincolnshire (tel 0754-2311).
ACCOMMODATION ASSISTANTS, BAR STAFF, WAITERS, WAITRESSES, KITCHEN STAFF, SHOP ASSISTANTS, QUALIFIED LIFEGUARDS, TECHNICIANS, NURSES (RGN), NURSERY NURSES (NNEB), CLEANERS, SECURITY STAFF, EXPERIENCED COOKS, SUPERVISORS, CLERICAL STAFF, REDCOATS, PORTERS, MAINTENANCE STAFF and many more (around 1000) to work in a Holiday Centre. Wages depend upon job. B. & L. provided for a small charge; staff may also live-out, in which case wages increase slightly. To work a 39-hour week. Applicants should be aged over 18 and of smart appearance. Training

will be given. Staff required from March to the end of October. Applications from mid-January to the Personnel Manager at the above address.

GROVE HOUSE: Bromesberrow Heath, nr Ledbury, Herefordshire HR8 1PE (tel 053 181-584).
GENERAL ASSISTANTS (1/2) to work in a guest house/riding stables. £25 p.w. B. & L. provided, plus plenty of free riding and occasional use of a car. Period of work between April and October for any length of time. Adequate riders and car drivers preferred. Applications to Mrs E. M. Ross at the above address. (O)

OXFORD SCHOOL OF DRAMA: Sansomes Farm Studios, Woodstock, Oxford OX7 1ER (tel 0993-812883).
COOK/HOUSEKEEPERS (2/3) to live and work in houses used to accommodate participants in summer drama courses in Oxford. Duties include providing breakfast and an evening meal. To work 7 days p.w. Wages of £100-120 p.w. plus full B. & L. Period of work mid-July to the end of August. Applicants must be responsible. Applications, enclosing photograph, c.v. and s.a.e., to the Administrator, at the above address, before the end of April. (O)

PEAK NATIONAL PARK CENTRE: Losehill Hall, Castleton, Derbyshire S30 2WB (tel 0433-20373). A residential Study Centre designed for those interested and involved in countryside conservation.
VACATIONAL ASSISTANT (1). £133 p.w. To work 37 h.p.w. including considerable weekend working, for which time off in lieu will be given. Should have experience and interest in some of the following: hill-walking, field leadership, cycling, sailing, local and natural history and practical crafts, as well as an outgoing personality, capable of communicating happily with individuals and families on holiday. The assistant will be required to help run and organize the summer holiday courses. Full driving licence essential and First Aid qualifications would be an advantage. B. & L. provided at approx. £12 p.w. M.p.w. approx 6-12 weeks, between mid-July and early October. Applications a.s.a.p. to Mr Peter Townsend, Director, Peak National Park Centre. (O)

ROB HASTINGS ADVENTURE LTD: 25 Southcourt Avenue, Leighton Buzzard, Bedfordshire LU7 7QD (tel 0525-379881). Runs high-adventure, multi-activity holidays in Denbigh, North Wales.
KITCHEN ASSISTANTS (8), TRAINEE INSTRUCTORS (8) and SPECIALIST INSTRUCTORS: FENCING (2), GOLF (2), CLIMBING (3), WHITEWATER CANOEING (3), RAQUETS (2), ARCHERY (2),

JUDO/KARATE (2), ART AND CRAFT (1), AEROBICS (1), SAILING (3), WINDSURFING (1), TEFL TEACHER (1). Wages from £38-75 p.w., depending on qualifications and experience. All specialist positions need qualifications and experience. Free B. & L. provided. One day off a week. Opportunities to use sports facilities and join in activities. Staff needed from beginning of July until 16 August. M.p.w. 5 week. No interview necessary. Applications from the New Year onwards to Rob Hastings, at the above address. (O)

ROCK LEA ACTIVITY CENTRE: Station Road, Hathersage, Derbyshire S30 1DD (tel 0433-50345). An outdoor pursuits centre in the Peak National Park that runs activity holidays for adults.
OUTDOOR PURSUITS ASSISTANTS (2) to teach sailing, canoeing, mountain biking, caving, pothling, walking, etc. Wages £3 per hour. Must have mountain activity centre experience and/or qualifications. Clean driving licence required for senior posts. Older staff with teaching qualifications preferred.
COOKS/CATERING ASSISTANTS (2). Wages £3 per hour. Basic food hygiene certificate and sense of humour needed.
ADMINISTRATIVE ASSISTANT (1). Wages negotiable. To help with office work and general administration.
AU PAIR (1). Wages negotiable. To help look after centre managers and their young child. An outdoor pursuits enthusiast is preferred.
Free B. & L. is provided for all positions. Work is available all year round. M.p.w. 1 month. Min. age for all positions is 18 years, with over 21's preferred. The centre operates a 7-day week and all staff are expected to work unsocial hours, with 1 weekend off out of every 3. The centre expects its staff to display professionalism at all times. Applicants must attend an interview, supply references, and be prepared to undergo a trial period of employment. Applications a.s.a.p. to Mr Iain Jennings, Managing Director, at the above address. (O)

Hotels and Catering

ALVASTON HALL HOTEL: Middlewich Road, Nantwich, Cheshire CW5 6PD (tel 0270- 624341).
WAITING STAFF (2). To work 10 shifts over 5 days p.w. Wages £90 p.w. To work over summer period. Min. age 18. No qualifications necessary, but must be presentable. Applications to Alison Jaggar, at the above address.

EASTGATE HOTEL: Merton Street. The High, Oxford OX1 4BE (tel 0865-248244).
WAITING STAFF (3), KITCHEN STAFF (1). To work approx. 40 hours p.w.

over 5 days. Some experience needed.
CHAMBER STAFF (1). To work $2\frac{1}{2}$ hours per day, 5 days p.w. Min. age 17. Experience helpful but not essential.
KITCHEN PORTER (1). Required one month only in June or July. Min. age 18.
BAR PERSON (1). Approx. 40 hours, 5 days p.w. Must be over 18, some experience preferred.
All staff receive £3 per hour. M.p.w. 2 months. Staff required from early June to late September. Limited accommodation available, meals on duty and uniforms provided. EC nationals welcome to apply. Applications from April/May to Sharon Jennings, General Manager, at the Eastgate Hotel. (O)

HOW CAPLE GRANGE HOTEL: How Caple, Herefordshire HR1 4TF (tel 098 986-208).
GENERAL ASSISTANTS (3). £80-90 p.w. Approx. 40 h.p.w. Free B. & L. Min. age 17 years. No experience necessary but must be keen and willing to work in all departments of the hotel. Must have own transport. Staff required from April to October (and also Christmas period). Preference given to applicants available in April. Applications to the Proprietor, How Caple Grange Hotel (please telephone to check for vacancy).

THE KING'S ARMS: Ombersley, Worcestershire (tel 0905-620142).
BAR STAFF (4) for general bar duties lunchtime and evenings. £3 per hour. 40 h.p.w. on a rota system. No accommodation available. Min. age 18 years. Staff required all year round. Applications a.s.a.p. to the Manager, The King's Arms. (O)

LONGMYND HOTEL: Cunnery Road, Church Stretton, Shropshire SY6 6AG (tel 0694-722244).
RESTAURANT STAFF (3). Wages to be arranged. Approx. 48 h.p.w. $5\frac{1}{2}$ days p.w. Free B. & L. Some experience necessary. M.p.w. 10 weeks between 1 July and 30 September. Applications in March to Richard Haswell, Longmynd Hotel. (O)

THE LYGON ARMS: Broadway, Worcestershire WR12 7DU (tel 0386-852255).
WAITING STAFF (2), CHAMBER STAFF (2), BAR STAFF (1). £65 p.w. To work 40 h.p.w. Min. age 16. Training will be given. Staff needed from May to October, m.p.w. 3 months. Free B & L provided. Applicants from EC welcome to apply. Must be available for interview. Applications from March to Kim Friedli, at the above address.

MARLOWE'S RESTAURANT: Marlowe's Alley, 17/18 High Street, Stratford-upon-Avon, Warwickshire CV37 6AU (tel 0798-204999).

WAITING STAFF £3 per hour including tips. Work available full or part time. Restaurant open noon-3pm and 6pm-midnight. Applicants must arrange own acommodation before applying. Period of work April-December. Applications to Mr George Kruszynskyj, Marlowe's Restaurant.

ROSE REVIVED INN & RESTAURANT: Newbridge, near Witney, Oxfordshire OX8 6QD (tel 0865-300221).
BAR STAFF (3), WAITERS/WAITRESSES (3), CHAMBER STAFF (1), WASHERS UP (2), KITCHEN ASSISTANTS (2). Wages and hours by arrangement. Tips extra. To work 5 days p.w. B. & L. available. Min. age 18 years. Silver service experience an advantage. M.p.w. 6 weeks at any time throughout the year. Applications to Mr A. B. Jefferson, Resident Manager, Rose Revived Inn & Restaurant. (O)

WELCOME BREAK SERVICE AREA (Trust House Forte): Peartree Roundabout, Woodstock Road, Oxford OX2 8JZ (tel 0865-54301).
GENERAL ASSISTANTS (12). £2.92 per hour starting rate. 5 day week. Hours: 7am-3pm and 3-11pm. No accommodation available. Min. age 16 years. M.p.w. 8 weeks between May and September. Applications from 1 April to the Personnel Office, Oxford Service Area.

WESTWOOD COUNTRY HOTEL: Hinksey Hill Top, Oxford OX1 5BG (tel 0865-735408).
GENERAL ASSISTANTS (2). £120 p.w. min. To work approx. 45 hours per $5\frac{1}{2}$ day week. Hours by arrangement with flexible day off. Free B. & L. Min. age 18 years. Tidy appearance required. Some experience in dining room (not necessarily full silver service) required, also chamber work. M.p.w. 6 weeks, May to October. Applications to Mrs M. Parker, Proprietor. (O)

WILLOW REACHES HOTEL: 1 Wytham Street, Oxford OX1 4SU (tel 0865-721545).
GENERAL ASSISTANT. £40-45 p.w. Approx. 40 h.p.w. B. & L. available (possibility of living out with wage adjusted accordingly.) M.p.w. 3 months between May and September. Weekend work also available. Applications from March to Mrs S. Sahota, Proprietor, Willow Reaches Hotel. (O)

WORLDS END LODGE: Staunton-on-Wye, Hereford HR4 7NF (tel 09817-308). An outdoor pursuits centre/youth hostel.
CLEANER/COOK (1). To work 44 hours, $5\frac{1}{2}$ days per week, o/t available. Wage to be negotiated. No experience necessary, but a knowledge of catering work useful. Must be outgoing and friendly. Positions cover all in-house work,

cleaning and cooking. Free B. & L. provided. Needed from beginning of May to end of September. M.p.w. beginning of June to end of August. Applicants must be available for interview. Applications (with c.v.) a.s.a.p. to Chris Charters or Dave Morris, at the above address. (O)

Outdoor

J. M. BUBB & SON: Pave Lane Farm, Newport, Shropshire TF10 9AX (tel 0952- 820213).
PICKERS AND PACKERS (20) for vegetables and dried flowers. Wages at Agricultural Wages Board hourly rate or at the going piece work rate. To work from 9am-5pm plus o/t. Camp site with facilities available. Min age 16. Period of work July to October. Applications to the above address. (O)

CAWLEY FARMS: Ashton Fruit Farm, Castle Ground, Ashton, Leominster, Herefordshire (tel 058 472-401).
FRUIT PICKERS (50-150). Pce. wk. rates. To work 7 days p.w. weather permitting. Hours 8am-10pm. Campsite available. M.p.w. 1 week between late June and early August. Harvests include strawberries, raspberries, blackcurrants and gooseberries. Applications by 1 June to the Manager, Ashton Fruit Farm. (O)

C. FRANCIS LTD: 13 Knight Street, Pincbeck, Spalding, Lincolnshire (tel 0775-723953).
SOFT FRUIT PICKERS (6). £90 p.w. To work 6-7 hours per day, 5 days p.w. Staff needed from 1 June to 1 October. M.p.w. 4 weeks. B. & L. available at approx. £50 p.w. Applications from January to Michael Bowser, at the above address. (O)

GROVE FARMS (HARWELL): Woodlands, Milton Hill, Abingdon, Oxfordshire OX14 4DP (tel 0235-831575).
FRUIT PICKERS, GENERAL FARM WORKERS. Wages and hours negotiable. Camping facilities may be available. Min. age 16. Staff required from July to October. Applications in April/May to the above address. (O)

HARBOROUGH DIRECT SERVICES: Central Depot, Springfield Street, Market Harborough, Leicestershire LE16 8BD (tel 0858-410363).
ASSISTANT GARDENERS. Approx. £134 p.w. plus bonus. No accommodation. To work 7.30am-4.30pm Mondays to Thursdays, 7.30am-12.30pm on Fridays. Required to undertake grounds maintenance duties throughout a large rural district. Period of work from May to September. Applications to Mr Peter James, D.S.O. Manager, at the above address. (O)

HILLTOP FRUIT FARM: Ledbury, Herefordshire HR8 1LN (tel 0531-2630/2291).
FRUIT PICKERS (100). Strawberry pickers paid pce. wk. rates. Ave. earnings £19-24 per day in 1991. Hours flexible, but usually 7am-3pm, or 5am-1pm in very hot weather. Staff needed for strawberry picking from approx. mid-June to mid-July. Plum, apple and pear pickers paid hourly at Agricultural Wages Board rates, plus bonus. To work from 8am-3pm/4pm. Plum, apple and pear pickers needed from approx. mid-August to mid-October. To work Sunday to Friday. Campsite provided, with showers and covered sitting area. Within walking distance of station, 1 mile from Ledbury. Min. age 18. Applications from May onwards to Mr or Mrs Bickham, Hilltop Fruit Farm. (O)

PENNOXSTONE COURT: Kings Caple, Hereford HR1 4TX (tel 043270-289).
STRAWBERRY PICKERS (35) wanted from mid-June to end September.
RASPBERRY PICKERS (15) wanted for month of July.
PLUM PICKERS (15) wanted from mid-August to end September.
Ave. £20 per, day based on pce. wk. rates. 6 days p.w. No B. & L., though plenty of camping available with full facilities. Applicants should be able to fit in with cheerful, friendly atmosphere. Min. age 18 years. Applications for all pickers to be submitted between April and first week in June, enclosing s.a.e. or IRC, to Mr N. J. Cockburn, Proprietor, Pennoxstone Court. (O)

REDBANK: Ledbury, Herefordshire HR8 2JL (tel 0531-3659).
STRAWBERRY PICKERS (many). Good pce. wk. rates offered to those willing to do some hard work. Friendly, cosmopolitan atmosphere, beautiful surroundings and 1 mile from town. Facilities provided include a campsite, showers and common room. Applicants must be over 16 and bring own tent. Period of work end of April to end of October. Applications (with s.a.e.) to Mr Angus Davison, at the above address. (O)

SIDDINGTON FARM: Leadington, Ledbury, Herefordshire HR8 2LN (tel 0531-2664).
STRAWBERRY PICKERS (30). Pce. wk. rates. Hours: 8am-2pm. Sunday to Friday inclusive. Some evening work. Campsite provided for those bringing their own camping and cooking equipment. Kitchen, TV room, toilets and showers are provided. No fruit picking experience necessary. Friendly working atmosphere. Period of work from third week in June for approx. 4 weeks. Applications to C. Houlbrooke, at the above address.

D. R. STOKES: Yew Tree Cottage, High Street, Longborough, Moreton on the Marsh (tel 0451-31126).

FRUIT WORKERS (20). £2.75 per hour. Work variable, including fruit picking, general orchard work, weeding, etc. Pce. wk. may be included. To work from 8am-5pm Monday-Friday, depending on availability and demand of fruit. Staff needed from mid-June to the end of August. M.p.w. 2 weeks. Camping area available. Applications from 1 May to R. S. Tonge, at the above address. (O)

UNIFORMATIC: Brockham, Birlingham, Pershore, Worcestershire WR10 3AA (tel 0386-750732).
ASPARAGUS CUTTERS/PACKERS (6). £3.50 per hour, with special bonus at the end of the season. To work 6 days p.w., guaranteed min. of 5 hours per day. Period of work from 20 April to 10 June. Accommodation available at a charge of £28, but must provide own food. Interview not always necessary. Applications from early April to Major Porter, at the above address. (O)

Sport

CONGLETON BOROUGH COUNCIL: Sandbank Leisure Centre, Middlewich Road, Sandbank, Cheshire CW11 9EA (tel 0270-767120).
CENTRE ASSISTANTS (4/6). Wages approx. £3.25 per hour if aged 18+; approx. £2.35 if 17 and approx. £2.11 if 16. Duties to include supervising swimming pool and organizing childrens' playscheme for 10-15 h.p.w. Min. age 17. Period of work from mid-July to the end of August. Applicants must hold Bronze Medallion with Advanced Resuscitation, or RLSS Lifeguard Bronze Medallion. Applications to the Personnel Manager, at the above address. (O)

NORTH KESTEVEN SPORTS CENTRE: Moor Lane, North Hykeham, Lincon LN6 9AX.
PART TIME SWIMMING POOL ATTENDANTS. £2.95 per hour. Uniform provided. Various hours, between 10am and 4.30pm weekdays, with opportunities to work evenings and weekends, including bank holidays. Duties: lifeguard, cleaning changing area. Must have RLSS Pool Bronze Medallion and Advanced Resuscitation certificate. Previous experience preferred. Ages: 18-39 years. Staff required July to September. Applications to K. Leggard, at the North Kesteven Sports Centre. (O)

NORTHFIELD FARM: Flash, nr Buxton, Derbyshire SK17 0SW (tel 0298-22543). Riding centre and working farm.
TREK LEADERS (2). Approx. £75 p.w. B. & L. free. To work 8.30am-5pm, $5\frac{1}{2}$ days per week. Work available from April to September/October. M.p.w. 2/3 months. Applicants must be competent riders, good with people, and preferably car drivers. Also, must be prepared to help out on the farm when needed. All applicants should be available for interview. Applications from

March to Mrs E. Andrews, Northfield Farm, at the above address. (O)

PGL YOUNG ADVENTURE LTD: Alton Court, Penyard Lane (874), Ross-on-Wye, Herefordshire HR9 5NR (tel 0989-764211). Over 2,500 staff needed to assist in the running of activity centres in Shropshire, Oxford and the Wye Valley.
INSTRUCTORS in canoeing, sailing, windsurfing, pony trekking, hill walking, fencing, archery, judo, rifle shooting, fishing, motorsports, arts and crafts, drama, English language and many other activities. Pocket money from £30 p.w. Full B. & L. provided. Min. age 18 years.
GROUP LEADERS to take responsiblity for small groups of children and ensure that they get the most out of their holiday. Pocket money from £30 p.w. Free B. & L. Min age 20 years.
Previous experience of working with children necessary. Vacancies available for short or long periods between February and October. Requests for application forms to the Personnel Department, PGL. (O)

RUSHCLIFFE LEISURE CENTRE: Boundary Road, West Bridgford, Nottingham.
POOL ATTENDANTS for lifeguard duties.
CENTRE ATTENDANTS for general duties.
Wages for above positions approx. £3.38 per hour. Applicants must hold RLSS Bronze Medallion.
CATERING STAFF. Wages approx. £3.10 per hour. RLSS Bronze Medallion necessary.
CHILDREN'S HOLIDAY ACTIVITY LEADERS. Wages approx. £3.24 per hour. Must be trained teachers.
Hours for the above positions by arrangement. Period of work July to August.
Applications to the Personnel Manager, at the above address. (O)

SURFACE WATERSPORTS: Rutland Water, Whitwell Bay Sailing Centre, Empingham, Leicesteshire LE15 8QS (tel 078 086-464). Situated on 3,000 acres of inland water. Also at Ferry Meadows, Ham Lane, Orton Waterville, Peterborough PE2 0UU (tel 0733-234418).
WINDSURFING INSTRUCTORS (2). £120 p.w. basic. Min. 40 h.p.w. with possible o/t. No B. & L. Must have RYA boardsailing or RYA sailing instructor's certificate or RYA sports boat handling or equivalent. Duties include rigging and de-rigging of sailboards and dinghies, windsurfing instruction and rescue work. Flexible attitude required. M.p.w. 2 months between April and September.
Applications from March to Mr Dave Hales, Proprietor, Surface Watersports. (O)

TENNIS COACHING INTERNATIONAL: Woodlands Tennis Centre, Thurleigh Road, Milton Ernest, Bedford MK44 1RF (tel 02302-2914).
TENNIS INSTRUCTORS (4). £135 p.w. Hours: 8.30am-12.30pm, 2.30-4.30pm or 7.30-9.30pm, over 6 or 6½ days p.w. Free B. & L. Candidates with LTA Part I, II or III coaching qualification preferred; however, county standard players also accepted. Knowledge of French, German or Spanish an asset. Also positions for teachers of languages with tennis experience, and domestic staff. Period or work 1, 2, 3, 4 or 5 weeks between 10 June and end of August, as well as the Easter vacation. Applications a.s.a.p. enclosing s.a.e. to Mr Peter Smith, Principal, Tennis Coaching International. (If reply not received within 3-4 weeks of application, positions may be presumed closed.) (O)

WHITE HORSE TRAIL RIDES: Sherbourne Cottage, Uffington, Oxon SN7 7RA (tel 036 782-783).
ESCORT RIDER/STABLE ASSISTANT (1). £40 p.w. To work approx. 40 h.p.w. including weekends, with 2 days off p.w. in lieu. Work involves escorting customers on horseback on long trail rides, and generally assisting with looking after the horses. Must have a full driving licence, and be experienced in horse-riding and care. Period of work 1 March to 31 October. M.p.w. 1 month. Age: 16+. Accommodation not available. Applicants must be able to attend an interview. Applications a.s.a.p. to David Morfee or Amanda Gooseman, at the above address. (O)

Language Schools

ANGLO-WORLD OXFORD: 108 Banbury Road, Oxford OX2 6JU (tel 0865-515808; fax 0865-310668).
NIGHT WARDENS (3) to supervise residential accommodation for an EFL summer course at an Oxford college. Wages approx. £95 p.w. plus free B. & L. and access to sports and library facilities. To work from 10pm-8am. Period of work from 28 June to 16 August. Tact and common sense are necessary. Min. age 21. Applications to the Principal at the above address.

CONCORD COLLEGE: Acton Burnell Hall, Shrewsbury, Shropshire SY5 7PF (tel 06944-632).
TEACHING STAFF (40) to teach EFL, dance, drama, physical and outdoor education and arts and crafts. Wages £420-805 per 4-week period, plus B. & L. Duties include residential & pastoral care of students aged 10-18. Period of work beginning of July to late August. Min. qualification usually a degree but undergraduates will be considered. PGCE or EFL qualifications an advantage. Applications to the Director of Summer Courses at the above address.

EUROPA SCHOOL OF ENGLISH: Glenfield, Boars Hill, Oxford (tel 0865-735370). English language tuition given at various locations within Oxford city limits.
PART-TIME TEFL TEACHERS (16) to teach weekday mornings. Approx £140 p.w. Must be graduates or undergraduates with classroom experience of TEFL.
ENGLISH TEACHERS (12) for residential course. Approx. £225 p.w. including free B. & L. Must be aged 22+ and have some sporting ability (tennis and sailing are most useful), and preferably some knowledge of TEFL. Periods of work: 3 week courses at Easter and during July and August.
ASSISTANT TENNIS COACHES to teach and supervise young foreign players, with some social tennis too. Applicants must have good club playing record and some coaching experience. Foreign applicants welcome. Period of work 2 weeks at Easter and 6-7 weeks in July and August. Applications for above positions to Mr A. Horwood, at the above address.
PART-TIME GENERAL DOMESTIC ASSISTANT to help with cooking, housework, etc. Live-in, with meals and study bedroom provided. £75 p.w. Hours by arrangement. Foreign applicants welcome. Period of work 15-14 June to 18 August.
Applications to Mrs J. M. Horwood, Europa School of English. Interviews for all positions are held between January and April.

LIVING LANGUAGE CENTRE: Highcliffe House, Clifton Gardens, Folkestone, Kent CT20 2EF (tel 0303-58536).
EFL TEACHERS for centre in Oxford. £150 p.w. depending on qualifications. Free accommodation available. Duties include teaching in the morning and afternoon. Some evening activities also. Period of work 12 July to 29 August. All teachers must be graduates with EFL qualifications. Applications to Mr Mackenzie-Bowie, Living Language Centre.

M M OXFORD STUDY SERVICES: 44 Blenheim Drive, Oxford OX2 8DQ (tel 0865-513788). Runs English Language Schools in Oxford.
EFL TEACHERS (35). From £175 p.w. plus B. & L. Must be graduates with experience of teaching English to foreigners. RSA Prep. certificate preferred. Also some help with social programme (sports and outings). M.p.w. 6 weeks between 1 July and 10 September.
SOCIAL/SPORTS ORGANIZERS (20). £95 p.w. for 6 days p.w. Full residential accommodation available or subsidised accommodation outside. Must be practical, responsible and able to work on own initiative. Experience with children and teenagers essential. Own transport desirable but not essential. General duties include helping with administration of activities programme (e.g. sports, discos, excursions, airport pick-ups, etc). Min. age 21. M.p.w. 6 weeks

from 28 June to 10 September.
Applications a.s.a.p. to M. E. Misirlizade, Course Director, M M Oxford Study
Services.

OXFORD HOUSE SCHOOL OF ENGLISH: 67 High Street, Wheatley, Oxford
OX9 1XT (tel 08677-4786 or 0865-874786).
EFL TEACHERS (4). Approx £200 p.w. To teach for 21 h.p.w. in groups of
up to 12, plus 1 afternoon supervising activities/sports and some evening and
social duties. B. & L. available at £80 p.w. half board. Applicants must have
good references, plenty of experience and TEFL training (e.g. RSA certificate).
Teaching from lower intermediate to advanced standard. Some small group
specialist teaching possible. M.p.w. 3 weeks between 3 July and 22 September.
Jobs suitable for native speakers only. Applications a.s.a.p. to Mr R. I. C.
Vernède, Principal, Oxford House School of English.

SEVERNVALE CENTRAL LANGUAGE ACADEMY: 23D Dogpole,
Shrewsbury, Shropshire SY1 1ES. English courses for foreign students held
in Shrewsbury.
EFL TEACHERS (5-10). £110-200 p.w. To teach 15-27 h.p.w., over 4 days (not
weekends). Accommodation (family full board or self-catering) can be arranged.
TEFL qualification and experience a necessity (e.g. RSA certificate). Period
of work June to September. Applications from February to Mr J. W. T. Rogers,
Principal, Severnvale Central Language Academy.

ST JOSEPH'S HALL: Junction Road, Oxford OX4 2UJ (tel 0865-711829).
EFL TEACHERS (30) for up to 30 hours teaching p.w. plus occasional extra
duties including giving informal talks, and supervising full day excursions and
evening duties. Wages £225 p.w. (min.) plus additional payments, e.g. £12 for
giving talks or £20 for supervising full day excursions. Applicants should have
a university degree and at least RSA Prep. Cert. qualifications; previous
experience of EFL work preferred.
SOCIAL MONITORS (6) for duties including supervising sports activities,
visits and excursions, meeting students at airports and accompanying them on
the school coach. Wages depend on the hours worked: average £130 p.w. To
work 2 out of the morning, afternoon and evening sessions per day on weekdays
and one at weekends. Applicants must be aged at least 18. Period of work by
arrangement between June and August. Applicants from America, Canada,
Australia and New Zealand will be considered. Accommodation not provided.
Applications to Mark Sandham, Course Director, at the above address.

THE SWAN SCHOOL OF ENGLISH: 11 Guild Street, Stratford-upon-Avon,
Warwickshire CV37 6RE (tel 0789-269161).

EFL TEACHERS (1/2). £210 p.w. Hours: 9am-5pm. 23 hours of teaching p.w. Must have min. 1 year of teaching experience. TEFL qualification essential. References and c.v. required. M.p.w. 3 weeks between June and September. Applicants from other English-speaking countries considered if available for interview. Applications from May to Mrs A. Holmes, Vice-Principal, The Swan School.

WARNBOROUGH COLLEGE: Boars Hill, Oxford OX1 5ED (tel 0865-730901; fax 0865-327796).
TEACHERS OF ENGLISH as a foreign language. Payment on an hourly rate. Teaching beginners, intermediate and advanced levels. Must have university degree, TEFL qualification and experience. Applications to the Director, English Language Programme, Warnborough College.

NORTH

Cleveland
Cumbria
Durham
Greater Manchester
Humberside
Isle of Man

Berwick-on-Tweed

Newcastle
Carlisle
Durham
Middlesbrough
Lake District
Scarborough
Douglas
York
Hull
Blackpool
Leeds
Grimsby
Liverpool Manchester Sheffield

Lancashire
Merseyside
Northumberland
Tyne and Wear
Yorkshire

'The North' describes a vast area, and the different regions it covers offer various hopes and hazards for job-hunting. The most common jobs arising during the summer season are those related to tourism. There are opportunities in the hotel and catering trade along the East Coast, particularly in Bridlington, Filey, Scarborough, Whitby, and further north, in South Shields, Whitley Bay and Berwick. In North Tyne, hotels will often provide accommodation. In South Tyne, bed and breakfast can usually be found, but further south, accommodation in seaside resorts is not easily come by. Hotel and catering work can be found inland too, in the Yorkshire dales, the Lake District, in holiday centres as well as hotels. The main centre on the West coast is Blackpool which has large numbers of vacancies for its many hotels, amusement arcades and fun parks. Morecambe and Lytham St. Annes are also popular tourist haunts, and the Royal Golf Club at Lytham St. Annes may take on people for summer tournaments.

Large factories, such as Rowntree Mackintosh in York, recruit staff over the summer and from September onwards to cater for Christmas sales. Joseph Terry in York, Hemsworth and Pontefract have vacancies making chocolate for Christmas. British Sugar in Scunthorpe recruit in September, as do Foxes Biscuits in Batley. Industries in the Durham area frequently take people on over the summer, particularly Glaxo Ltd, Mattesons and Mono Containers.

KP foods in Cleveland may also employ people to cover holiday shortages. On a small scale, fruit pickers are needed in Northumberland at farms, such as Whinnetley and Brockbushes, and also around the Scunthorpe area.

Various Local Authorities such as Gateshead, South Tyneside and Sunderland may have work on playschemes, or need holiday cover in their many clerical departments; the Civil Service may also take on casual appointments. Newcastle and other large towns are the best places to try for retail, and other places recommended for temporary summer work are Alwick, Banburgh, Corbridge, Haydon Bridge, Hexham, Seahouses, Barnard Castle, Durham and Redcar.

Jobcentres report that speculative approaches made direct to companies tend to be the most successful, although most Local Authority vacancies continue to be advertised through Jobcentres. The best approach would probably be to use a combination of the local Jobcentre services with direct independent approaches.

Business and Industry

GOOD NEWS TRAVEL: Freetown Way, Hull (tel 0482-26755).
PSV DRIVERS (6) to work in Britain (and/or abroad). £30 per day plus tips and living expenses. Hours by arrangement. Period of work June to September. Applicants should be aged 21 or over with a full PSV drivers' licence (manual). Applications to the Personnel Manager at the above address. (O)

JOHN ARDERN RESEARCH: 12 Cateaton Street, Hanging Bridge, Manchester M3 1SQ (tel 061-832 4209).
Students and others interested in market research should contact John Ardern, Senior Research Partner, **as early as possible**.

LISHMAN SIDWELL CAMPBELL & PRICE: Becket's House, Market Place, Ripon, North Yorkshire HG4 1BZ. Opportunities also at Harrogate, Boroughbridge, Wetherby, Knaresborough, Northallerton, Darlington, Leeds, York, Thirsk and Bradford.
CLERKS (8). Wages vary according to age, experience, etc. Hours: $7\frac{1}{2}$ hours per day, 5 days p.w. Applicants should be studying for accountancy qualifications. Applications to Mr B. Price, FCA, FCCA, FBIM.

Children

FULWOOD LEISURE CENTRE: Black Bull Lane, Fulwood, Preston, Lancashire PR2 4YA (tel 0772-716085).
PLAYLEADERS. Approx. £2.26 per hour. To work 9am-5pm Monday to Friday. Required to supervise and become involved with a wide range of sports,

games, arts and crafts for 5-15 year olds. No specific qualifications necessary. Period of work 9 July to 31 August. Application forms available from the above address, or write giving full details.

PRESTON BOROUGH COUNCIL: Guild Hall, Lancaster Road, Preston, Lancashire (tel 0772-203456).
SUPERVISORS (12) to be in charge of play leaders at 11 sites.
PLAYLEADERS (60) to organize a wide range of activities, including sports, games, art and craft, and drama, and to take the children on trips off site. Wages to be arranged. Period of work mid-July to end of August. Approx. 30 h.p.w., Mondays to Fridays. Min. age 18. Contact the Personnel Department at the above address for an application form.

ROSSENDALE BOROUGH COUNCIL: 35 Kay Street, Rowtenstall, Rossendale, Lancs BB4 7LS (tel 0706-217777).
PLAYSCHEME LEADERS (9). £95 p.w. To work from 20 July to 17 August.
PLAYSCHEME WORKERS (27). £85 p.w. To work from 20 July to 24 August.
PLAYSCHEME ORGANISER. £130 per week plus car allowance. To work from 22 June to 14 August.
Hours from 8.30am-4pm Monday-Friday. Applicants should have empathy with children, good organizational skills, patience and tact. Applications to the Personnel Officer at the above address.

Holiday Centres and Amusements

ALLEN (PARKFOOT) LTD: Howton Road, Pooley Bridge, Penrith, Cumbria CA20 2NA (tel 07684-86309). Caravan site.
BAR STAFF to help the head barman, and collect and wash glasses. Hours from 6pm-midnight. Min. age 18 years.
KITCHEN ASSISTANTS (2) to help the head cook prepare meals, clear tables, operate the dishwasher and work the till. Hours 8am-2pm and 6pm-11pm.
COOK/CHEF. For preparing cooked breakfasts, lunches and evening meals. Hours 8am-2pm and 6-11pm. Wages negotiable according to experience. Accommodation can be arranged if necessary. Period of work Easter, May Bank Holidays and from July to mid-September. Applications, enclosing colour photo, details of work experience and dates of availability, to Mrs B. Mowbray or Mrs F. Bell, Parkfoot Caravan Park. (O)

BLACKPOOL WINTERGARDENS AND OPERA HOUSE: Church Street, Blackpool, Lancashire FY1 1HW (tel 0253-25252).
BAR STAFF. £2.60 per hour. To work up to 39 hours over 6 days per week, including evenings and weekends. Should be aged over 18. Experience beneficial,

and applicants should be pleasant and smart.
CATERING STAFF: £2.74 per hour, £2.50 if aged 16-18 years.
THEATRE USHER/ETTES. Wages on commission. To work 5 or 6 evenings a week, including weekends. No experience necessary but applicants should be pleasant and smart.
STAGE HANDS. £2.75 per hour. To shift scenery, props, etc. Some experience beneficial.
BOX OFFICE CASHIERS. £2.89 per hour. To work 40 hours over 6 days per week, including weekends. Should have some experience of handling cash, dealing with customers and a pleasant telephone manner.
PLAY ASSISTANTS. £2.68 per hour. Should have some experience of working with children. Some knowledge of First Aid would be useful.
All rates of pay reviewed in April. Must be available for 3 months between July and November. A work permit is essential for those applying from overseas. Applications in June to the Personnel Manager, Blackpool Wintergardens.

BROWN RIGG VENTURE CENTRE: Bellingham, Hexham, Northumberland NE48 2HR (tel 0434-220272).
GENERAL ASSISTANTS. £15-30 p.w. Free B. & L. Min. age 17 years. M.p.w. 4 weeks between May and October. Applications to Mr Donald R. MacLeod, Proprietor, Brown Rigg. (O)

CAMELOT ADVENTURE THEME PARK: Charnock Richard, Chorley, Preston, Lancashire PR7 5PL (tel 0257-453044).
RIDE OPERATORS and RETAIL/CATERING/JANITORIAL/ADMISSIONS/ ARCADE STAFF. Wages according to age. To work up to 39 h.p.w. No accommodation available. Min. age 16. Applications a.s.a.p. to the Personnel Manager, Camelot Adventure Theme Park.

FARSYDE STUD & RIDING CENTRE: Robin Hood's Bay, Whitby, North Yorkshire YO22 4UG (tel 0947-880249).
GENERAL ASSISTANTS (2) for support duties for residential riding holidays. £2.50 per hour. Min. of 20 h.p.w. £30 p.w. for accommodation in house, cottage or caravan. Applicants must be willing, self-motivated, cheerful, non-smokers, adaptable, able to relate well to teenagers and adults, and enjoy country life. M.p.w. 6 weeks between May/June and September/October. Applications to Mrs A. Green, Owner/Manager, Farsyde Stud & Riding Centre. (O)

FLAMINGOLAND ZOO AND FUN PARK: Kirby Misperton, North Yorkshire YO17 04X (tel 065 386-287).
BAR STAFF (10), RIDE OPERATORS (15), SECURITY STAFF (5). Approx.

£140 p.w.
CATERING STAFF. Approx. £135 p.w.
Rates of pay shown for 21 years and above. To work 6 days p.w. plus holiday
entitlement. B. & L. available at £15-25 p.w. Staff needed from mid-July to
mid-September. M.p.w. 4 weeks. Applications from mid-June to Steve
Crampton, General Manager, at the above address. (O)

M. B. & J. GOODWIN LTD: Low Skirlington Caravan Park, Skipsea, nr
Driffield, Humberside YO25 8SY (tel 026 286-213/466).
ASSISTANT COOK, BAR ASSISTANT to work on a holiday caravan site.
£90 p.w. or by arrangement. Normal hours include weekends and evenings.
Free accommodation provided in a caravan. Period of work from June to
September. Applications to M. B. & J. Goodwin Ltd. (O)

HOLKER ESTATES LTD: Cark-in-Cartmel, nr Grange-over-Sands, Cumbria
(tel 053 95-58328). Manages Holker Hall, a stately home with gardens,
exhibitions and deer park.
PART TIME ASSISTANTS (6-10) for work in cafe, hall or car park. Approx.
£2.70 per hour. Must be friendly and helpful. Staff needed from Easter to end
of October. M.p.w. 4 months. No accommodation available. Applicants must
be available for interview. Applications from end of January to Mrs C. Johnson,
at the above address. (O)

LIGHTWATER VALLEY THEME PARK: North Stainley, Ripon, North
Yorkshire HG4 3HT (tel 0765-635321).
CATERING STAFF (50), CLEANING STAFF and GENERAL ASSISTANTS
(50), KIOSK SALES STAFF (50), RIDE STAFF (80). To work full/part time
from Easter to the end of the season. Wages to be arranged. The amount of
work depends on the number of visitors, but full time work is generally available.
Applications to the General Manager, at the above address, as soon as possible.

NORTH YORK MOORS ADVENTURE CENTRE: Park House, Ingleby
Cross, nr Osmotherley, Northallerton, North Yorkshire DL6 3PE (tel 060
982-571).
INSTRUCTORS/GENERAL ASSISTANTS (2) to help with day to day running
of activity centre, e.g. equipment repairs, general building work, etc. Driving
licence required. To instruct in rock climbing, canoeing, caving, orienteering
and camping. Min. age 19 years.
COOK'S ASSISTANT (1) to help with catering for visitors (guests do their
own washing up). Possibility of helping with instruction or joining in with
outdoor pursuits.

Wages and hours by arrangement. Free B & L. Period of work May to end of September. Applications, with s.a.e., to Mr Ewen Bennett, North York Moors Adventure Centre. (O)

OUTWARD BOUND CITY CHALLENGE: 10 Rodney Street, Liverpool L1 2TE (tel 051-707 0202). Courses, based in Coventry or Liverpool, for young people aged 17-24 who wish to take part in intensive voluntary service placements within the community.
TUTORIAL STAFF (approx. 10) needed to run residential training courses. Tutors liaise with placements and run evening group sessions to draw out learning points from the experiences of the participants. Wages negotiable according to experience. Full B. & L. provided. Tutors must be prepared to live at the residential base for the duration of the course, and work long hours with little free time. Periods of work are approx. 29 May-16 June and/or 31 July-16 August in Coventry, or 17 June-4 August and/or 11 September-29 September in Liverpool. Min. age 23. Applicants must have teaching/social work/youth work qualifications and experience, and need a good understanding of group work and counselling. A clean driving licence would also be an advantage. Applications to the above address.

Hotels and Catering

ALNMOUTH HOTELS LTD: The Schooner Hotel, Northumberland Street, Alnmouth, Northumberland NE66 2RS (tel 0665-830216). Alnmouth Hotels Ltd runs two 24-bedroom hotels.
WATIING STAFF (3), CHAMBER STAFF (2) and BAR PERSONS (2). £3 per hour gross on set shifts. To work 40-45 h.p.w. There is a high tipping potential. Accommodation is available at a cost of not more than £2.55 per day. M.p.w. 4 weeks, between mid-June and mid-September. Applications a.s.a.p. to J. Orde, The Manager, Alnmouth Hotels Ltd. (O)

THE BLACK BULL: Reeth, Richmond, North Yorkshire DL11 6SZ (tel 0748-84213). Small country pub and hotel.
WAITING STAFF (3). Duties will include preparation of salads and sandwiches and microwave cookery.
BAR STAFF (1). £2.60 per hour for 39 h.p.w. basic, with some o/t possible. Two days off p.w. B. & L. available at £15 p.w. M.p.w. Easter to Spring Bank Holiday or mid-July to end of September/October. Applicants should preferably be available for interview. Applications enclosing s.a.e., from 1 March, to Mrs E. M. Sykes, Proprietor, at the above address.

BRACKENRIGG HOTEL: Watermill, Penrith, CA11 0LP (tel 0768-486206). GENERAL ASSISTANTS (3) for bar work, waiting at table and some cleaning work. Wages by arrangement. Accommodation is provided (may be necessary to share a room). To work 45 h.p.w. over 5 days. Hours vary every day and o/t is paid. Two days off per week. Period of work from May to November. Applicants should be aged over 18. Training is provided so experience is not necessary. Applications to the Manager at the above address. (O)

BRATHAY HALL TRUST: Ambleside, Cumbria LA22 0HP (tel 053 94-33042). A residential training centre. DOMESTIC/GENERAL ASSISTANTS. Up to 10 needed for general and domestic work such as washing up, potato peeling and housework on a grand scale. Wages £55 p.w. Applicants must be prepared to work hard, but there are opportunities to take part in outdoor activities. To work 40 h.p.w. with 2 consecutive days off. Free B. & L. Min. age 17. Staff needed all year round. M.p.w. 3 months. Applicants must be available for interview. Applications anytime to Miss Denise Spooner, Housekeeper, at the above address. (O)

CHADWICK HOTEL: South Promenade, St. Annes-on-Sea, Lancashire FY8 1NP (tel 0253-720061). GENERAL ASSISTANTS (2). £128 p.w. 5 days p.w. Approx. 44 h.p.w. Hours: 7.30am-2.15pm, 5-9pm. No accommodation available. Min. age 18 years. Post suitable for second year catering students or similar, with 2 years experience and good references. M.p.w. 10 weeks between April and 1 November. Applications from February to Mr Corbett, Manager, Chadwick Hotel. (O)

CRAIGLANDS HOTEL: Cowpasture Road, Ilkley, West Yorkshire (tel 0943-607676). WAITING STAFF (2), BAR PERSON (1), CHAMBER STAFF (2), GENERAL ASSISTANTS (2), GARDENER (1). Wages approx. £2.56-3.00 per hour, depending on experience. Period of work from June to early September, or longer. To work 35-39 h.p.w. Min. age 16. Applicants need good social skills, to be punctual, and to have a smart appearance, and a good sense of humour. Applications to the above address. (O)

FEVERSHAM ARMS HOTEL: Helmsley, Yorkshire YO6 5AG (tel 0439-70766). GENERAL ASSISTANTS. From £90-100 p.w. depending on age (plus tips). Approx. 8 hours per day, 5 days p.w. Free B. & L. (share room), with central heating and colour TV. Accommodation available for women only. Age 18-25 years. Non-smokers. Good health important. Must be cheerful, hard working country lover. Use of hotel tennis court and swimming pool. M.p.w. 12 weeks between February and December. Preference given to those who can stay longer. Applications a.s.a.p. to Mrs Rowan de Aragues', Feversham Arms Hotel.

FORTE POST HOUSE HOTEL: Tadcaster Road, York YO2 2QF (tel 0904-707921).
GENERAL WAITING STAFF. £2.90 per hour. To work hours as required: generally 40 per week, straight or split shifts. No board or accommodation available. M.p.w. 10-12 weeks between Easter and October. Applicants should be aged 18 or over, of smart appearance and an outgoing personality, and should have relevant previous experience. Overseas applicants must have a good knowledge of English. Applications to Mr Neil Swain, Personnel Manager, Forte Post House Hotel. (O)

THE GRASMERE HOTEL: Grasmere, nr Ambleside, Cumbria LA22 9TA (tel 053 94-35277). A very busy 12-bedroom hotel.
ASSISTANT COOK (1). £130 p.w.
GENERAL ASSISTANT (1). £110 p.w. Duties include waiting, bar work, housekeeping, reception, office work and some kitchen work.
All positions work 40 h.p.w. 5 days p.w. Living-in accommodation available for women only. Own room with TV provided. Min. age 18. Preferably college trained or at least 1 year's experience. M.p.w. 6 months, April to October. Applications to Mr Ian Mansie, Proprietor, at the Grasmere Hotel.

KING'S ARMS HOTEL: Market Place, Askrigg, Wensleydale, North Yorkshire DL8 3HQ (tel 0969-50258).
GENERAL ASSISTANTS (2). £100 p.w. plus share of tips. To work 40 h.p.w. B. & L. available for £20 p.w. Min. age 18 years. Previous hotel experience essential. M.p.w. 6 months between May and November. Applications from April to Mr or Mrs Hopwood, Proprietors, King's Arms Hotel. (O)

LEEMING HOUSE HOTEL: Watermillock, Ullswater, nr Penrith, Cumbria CA11 0JJ (tel 07684-86622).
WAITERS/WAITRESSES (4). Silver service experience needed.
BARMEN/PORTERS (2). Previous bar work experience required.
CHAMBER STAFF (4).
All staff paid £95 p.w. To work 5 days p.w. with consecutive days off. Accommodation provided (some shared) plus all meals. Ages: 18-25 years. M.p.w. 12 weeks between 1 March and 5 November. Applications from 1 February to the Personnel Manager, Leeming House Hotel. (O)

LINDETH FELL HOTEL: Bowness-on-Windermere, Cumbria LA23 3JP (tel 09662-3286). A country house hotel.
GENERAL ASSISTANTS (3). £100 p.w. To work 40 h.p.w. Duties include helping in the dining room, bedrooms and bar. B. & L. provided. M.p.w. June to September between 1 March and 15 November. Applicants must be available for interview. EC nationals welcome. Applications from 1 January to P. A. Kennedy, owner, at the above address. (O)

MALLYAN SPOUT HOTEL: Goathland, near Whitby, Yorkshire (tel 094 786-341/206). Hotel with predominantly young staff, in beautiful quiet countryside.
WAITERS/WAITRESSES (2), KITCHEN ASSISTANTS (2), BEDROOM STAFF. £90 p.w. To work 40 h.p.w over 5 days p.w. Free B. & L. Intelligent workers preferred. M.p.w. 6 months between March and November. Applications with s.a.e. to Mrs Heslop, Mallyan Spout Hotel. (O)

THE MANOR COUNTRY GUEST HOUSE: Acaster Malbis, York YO2 1UL (tel 0904-706723 from 9am to 9pm).
WAITERS/WAITRESSES, GARDEN/WOODLAND WORKER. Wages to be arranged. Scale charge made for full B. & L. Min. age 16 years. No experience necessary. M.p.w. 6 weeks between mid-March and end of October. Applicants able to work at Easter particularly welcome. Interview necessary. Single applicants **only**, enclosing s.a.e. and returnable photograph (essential) to the Manageress, The Manor Country Guest House.

MOTEL LEEMING LTD: Bedale, North Yorkshire DL8 1DT (tel 0677-23611). Part of Leeming Service Area (A1/A684 Intersection).
GENERAL ASSISTANTS (2). 5 days p.w. Must be hotel or catering students.
KITCHEN ASSISTANTS (3). Split and straight shifts over 5 days. Must be catering students.
RECEPTIONIST. Must have hotel experience.
SENIOR WAITING STAFF (2). Wages plus tips. Split shifts, 5 days p.w. Must be hotel or catering student with experience in silver service.
OTHER WAITING STAFF (3). Wages plus tips. 5 days p.w. Must have experience in silver service.
BARMAN/MAID (1). Split shifts. 5 days p.w. Must have previous bar and cash handling experience.
SHOP ASSISTANTS (2). Straight shifts, 5 or 6 days. Must have cash handling experience.
CAFE ASSISTANTS (6). Straight and split shifts over 5 days.
CAFE ASSISTANTS-NIGHT SHIFT (2). Straight shifts, 5 nights p.w.

Wages to be arranged. B. & L. available. Min. age 18 years. M.p.w. 8 weeks between June and October. Applications from April to C. A. Les, Motel Leeming Ltd. (O)

PENNINGTON ARMS HOTEL: Ravenglass, Cumbria (tel 0229-222/626). GENERAL ASSISTANTS (4) to wait at table, work in the bar, clean, do laundry and wash up. £65-90 p.w. 39-50 h.p.w. Hours: 7am-2pm/4pm and 6-11pm (split shifts); noon/2pm-11pm. Must work 3 evenings p.w. possibly 4. Free B. & L. Must be willing to share accommodation. Min. age 18 years. M.p.w. 8 weeks between April and October. Applicants should be hardworking and have common sense. Applications including s.a.e. and photo from February to the Pennington Arms Hotel. (O)

POST HOUSE HOTEL: Clayton Road, Newcastle, Staffordshire (tel 0782-717171).
LOUNGE WAITER/WAITRESS (1), RESTAURANT WAITERS/WAITRESSES (3). To work early and late shifts.
BANQUETING WAITERS/WAITRESSES (3). To work late shifts of 3/4 hours. Wages approx. £2.60 per hour. Accommodation is available. Period of work from the end of June to mid-September. Applicants should be aged at least 18. training will be given. Applications to the Personnel Manager, at the above address.

PREMIER HOTEL: 66 Esplanade, Scarborough, North Yorkshire (tel 0723-361484).
CHEF or EXPERIENCED COMMIS CHEF, and TRAINEE COMMIS CHEF. Must be able to work unsupervised.
GENERAL ASSISTANTS (6) for dining room, bedrooms, general cleaning, bar, kitchen and reception duties. Experience not essential. Wages as per Catering Wages Act plus tips. To work 6 days p.w. B. & L. provided. The hotel particularly welcomes catering students and hotel management students wishing to gain experience in catering. Applications from February onwards to Mr & Mrs R. Jacques, Proprietors, Premier hotel.

THE QUEEN'S HOTEL: Main Street, Keswick, Cumbria CA12 5JF (tel 07687-73333). A 35-bedroom hotel in the heart of the Lake District.
CHAMBER STAFF (1), WAITING STAFF (1), BAR STAFF (2). £100 p.w. 40 h.p.w. No qualifications or experience necessary. Free B. & L. provided. M.p.w. 8 weeks between July and the end of August/September. Applications a.s.a.p. to Mr Peter Williams, Proprietor, The Queen's Hotel. (O)

RED HOUSE HOTEL: nr Keswick, Cumbria CA12 4QA (tel 07687-72211). GENERAL ASSISTANTS. £350+ per month live-in. No experience necessary, but cheerful extroverts preferred. Applicants should be able to work for several months and not just over the summer vacation. Applications **not** before 1 May to V. W. Moor, Red House Hotel. (O)

RED LION INN: Cloughton, Scarborough, Yorks (tel 0723-870702).
BAR TENDER to serve drinks, etc.
KITCHEN ASSISTANT to cook simple meals and manage a small kitchen efficiently.
CHAMBER ASSISTANT to work 2 hours every morning. Wages by arrangement. Accommodation not available. Period of work July to September. Applicants should be aged under 25. Applications to Mrs C. M. Wood or Mr M. Culling at the above address. (O)

THE SAWREY HOTEL: Far Sawrey, Ambleside, Cumbria LA22 0LQ (tel 096 62-3425).
GENERAL ASSISTANTS (4). Wages £85 p.w. plus tips. Hours 8am-3pm, 7.30pm-9.30pm, 5 days p.w. No experience necessary. Car drivers with clean licence preferred. Min. age 18 years. Applications from February to Mr and Mrs Brayshaw, The Sawrey Hotel. (O)

SHARROW BAY HOTEL: Lake Ullswater, Penrith, Cumbria (tel 07684-86301/86483).
STILLROOM ASSISTANTS (3). Approx. £130 p.w. 54 h.p.w. 6 days p.w.
GENERAL ASSISTANTS (up to 6). Min. £130 p.w. hours as above. To work in bedrooms. Free B. & L. Age: 17-30 years. Must have domestic interests and lots of common sense and enjoy living in the country and working in a team of perfectionists. M.p.w. 9 months from early March to end of November. References required. Applications from January to Mr N. R. Lawrence, Manager, Sharrow Bay Hotel. (O)

THE SUN INN and THE GEORGE & DRAGON: Main Street, Dent, Cumbria LA10 5QL.
COOKS/BAR PERSONS. Good hourly rate, plus bonus on bank holidays. Accommodation provided. To work 40 h.p.w. Period of work July to September. Min. age 18. Applications to Mr Martin Stafford, Dent Brewery, Hollins, Cowgill, Dent, Cumbria LA1 5TQ (tel 05875-326). (O)

SWALLOW HILLTOP HOTEL: London Road, Carlisle CA1 2PQ (tel 0228-29255). A busy 3-star, 97-bedroom hotel within easy reach of the Lakes

and Scotland.
HOUSEKEEPING STAFF (2). Wages to be arranged. To work 27 hours over
a 5 day week. Experience preferable.
WAITING STAFF (3). Wages to be arranged. To work 39 hours (not guaranteed)
over a 5 day week. Should have experience and social skills.
PORTER. Wages to be arranged. Max. hours 39, over 5 days. Should be
physically fit and have social skills.
All staff must be presentable. M.p.w. 12 weeks, between May and September.
No accommodation available. Applications from January to Miss Linda Moore,
Operations Manager, at the above address. (O)

WASHINGTON MOAT HOUSE: Stone Cellar Road, High Usworth,
Washington, District 12, Tyne and Wear (tel 091-417 2626).
SILVER SERVICE WAITING STAFF (20). £2.60 per hour. Hours as required.
Must be able to silver serve. Min. age 16.
BAR STAFF. Must have previous experience. Hours as required. Min. age 18.
No accommodation available. Staff needed from July to December. M.p.w. 4
weeks. Applicants must be available for interview. Applications from January
to Miss J. Cahill, at the above address. (O)

THE WHITE HORSE FARM HOTEL: Rosedale Abbey, nr Pickering, N. Yorks
YO18 8SE (tel 075 15-239). Country hotel in the centre of the North York Moors
National Park.
GENERAL ASSISTANTS (4). To work in bar, dining room, kitchens and
bedrooms. £100-120 p.w. and free accommodation. Approx. 48 h.p.w. Female
staff preferred for live-in accommodation. Min. age 18 years. M.p.w. 1 June-30
September. Applications from 1 March to Clare Proctor, Proprietor, The White
Horse Farm Hotel. Replies will **only** be sent to applicants who send a s.a.e. (O)

WHITWELL HALL COUNTRY HOUSE HOTEL: Whitwell-on-the-Hill,
Yorkshire YO6 7JJ (tel 065 381-551).
GENERAL ASSISTANTS (2). To work in the dining room and reception in
the evening. £105 p.w., less a charge for accommodation. To work 45 hours
per 5 day week. Must be experienced. Period of work from June to end of
September. Applications including s.a.e. to Mrs P. F. Milner, Whitwell Hall.

Outdoor

FRUIT OF NORTHUMBRIA LTD: Whinnetley Farm, Haydon Bridge,
Northumberland NE47 6EA (tel 0434-688882).
FRUIT PICKERS (500). Pce. wk. rates, paid on a daily basis. Picking mainly

strawberries. To work in the mornings. Staff needed from approx. 15 June until the end of August. No accommodation available. Applications from May onwards. (O)

LANCASHIRE FRUIT GROWERS: The Gravel, Mere Bow, nr Preston (tel 0772-814804).
FRUIT PICKERS (20). Pce. wk. rates: 10p per lb strawberries, 15p per lb raspberries. To work 6-8 hours per day, 7 days p.w. Min. age 16. No accommodation available. Staff needed from mid-June until mid-August. M.p.w. 2 months. Applications from 1 June to Mr Fairclough, Manager. (O)

Sport

ALSTON TRAINING & ADVENTURE CENTRE: Alston, Cumbria CA9 3DD (tel 0434-381886).
ASSISTANT OUTDOOR ACTIVITY INSTRUCTORS. Free B. & L. provided and free training given. Should have current driving licence. MLC or Canoe qualification useful. Domestic staff also required. Period of work 1 July to 30 September. For further details contact Mr Dave Simpson, Head of Centre, A.T.A.C., at the above address.

BEARSPORTS OUTDOOR CENTRES: Windy Gyle, Belford, Northumberland NE70 7QE (tel 0668-213289).
OUTDOOR PURSUITS INSTRUCTORS and TRAINEES, DOMESTIC ASSISTANTS (12). Pocket money and free B. & L. Long hours, with 1 day off per week. Min. age 18. Must be friendly and interested in outdoor pursuits. Training given. Staff needed all year round. M.p.w. 1 month. Applications any time to Peter Clark, at the above address. (O)

BROWN RIGG VENTURE CENTRE: Bellingham, Hexham, Northumberland NE48 2HR (tel 0434-220272).
RIDING, CANOEING, DINGHY SAILING and BOARDSAILING INSTRUCTORS. From £50 p.w. Free B. & L. Water sports take place on Kielder Water Reservoir. Min. age 20 years. M.p.w. 4 weeks between May and October. Applications, stating relevant qualifications, to Mr Donald R. MacLeod, Brown Rigg. (O)

CAMP WINDERMERE: Low Wray, Ambleside, Cumbria (tel 05394-32163).
A camp catering mainly for children within the ages of 10-17.
OUTDOOR PURSUITS INSTRUCTORS (12). Required to assist qualified instructors and act as camp counsellors. Applicants should ideally have experience in canoeing, walking, sailing and climbing, but this is not essential.

Free B. & L. is provided in return for enthusiastic and hard work. Staff will be given one day off a week. Instructors are required from May to September, the m.p.w. being 1 month. Applications after 1 January, to the Chief Instructor, Camp Windermere.

NORTHUMBRIA HORSE HOLIDAYS: East Castle, Annfield Plain, Stanley, Co. Durham DH9 8PH (tel 0207-230555/235354). A horse-riding centre that offers fully catered holidays for riders of all abilities.
POST TRAIL LEAERS (6). £50 p.w. Outgoing, pleasant personality needed, plus good horse-riding skills and knowledge.
RIDING INSTRUCTORS (4). £75 p.w. Must have British Horse Society Instructors Certificate.
HOTEL STAFF (10) to work as cleaners, waiting and bar staff, and cooks. Wages from £40 p.w. Must be able to work to a high standard. Free B. & L. is available. Period of work Easter to end of October, with m.p.w. 1 month. Applications a.s.a.p. to H. Dodd or J. M. Davies, at the above address. (O)

THE VENTURE CENTRE: Lewaigue Farm, Maughold, Isle of Man (tel 0624-814240). Adventure training centre giving introductory instruction in outdoor activities to children aged 9-15.
INSTRUCTORS (3). Wage according to experience. Hours depend on groups under instruction; 7-day week at times. Free B. & L. Min. age 23 years. Essential training given to suitable candidates. M.p.w. 2 months between March and September. Applications a.s.a.p. to Mr D. Read, Director, The Venture Centre. (O)

WATERSPLASH WORLD: North Bay, Scarborough, Yorkshire (tel 0723-372744).
LIFE GUARDS (10). £2.10 per hour. Must have life saving certificates.
LOCKER ATTENDANTS 96). £1.90 per hour.
Approx. 45 h.p.w. Applications from either sex are welcome. Period of work from the end of May to mid-September. No accommodation provided. Applications to Mr Samples, Watersplash World. (O)

WEAR VALLEY DISTRICT COUNCIL: Civic Centre, Crook, County Durham (tel 0388-765555 ext 213).
RELIEF POOL/LEISURE ATTENDANTS to supervise the pool and clean buildings at one of four complexes. Hours by arrangement. Period of work July-September. Min. age 18. Applicants must hold at least the RLSS Bronze Medallion and must be prepared to undergo a water test. Applications to Jeanette B. Thompson at the above address.

YMCA NATIONAL CENTRE: Lakeside, Ulverston, Cumbria LA12 8BD (tel 053 95-31758).
DAY CAMP LEADERS (25). £15 p.w. plus travelling expenses. To work $5\frac{1}{2}$ days p.w. Hours: 9am-5pm. Free B. & L. Min. age 18 years. Some experience of outdoor activities, and an interest in working with children necessary. The work involves leading groups of children aged 8-13 years in a wide range of activities, from environmental awareness to rock climbing. M.p.w. 7 weeks between early July and end of August. Application forms available from November 1991, from Jim Dobson, Centre Manager, YMCA National Centre. (O)

Language Schools

EAST ANGLIAN SCHOOL OF ENGLISH: Burebank College, Aylsham, Norfolk (tel 0263-733203).
ASSISTANT TEFL TUTORS for work in Yorkshire. For details of work see entry in East Anglia chapter.

SCOTLAND

Scotland's unemployment problem is similar — if not worse — to that in England, and yet the hotel and catering field remains a fairly reliable source of work; and vacancies can also be found in the retail and distribution industries.

The hotel industry in the Highlands and Islands is remarkably buoyant and (subject to weather) offers employment from Easter until the end of October. Many hotels are in isolated areas, so a considerable number of staff have to be recruited from outside. However, you must be prepared to live and work in a remote area for the whole season. Jobcentres in Inverness and Fort William can usually help with this type of work.

Fruit picking is another industry which employs a large number of staff over the summer season. Perth and Tayside are the most popular areas for this type of work. The season usually lasts from the end of June until mid-September. Weather conditions can affect both the length of the season and demand for labour. Details can be obtained from the Jobcentres in Blairgowrie and Perth.

Edinburgh attracts a considerable number of tourists each year, particularly over the festival (late August), and there are always opportunities for bi-lingual staff to act as guides. Hotels recruit for a wide range of jobs and large department stores employ additional sales staff. The District Council engages assistant or experienced gardeners and general attendants over the summer months. There is also a large demand for clerical staff, and there are usually plenty of vacancies displayed in the Edinburgh Jobcentre.

Although there are numerous opportunities for temporary work in Edinburgh, accommodation is rarely provided and can be difficult to find.

Business and Industry

ARRAN PROVISIONS LTD: The Old Mill, Lamlash, Isle of Arran, Scotland KA27 8JU (tel 07706-606).
PACKING AND PROCESS OPERATIVES (20). The work involves either packing jars of mustard and preserves into gift packaging and boxes, or making the produce and filling jars. Wages £2.68 per hour. To work 7.30am-4.30pm Mondays to Fridays; o/t available throughout the summer. Period of work from June to October/November. No accommodation provided. Applications to L. J. Campbell at the above address.

JIM NEARY SELF DRIVE HIRE: 15 Fairley Street, Glasgow G51 (tel 041 427-5475).
CAR CHECKER, CAR DRIVER, RENTAL RECEPTIONIST. £1.50 per hour. To work from 8.30am-5pm with one hour for lunch, 5 days p.w. Min. age 21. Applicants must have held driving licence for at least a year. Period of work May to September. M.p.w. by arrangement. No B. & L. available. Applications to Mrs Moir or Mr Neary at the above address.

Children

LOTHIAN PLAY FORUM: Room 9, Dalry Primary School, Dalry Road, Edinburgh EH11 2BU (tel 031-337 6208). Community Education Service, funded by the Lothian Regional Council.
PLAYSCHEME HELPERS (approx 30). Wages nominal. To work Monday to Friday, 10am-noon and 2-4pm. Applicants should have experience of working with primary school age children in varied skills. Duties include assisting with outings, swimming, outdoor activities, painting, drawing, etc. **No meals or accommodation are provided**. It is stressed that rented accommodation is both very hard to find and very expensive in Edinburgh, even though the period of work is before the Festival, namely May/June and the beginning of August. M.p.w. 2 weeks. Applications should be sent by the first week of June to Betty Kennedy, at the above address.

Holiday Centres and Amusements

CRUNACHY CARAVAN PARK: Taynuilt, Argyll (tel 086 62-612).
ASSISTANT to maintain grass by cutting, with a sit-down mower, and patching any worn areas; also to clean toilet areas. £2 per hour. To work 7 hours per day, 6 days p.w. Period of work from April to August. Only applicants who can work the full period will be considered. Accommodation provided, and free site available for own caravan. Applications to Mr Angus Douglas at the above address.

GLENCOE OUTDOOR CENTRE: Glencoe, Argyll PA39 4HS (tel 08552-350).
DOMESTIC/SPORTS ASSISTANTS (4). £20 p.w. To work 8 hours per day. 5 days p.w. Four days p.w. domestic work (split shifts, afternoons free) and one day assisting the team of instructors. Plenty of opportunity to take part in activities during free time. B. & L. provided. M.p.w. 2 months between January and end of September. Min. age 18. Applicants should be committed Christians willing to work hard as part of a Christian team. An interview is usually required. Applications a.s.a.p. to Debbie Williams, Director at the above address. (O).

KINDROGAN FIELD CENTRE: Enochdhu, Blairgowrie, Perthshire PH10 7PG (tel 025 081-286).
GENERAL ASSISTANTS. £56 p.w., including B. & L. Approx. 35 hours p.w. mainly split shifts. Work available March to the end of April. M.p.w. 6 weeks. Duties include working in kitchen/pantry area of main house. Ideal for students of environmental subjects interested in using the library and laboratory facilities, and there will be opportunities to join in some field courses and assist in scientific work. EC applicants welcome. Applications to Mrs Heather Harney, House Manager, Kindrogan Field Centre.

LOCH MORAR ADVENTURE CENTRE: Bracora, By Mallaig, NW Scotland PH40 4PE (tel 0687-2164).
GENERAL ASSISTANTS (2). To help with sailing dinghies, canoes, fishing boats, general maintenance of equipment, and cooking and cleaning. £35 p.w. plus free accommodation. To work 3 hours morning and evening. Extra work (as overtime) acting as crew or giving instructions for those with experience of canoeing and sailing. Staff needed from Easter to October. Interview necessary. Applications a.s.a.p. to H. R. Jenkins, at the above address. (O)

MRS R.T.S. MACPHERSON: 27 Archery Close, London W2 2BE (tel 071-262 8487).

HOLIDAYS HELPERS required for a Highland home, to help with garden and outdoor work, such as painting fences and gates, cooking, and picking fresh fruit. B. & L. provided. Two character references essential. Wages negotiable. Applications to Mrs R. T. S. Macpherson at the above address.

TUMMEL VALLEY HOLIDAY PARK: Tummel Bridge, By Pitlochry, Perthshire PH16 5SA (tel 088 24-221).
BAR STAFF (4), WAITING/GENERAL ASSISTANTS (2). £2.74 per hour plus tips. Accommodation provided, for which 20p per hour is deducted from wage. 6 days p.w. Variable hours, work as required. No o/t though bank holidays are paid at double time. Min. age 18 years. No experience needed. Period of work April to October. Applications to the General Manager, Tummel Valley Holiday Park.

Hotels and Catering

ARDENTINNY HOTEL: Ardentinny, Loch Long, Argyll PA23 8TR (tel 036 981-209).
GENERAL STAFF. £75 p.w. To work 39 h.p.w. plus o/t, including Sundays. Free B. & L. provided. M.p.w. April o October or May to september. Applicants should be happy, hardworking and honest. Applications early in the year to Mr John Horn, at the above address.

BADENOCH HOTEL: Aviemore, Inverness-shire PH22 1PF (tel 0479-810261).
RESTAURANT WAITING STAFF (4) for silver service work. To work split shifts over a 5-day week. Applicants should be aged 17 or over and have at least one year's experience.
BAR STAFF (3) to work in cocktail and disco bars. To work 5 days on, 2 days off. Applicants should be aged 18 or over and have at least one year's experience.
RECEPTION STAFF (2). Duties include operating a switchboard and electronic adding machine, typing, taking reservations and dealing with the restaurant analysis. Applicants should be aged 18 or over with at least one year's experience.
HOUSE STAFF (8) to take care of all aspects of chamber work. Should have at least 4 month's experience.
Wages £2.50 per hour plus tips. O/t available at time and a half. B. & L. provided. To begin work in May. Applications to Kirsty Wilson, Assistant Manager, at the above address. (O)

BAREND PROPERTIES LTD: Sandyhills, Dalbeattie, Kirkcudbrightshire (tel 038 778-663).

COOKS (2). £140-180 pw. $5\frac{1}{2}$ days p.w. To cook in a small, high quality restaurant in south-west Scotland. Need ability to cook and intelligence.
BAR STAFF (2). Approx. £100 p.w. $5\frac{1}{2}$ days p.w. To work in a bar on a holiday site.
Free B. & L. provided. Period of work 1 April to 31 October. Applications, at any time, to Mrs Gourlay, at the above address. (O)

THE CEILIDH PLACE: West Argyll Street, Ullapool, Ross & Cromarty IV26 2TY (tel 0854-612103). Runs hotel, restaurant, clubhouse, coffee shop, bookshop, art exhibitions, summer programme of events, mostly musical. Proprietors are members of CND, Greenpeace, the ANC and NSC.
COOKS (6). 1 vegetarian, 1 pastry and baking, 2 qualified with experience, and 2 with natural skill and enthusiasm.
HOUSESTAFF (2). Must be fit.
WAITERS/WAITRESSES to serve breakfast and dinner.
RECEPTIONISTS (2). Computer knowledge essential.
DISHWASHERS AND GENERAL ASSISTANTS (2). Must have ambition to keep things clean and tidy.
COFFEE SHOP ASSISTANTS (4). Serving food and drink and clearing tables.
Basic wage of £75 p.w. with B. & L. Higher rates paid depending on skills and responsibility. Work available between February and December. M.p.w. 12 weeks, (no shorter period considered). For further information and an application form write to Mrs J. Urquhart at the above address.

CLACHAIG INN: Glencoe, Ballachulish, Argyll PA39 4HX (tel 08552-252). Climbing and hill-walking centre in Glencoe.
GENERAL ASSISTANTS required for busy country inn set in the mountains of northwest Scotland. Wages to be arranged. Duties include bar work (handling both drinks and food), waiting, cleaning and odd jobs. Accommodation provided. Applicants must enjoy country life. Foreign applicants with a good command of the English language welcome. Applications to Mr Guy Daynes, at the above address. (O)

CLIFTON HOUSE HOTEL: Nairn, Nairnshire (tel 0667-53119).
WAITERS, WAITRESSES, HOUSE and KITCHEN ASSISTANTS (6-7). Wages and hours by arrangement. B. & L. provided, charge to be discussed. Experience preferable but not necessary. M.p.w. 4 weeks between March and October. Applications in writing to Mr J. Gordon Macintyre, Proprietor, Clifton House. (O)

COUL HOUSE HOTEL: Contin, Ross-shire IV14 9EY (tel 0997-421487). Country house hotel in northern Highlands specializing in rambling, birdwatching, fishing and golf.
WAITER/WAITRESS, KITCHEN and BAR STAFF. From £380 per month live in, £455 live out. To work 5 days per week. M.p.w. end of April to end of September (no shorter periods considered). Suitably qualified foreign applicants welcome. Applications a.s.a.p. before end of February, to Mr M. A. Hill, Coul House Hotel. (O)

CRAIGARD HOTEL: Boat of Garten, Inverness-shire (tel 047 983-206). HOUSE STAFF (2), CHAMBER STAFF (3). Experience preferred. WAITING STAFF (3), KITCHEN ASSISTANT (1). Experience not essential. Basic wage £70 p.w. Free B. & L. provided for all positions. Must provide own overall, white blouse, black skirt (females), white shirt, black/grey trousers (males). Min. age 18. Fares within the UK paid if full period worked. All staff must be available from June to end of September, preferably until mid-October. Applications with photograph from January to Mrs P. Sanders, Craigard Hotel. (O)

CRAW'S NEST HOTEL: Bankwell Road, Anstruther, Fife KY10 3DA (tel 0333-310691).
KITCHEN HANDS (2). £105 p.w. plus end of season bonus. To work 5 days p.w. No experience necessary.
WAITING STAFF (3). £105 p.w. To work 5 days p.w. Silver service. Some experience would be useful, though is not essential.
Free B. & L. M.p.w. 3-4 months between May and September. Applications a.s.a.p. to Mr I. Birrell, Craw's Nest Hotel. (O)

THE CRINAN HOTEL — SCOTLAND

Waiting Staff (8)	**Bar Staff (6)**
Room Attendants (6)	**Receptionist (1)**

To work in a fishing village and sailing centre in an extremely beautiful location. £85 per week plus tips and free board and lodging. Period of work at least 10 weeks between April and October.
Send applications to or telephone **Mr N. A. Ryan, Managing Director, The Crinan Hotel, Argyll, Scotland PA31 8SR. Tel: (054 683) 261. Fax: (054 683) 292.**

CRINAN HOTEL: Crinan, nr Lochgilphead, Argyll PA31 8SR (tel 054 683-261). Fishing village and sailing centre in a beautiful location.
WAITING STAFF (8). Split shifts for mealtimes.
BAR STAFF (6). Split shifts.
ROOM ATTENDANTS (6). Hours: 7am-3pm.
£85 p.w. plus tips. Free B. & L. Min. age 18 years. Experience helpful but not essential. M.p.w. 10 weeks between April and October. Interviews held at Easter. Applications from February to N.A. Ryan, Managing Director, Crinan Hotel.

DALMUNZIE HOUSE HOTEL: Glenshee, Perthshire PH10 7QG (tel 025 085-224). Country house hotel on 6,000-acre estate in a remote mountain situation.
GENERAL HOTEL STAFF (6). Wages and hours by arrangement according to type of job. To work $5\frac{1}{2}$ days p.w. B. & L. provided. Min. age 18 years. Period of work January to late October. Only applications enclosing s.a.e. will receive a reply. Applications to Simon and Alexandra Winton, Proprietors, Dalmunzie House Hotel. (O)

DRUIMNACROISH COUNTRY HOUSE HOTEL: Dervaig, Isle of Mull, Argyll PA75 6QW (tel 06884-274).
GENERAL ASSISTANTS (2). £90+ p.w. for approx. 35 hours per week. Free B. & L. provided. Duties include cleaning, waiting, gardening, picking fruit and vegetables, laundry, etc. Hours are adaptable and free time is always given as generously as possible. Applicants must be loyal, responsible, clean, honest, willing, cheerful and conscientious. M.p.w. preferably 6 months, between mid-April and mid-October. As the hotel is in a remote situation, own transport is advisable. Applications from March onwards to Mrs Wendy McLean, at the above address. (O)

DRUMOSSIE HOTEL: Perth Road, Inverness (tel 0463-236451).
WAITING STAFF (3). £85 p.w. live in. To work 39 h.p.w. 5 days p.w. Must have pleasant personality and an interest in people. Staff required from May to October. Applications to the Manager, Drumossie Hotel. (O)

DUISDALE HOTEL: Isle Ornsay, Isle of Skye (tel 047 13-202).
GENERAL ASSISTANTS (4). Wages by arrangement. Free B. & L. Min. age 20 years. Previous experience preferred. M.p.w. 3 months between April and October. Applications to Mrs M. A. Colpus, Proprietor, Duisdale Hotel. (O)

DUNDONNEL HOTEL: By Garve, Wester Ross, Ross-shire (tel 085 483-234). Busy 24-bedroom hotel just south of Ullapool in an area of outstanding mountain scenery. ASSISTANT CHEF/COOK (with experience), COMMIS CHEF/COOK, DINING ROOM STAFF (3), one to take charge, GENERAL ASSISTANTS (3) for kitchen and stillroom, BAR STAFF (2), CHAMBER STAFF (2), PETROL STATION ATTENDANT. From £95 per 5½-day week, with higher rates for skilled and senior personnel, plus free B. & L. in excellent accommodation (own room). M.p.w. 12 weeks, but longer period preferred. Most posts from Easter to October, with some from mid-May to end of September. Applications with s.a.e. and photograph, including details of any previous work experience and dates of availability, to Mr and Mrs S. W. Florence, Dundonnel Hotel.

DUNTULM CASTLE HOTEL: Duntulm, Isle of Skye (tel 047 052-213). Country house hotel in beautiful location. WAITING STAFF (2), CHAMBER STAFF (2), COOK, RECEPTIONIST/BAR ASSISTANT, KITCHEN ASSISTANT. Wages negotiable. Free B. & L. Hours by arrangement. Previous experience preferred. Would suit country lovers. Applications to Mr or Mrs MacDonald, Proprietors, Duntulm Castle Hotel. (O)

EWINGTON HOTEL: 132 Queen's Drive, Queen's Park, Glasgow G42 8QW (tel 041 423-1152). Busy city hotel. WAITERS/WAITRESSES, KITCHEN STAFF, CHAMBER STAFF and RECEPTIONIST (5 altogether). £80 p.w. To work 5 days p.w. 40 hours p.w. approx. Some hotel experience required. No live in accommodation is available. M.p.w. 6 weeks between June and October. Applications from March to Mrs Edward, Ewington Hotel. (O)

FERNHILL HOTEL: Portpatrick, nr Stranraer, Wigtownshire (tel 077 681-220). WAITER/WAITRESSES (2), BAR STAFF (1), CHAMBER STAFF (1). £84 p.w. plus tips. To work 40 h.p.w. 5 days on, 2 days off. O/t available at £3.99 per hour. Free B. & L. provided. Experience is not essential but must be willing workers and interested in the job. M.p.w. 2/3 months: 1 April to end of June, or mid-August to the end of October. Applications after 1 March to Mrs Anne Harvie, Fernhill Hotel. (O)

THE FRIGATE: Shore Street, Ullapool, Ross & Cromarty. A busy seafront

cafe, bakery, health food shop, and tearoom.
GENERAL ASSISTANTS (6). Basic wage of £75 p.w. plus free B. & L. M.p.w.
12 weeks, between March and October. For further information and an
application form, write to Mr John Grant, at the above address.

THE GALLEY OF LORNE HOTEL: Ardfern By Lochgilphead, Argyll PA31
8QN (tel 08525-284).
GENERAL ASSISTANTS (2). Weekly wage depending on experience, plus
tips. Hours by arrangement. Free B. & L. available. Work as general assistant
includes bar work, waiting and general duties. Students must be reliable,
intelligent and have a sense of humour. Period of work from mid-May to
September. Applications to Mr Hanbury, at the above address. (O)

THE GLENEAGLES HOTEL: Auchterarder, Perthshire PH3 1NF (tel
0764-62231).
FOOD SERVICE STAFF (6). Wages approx. £150 p.w. if living out, £110 p.w.
if living in. To work $42\frac{1}{2}$ hours per 5 day week. Applicants should be aged
over 18. Applications to the Personnel Manager, at the above address. (O)

GLENISLA HOTEL: nr Alyth, Perthshire PH11 8PH (tel 057 582-223).
BAR PERSON/WAITER/WAITRESS (2). Wages approx. £75.80 p.w. plus good
tips. Free B. & L. Hours 8am-3pm or 3-11pm, 5 days p.w. Period of work May-
October. Experience of bar work or waiting at table an advantage but not
essential. Applicants need a good sense of humour. Application to Mr Michael
Bartholomew, at the above address. (O)

HUNTLY ARMS HOTEL: Aboyne, Royal Deeside, Aberdeenshire AB34 5HS
(tel 03398-86101).
WAITING STAFF (4), BAR STAFF (2), CHAMBER STAFF (2). Experience
not necessary, training given.
2nd CHEF/COOK. Experience essential.
All wages depend on experience and ability. To work 40 h.p.w. O/t available
at £3.40 per hour. Accommodation available. References essential. Min. age
16 years. M.p.w. 8 weeks between 31 April and October; employees must stay
until end of September. Applications to Mr M. Chapman, Director, Huntly
Arms Hotel. (O)

KNOCKINAAM LODGE HOTEL: Portpatrick, Wigtownshire OG9 9AO (tel
077 681-471). Small country house hotel.
GENERAL ASSISTANT to perform duties such as reception and bar work
and waiting at table. Wages by arrangement. Accommodation provided. Previous

experience useful but must be willing to work hard, be intelligent, sympathetic, caring and have a sense of humour. Applicants from EC welcome. Applications to Mr M. Frichot, Knockinaam Lodge Hotel.

LEDGOWAN LODGE HOTEL: Achnasheen, Wester Ross IV22 2EJ (tel 044 588-252).
COCKTAIL BAR, HOUSE, PANTRY, KITCHEN and WAITING STAFF. Average gross wage £150 per working 6-day week, depending on age and experience. To work approx. 60 h.p.w. 1 day off p.w. Accommodation available in private rooms. M.p.w. 12 weeks between Easter and October. Applications a.s.a.p. enclosing photograph, age and references if possible to Mr G. T. Millard, Ledgowan Lodge Hotel. (O)

LOCH INSH WATERSPORTS AND SKIING CENTRE: Kincraig, Inverness-shire (tel 0540-651272). An outdoor centre offering accommodation and activity holidays.
RESTAURANT STAFF. Wages variable. To work a 5 or 6-day week. no experience needed. B. & L. provided either free, or at a charge of up to £25 p.w. Work available all year round, with m.p.w. 3 months. Interviews necessary. Applications to Clive Freshwater, at the above address. (O)

LOCH NESS LODGE HOTEL: Drumnadrochit, Inverness-shire (tel 045 62-342).
SUPERIOR HOTEL ASSISTANTS (up to 20). Wages from £75 p.w. To work approx. 42 h.p.w. for all positions. Free B. & L. M.p.w. between 1 March and 1 November. Applications with c.v. and photograph, from mid-January, to Mr and Mrs Skinner, Loch Ness Lodge Hotel. (O)

McTAVISH'S KITCHENS (OBAN) LTD: Restaurants in the West Highland resort towns of Oban and Fort William. There are a considerable number of vacancies, particularly for students, between April and October.
WAITING STAFF, SELF-SERVICE ASSISTANTS, KITCHEN ASSISTANTS, COOKS, BAR STAFF and CLEANERS. Meals and accommodation provided without charge — o/t paid. Late season employment — August to October — also available.
If interested in any of the above positions write, enclosing s.a.e., to: McTavish's Kitchens, 8 Argyll Square, Oban, Argyll, or McTavish's Kitchens, High Street, Fort William, Inverness-shire.

NORTH BRITISH TRUST HOTELS LTD: 1 Queen Charlotte Lane, Edinburgh EH6 6BL (tel 031 544-7173).

GENERAL ASSISTANTS (12), BAR STAFF (6), WAITING STAFF (3), CHAMBER STAFF (3). £65-85 p.w. plus free B. & L. To work 40 h.p.w. M.p.w. 5 months between May and October. Applications from April to the Personnel Manager, North British Trust Hotels Ltd. (O)

ONICH HOTEL: Onich, Inverness-shire PH33 6RY (tel 085 53-214). Modern family-run hotel with 25 bedrooms, situated on Loch Linnhe overlooking Glencoe Mountains.
BAR STAFF (2), WAITING STAFF (3), COOKS (2), PORTERS/WINE WAITERS (2).
From £90 p.w. To work $5\frac{1}{2}$ days p.w., 8 hours per day. Free B. & L. Must be of tidy appearance and have a pleasant and helpful manner. M.p.w. 3 months between late April and late October; preference given to those who can work whole period. Applications from 1 January, with photograph, to Mr Young, Onich Hotel. (O)

PALACE HOTEL: Breadalbane Terrace, Aberfeldy, Perthshire PH15 2AG (tel 0887-20359).
GENERAL ASSISTANTS (4). £95 p.w.
KITCHEN PORTER, STILLROOM ATTENDANT. £95 p.w. To work 42 h.p.w. split shifts.
PUBLIC BARMAN. £110 p.w.
HOUSE STAFF. £100 p.w.
To work 7am-2pm and 7-10pm. To work a 6-day week. All positions live-in, with free B. & L. M.p.w. 5 months between 1 May and 30 October. Applications in writing from 1 March to Mr S. Vincent, at the Palace Hotel. (O)

RAASAY OUTDOOR CENTRE: Isle of Raasay, By Kyle, Ross-shire IV40 8PB (tel 047 862-226).
KITCHEN ASSISTANTS (2), COOKS (2), HOUSEKEEPERS (2), RECEPTIONIST (1). Wages negotiable. To work a 6-day week. No qualifications necessary, but experience is preferable. B. & L. is provided, the charge for which is negotiable. M.p.w. 4-6 weeks, with work available from March to November. An interview is generally necessary, although applicants may alternatively work a probationary week. Applications from February to Lyne Rowe, Raasay Outdoor Centre, at the above address. (O)

SCOTTISH HIGHLANDS HOTELS: 98 West George Street, Glasgow G2 1PW (tel 041 332-3033).
CHEFS, WAITING STAFF, CHAMBER STAFF, BAR STAFF to work in 3 star hotels in Lairg and Pitlochry. £100 p.w. To work 40 h.p.w. Free B. & L.

provided. Staff needed from May to September/October. M.p.w. 8 weeks. Min. age 18. Interview not always necessary. (O)

STAKIS BADENOCH HOTEL: Aviemore Centre, Inverness-shire PH22 1PF (tel 0479- 810261).
WAITERS/WAITRESSES (6-7), PORTERS (2), KITCHEN PORTERS (4), HOUSESTAFF (7-8), BAR STAFF (4-5), CHEFS (2-3). £2.50 per hour, 39 h.p.w. over 5-day week. Min. age 18. Experience an asset and preference given to flexible, cheerful and willing personalities. B. & L. available at £20 p.w. M.p.w. 3 months between mid-May and end of September. Two references and photograph with c.v. to the Personnel Manager from February onwards. (O)

SUMMER ISLES HOTEL: Achiltibuie by Ullapool, Ross-shire IV26 2YQ (tel 085428-282). A renowned hotel on the west coast of Scotland set in magnificent scenery.
COOK (1). To take charge of food in licensed cafe. Must be experienced.
ASSISTANT COOK (1). To assist head chef and cook breakfasts. Training given but must have natural aptitude and enthusiasm. Excellent opportunity to learn.
HOUSE/KITCHEN STAFF (3). Room cleaning, laundry, dishwashing.
GENERAL ASSISTANTS (4). For dining room, bar and reception work, and some housework.
BAR STAFF (2). CAFE ASSISTANTS (2). To share serving, cleaning and dishwashing. Wages £115 min. for 45 h.p.w. (6 days), with higher rates for skilled and senior personnel. Free B. & L. M.p.w. 3 months between Easter and mid-October. Preference given to those prepared to work the whole season. The jobs are suited to those prepared to work hard and make the most of their free time. Applications, with s.a.e. and photograph, to Mr Mark Irvine, Summer Isles Hotel.

TIRORAN HOUSE HOTEL: Isle of Mull, Argyll PA69 6ES (tel 068 15-232). DOMESTIC STAFF (5) to undertake the full range of domestic duties in a small country house hotel, including waiting, cleaning rooms, working in the laundry, helping with food preparation, etc. £105 p.w. plus B. & L. for females only. 60 working hours p.w. min. on a rota system that allows one full day off p.w., plus most afternoons and odd mornings. M.p.w. 12 weeks between 30 May and early October. No special qualifications or experience required, but applicants must be non-smokers and should be intelligent, have a sense of humour and be prepared to work hard to high standards. Applications a.s.a.p. to Wing Commander and Mrs Robin Blockey, Proprietors, Tiroran House Hotel. (O)

WAVE YACHT CHARTERS: 1 Hazel Drive, Dundee DD2 1QQ (tel 0382-68501).
COOK/DECKHAND (1). Wages from £100 p.w. Free B. & L. To prepare mels on boad yacht. Cordon Bleu cooking qualification needed, and sailing experience preferred. Age: 18-35 years. Reasonable amount of time off when boat is in harbour. Period of work 1 April to 30 september. Applications at any time to Mrs Bruce, at the above address. (O)

WOODLEA HOTEL: Moniaive, Dumfries-shire DG3 4EN (tel 084 82-209). GENERAL ASSISTANTS (2). Approx. £85 p.w. for employees over 18. Tips in addition. To work 39 h.p.w. with 2 days off p.w. B. & L. available for females only. Expected to help in all aspects of hotel including serving in the bar, toilet cleaning, kitchen and dining room work. Staff welcome to use swimming pool and other sports facilities when not in use by guests. M.p.w. 3 months preferably to end of September. Period of work Easter to end of October. Applications enclosing s.a.e., 2 references, personal details, a recent photograph and dates of availability, to Mr M. R. McIver, Woodlea Hotel. (O)

Medical

BRUNTSFIELD HELPING HANDS (EDIN.) LTD: 45 Barclay Place, Edinburgh EH10 4HW (tel 031-228 1382).
NURSES and NURSING AUXILIRIES can be placed throughout the Edinburgh area all year round. Placements may be in hospitals, nursing homes, industry or private homes. Applicants must register in person. Applications to Bruntsfield Helping Hands (Edin.) Ltd.

Outdoor

ARDMAIR POINT CARAVAN SITE/BOAT CENTRE: Ardmair Point, Ullapool, Ross-shire (tel 0854-2054).
BOAT CENTRE ASSISTANT (1). Boat handling and glass fibre experience preferred. Duties include renting small boats and equipment, assisting with repair of fibreglass boats, and the servicing and repair of outboard engines.
CARAVAN SITE ASSISTANTS (4). Duties include reception/shop work, cleaning and grass cutting; a large proportion of the work is out of doors which also involves some tractor driving. Easter work (general pre-season work) is also available for 2 people.
Wage £3.50 per hour. To work 45 hours, $5\frac{1}{2}$ days p.w., with shifts covering 8am-10pm. Accommodation available for women only. Min. age 18 years. All jobs best suited to people interested in water sports and/or outdoor pursuits. For further details and application form send s.a.e. to the above address. (O)

BARNYARDS FARM: Beauly, Inverness-shire IV4 7AT (tel 0463-782866). An international farm camp in the Highlands, 12 miles from Loch Ness. RASPBERRY PICKERS required from early July until late August. Pce. wk. rates paid daily. To work from 7.30am-4.30pm. Free caravan accommodation provided (£10 deposit — refundable when leaving). Also free campsite facilities, but campers must bring own camping equipment. All pickers have use of kitchen, hot showers, toilet, etc., but should bring own cooking and eating utensils and bedding. The farm is 10 minutes walk from Beauly services — shops, pubs, etc. Applications with s.a.e. to Mr D. Courts, Barnyards Farm, Beauly. (O)

MR S. CAMPBELL: Cairntradlin, Kinellar, Aberdeenshire AB2 0SA (tel 0224-790288).
STRAWBERRY/RASPBERRY PICKERS (15). Pce. wk. rates paid daily. To work 6-8 hours per day, 6 days p.w., weather and crop conditions permitting. Self-catering accommodation provided in farm buildings, with male and female dormitories, kitchen, toilets and showers. Camping area also available for those with camping equipment. Applicants must bring eating utensils, warm sleeping bags and warm clothing. £15 will be charged for use of facilities, refundable to those who stay for a period of three weeks. Period of work: 11/12 July for 4-5 weeks. Applications to Mr S. Campbell, at the above address. (O)

W. HENDERSON: Seggat, Auchterless, Turrif, Aberdeenshire AB5 8DL (tel 08884-223).
STRAWBERRY PICKERS/PACKERS. Pce. wk. rates. To work 7 hours per day, 6 days p.w. Self-catering accommodation available free; must bring own sleeping bag. Situated 1 mile from main road with regular bus service between Aberdeen and Inverness. Period of work mid-July to mid-August. M.p.w. 4

weeks. Applications from 30 January onwards to Mr W. Henderson, at the above address. (O)

JOHN STUART (MURRIAL) LTD: Murrial, Insch, Aberdeenshire AB5 6NU (tel 0464- 20296). Mixed farm 27 miles from Aberdeen.
STRAWBERRY PICKERS and GENERAL FARM HANDS (6). Pce. work rates (12p per lb) for picking, £2.50 per hour for other work such as weeding or grading strawberries. Must be willing to work hard from 8am-4.30pm, with Saturdays free. Self-catering accommodation in caravans or cottage. Period of work from beginning of July and mid-August. Applications a.s.a.p. to Mrs Christina Stuart. If no reply within 10 days, assume all jobs have been taken. (O)

NAIRN VALLEY FRUIT GROWERS: Cantraybruich, Culloden Moor, Inverness IV1 2EG (tel 0463-790260).
RASPBERRY PICKERS (25). Pce. wk. rates (in 1991 the rate was 12 pence per pound for raspberries). A good picker should earn £8 per day at the beginning and end of season and up to £15 per day during the peak picking days. To work 40 h.p.w. 7 days p.w. Free campsite equipped with showers, toilets, kitchen and rest area with TV in farm buildings. Campers must bring their own tents and cooking utensils. Transport provided for shopping, etc., in Inverness 7 miles away. Min. age 18 years. M.p.w. 1 week between 15 July and 20 August. Applications from 1 May enclosing s.a.e. to Mr D. W. M. Fraser, Nairn Valley Fruit Growers. (O)

NEWTON OF LEWESK: Old Rayne Insch, Aberdeenshire AB52 65W (tel 04645-250).
STRAWBERRY PICKERS (10-12) to work from 1 July-15 August. Pce. wk. rates. Accommodation provided. To work 6-8 hours per day, 6/7 days p.w., weather permitting. Applications to Messrs G. & B. Walker at the above address.

PERIMETER FARMS LTD: By Lentran, Inverness-shire. International farm camp in the Highlands near Loch Ness on a beautiful site overlooking the Beauly Firth.
RASPBERRY PICKERS. Highest pce. wk. rates paid daily. Some packing work also. Travelling allowance paid to the Highlands. Applications from March to Perimeter Farms, Yeld lane, Kelsall, Cheshire CW6 0JD.

Sport

BAREND PROPERTIES LTD: Sandyhills, Dalbeattie, Kirkcudbrightshire (tel 038778-663).
TREK LEADER (1). £75 p.w., 6 days p.w. To look after the horses and take out riders for 1 or 2 hour treks. Min. age 18 and experience necessary. Free B. & L. provided. Period of work 1 April to 31 October. Applications at any time to Mrs Gourlay, at the above address. (O)

CAIRDSPORT LTD: Aviemore Centre, Inverness-shire PH22 1PL (tel 0479-810296).
DRY SKI SLOPE INSTRUCTOR (1). Must have BASI qualifications.
SAILING INSTRUCTORS (2). Must have RYA qualifications.
SHOP ASSISTANTS (3). To work split shifts. No o/t available. No experience necessary. Wages £110 p.w. To work 39 h.p.w. Staff required from 1 July to end of August. M.p.w. 6 weeks. B. & L. provided at a charge. Interviews necessary. Applications to Scott Bruce, Cairdsport Ltd, at the above address. (O)

CRAOBH HAVEN WATERSPORTS LTD: Craobh Haven, by Lochgilphead, Argyll PA31 8QR (tel 08525-664).
WATERSPORTS INSTRUCTORS (5). £40 p.w. plus free B. & L. Hours as necessary. Experience of watersports (canoeing, windsurfing, dinghy sailing, etc.) essential and qualifications preferable. Trainee positions are also available. Staff required on a seasonal basis. Apply as early as possible to the Manager, Craobh Haven Watersports Ltd. (O)

GALLOWAY SAILING CENTRE: Shirmers Bridge, Loch Ken, Castle Douglas DG7 3NQ, S. W. Scotland (tel 06442-626).
SAILING INSTRUCTORS: DINGHY (5), WINDSURFERS (3). Courses start at 10am and finish 5pm. Must be RYA qualified or have a similar level of competence.
COOK/GENERAL HELP (1). No special qualifications needed. Experience an advantage.
Wages negotiable, hours variable. Applicants should be versatile and good with

people, and should be prepared to accept responsibility. Knowledge of DIY an advantage. B. & L. available. Period of work from May to September, with m.p.w. negotiable. Applications to Mr. R. Herman, Principal, at the above address. (O)

LATHERON PONY CENTRE: Latheron, Caithness KW5 6DT (tel 059 34-224).
PONY TREK LEADERS (1-2). £25 p.w. plus tips 6 days p.w. Some experience with horse and ponies required. Free B. & L. M.p.w. July-August, work available from April to September. Applications from March to Mrs Camilla Sinclair, Owner, Latheron Pony Centre.

LOCH INSH WATERSPORTS & SKIING CENTRE: Kincraig, Inverness-shire (tel 0540-651272). An outdoor centre offering accommodation and activity holidays. Watersports take place between May and October, and skiing between December and April.
WATERSPORTS INSTRUCTORS. RYA and BCU qualified, or trainee instructor standard.
SKIING INSTRUCTORS. BASI-qualified, or trainee instructor standard.
Wages variable. To work a 6-day week. B. & L. provided either free, or at a charge of up to £25 p.w. M.p.w. 3 months, with work available all year round. Interview necessary. Applications to Clive Freshwater, at the above address. (O)

PGL YOUNG ADVENTURE LTD: Alton Court, Penyard lane (874), Ross-on-Wye, Herefordshire HF9 5NR (tel 0989-764211). Over 2,500 staff needed to assist in the running of activity centres in Perthshire.
INSTRUCTORS in canoeing, sailing, windsurfing, pony trekking, hill walking, fencing, archery, judo, rifle shooting, fishing, motorsports, arts and crafts, drama, English language and many other activities. Pocket money from £30 p.w. Full B. & L. provided. Min. age 18 years.
GROUP LEADERS to take responsibility for small groups of children and ensure that they get the most out of their holiday. Pocket money from £30 p.w. Free B. & L. Min. age 20 years. Previous experience of working with children necessary. Vacancies available for short or long periods between February and October. Requests for application forms to the Personnel Department, PGL. (O)

PORT EDGAR SAILING CENTRE: South Queensferry, Edinburgh EH30 9SQ (tel 031-331 3330). Scotland's largest sailing school.
DINGHY SAILING, WINDSURFING AND/OR CANOEING INSTRUCTORS (6). £140 p.w. basic. To work 10 sessions of approx. 35 hours. O/t rates for weekends. Limited accommodation available for £12 approx. p.w.

RYA or BCU instructor qualifications preferred. M.p.w. 6 weeks between April and late October. Applications from 1 January to Mr Oliver Ludlow. (O)

RAASAY OUTDOOR CENTRE: Isle of Raasay, By Kyle, Ross-shire IV40 8PB (tel 047 862-266).
INSTRUCTORS (12). To teach canoeing, surfing, sailing, climbing, abseiling, orienteering, etc.
Wages negotiable. To work a 6-day week. Qualified applicants preferred.
VOLUNTARY INSTRUCTORS (6). To participate in the teaching of the above activities. No wage, but approx. £15 pocket money p.w. is given. To work a 6-day week. Qualified applicants preferred. Work available between March and November. M.p.w. 4-6 weeks. Free B. & L. provided. Applicants may attend an interview, or may alternatively work a probationary week. Applications from February to Lyne Rowe, Raasay Outdoor Centre, at the above address.

SKYE AND LOCALSH DISTRICT COUNCIL: Isle of Skye Swimming Pool, Park Road, Portree, Isle of Skye (tel 0478-2655).
SEASONAL LEISURE ATTENDANTS (1/2) for lifeguarding duties at the pool, and to help outside on the sports field. Wages approx. £3.38 per hour. Hours by arrangement. Accommodation is not available. M.p.w. June-August. Applicants must be aged over 18 and hold a current RLSS Bronze Medallion. Applications to the Personnel Department, at the above address.

TIGHNABRUAICH SAILING SCHOOL: Tighnabruaich, Argyllshire. Large sailing school in the West Highlands.
SAILING INSTRUCTORS (10), BOARDSAILING INSTRUCTORS (2). £42-50 p.w. Hours: 9.30am-5.30pm, 6 days p.w. Free B. & L. RYA Instructors' Certificate preferably but good sailors who can train for certificate also considered. M.p.w. 3 weeks (longer period preferred) between April and end of September. Applications from January onwards to the Sailing Master, Tighnabruaich Sailing School. (O)

Language Schools

THE EDINBURGH SCHOOL OF ENGLISH: 271 Canongate, The Royal Mile, Edinburgh EH8 8BQ (tel 031-557 9200). Arranges English language summer courses for school children (10-18 years) in Aberdeen, Edinburgh, Dundee and Durham.
ACTIVITY LEADERS to be responsible for the smooth running of the afternoon, evening and weekend leisure programme. The job involves taking students on various cultural visits and organizing and supervising sports. Applicants need sound knowledge of one of the above locations. One leader

is employed for every 10 students. Some leaders are required to live and supervise in a hall of residence in addition to the above. Hours by arrangement. B. & L. available for a few applicants only. Courses are run between mid-June and early September, and also during April. M.p.w. 3 weeks. Applicants should be English speakers aged over 21. Should also be enthusiastic and energetic, with good organizational abilities. They should also get on well with teenagers and be interested in sports and/or cultural visits. Applications to Mrs Margot Huggins at the above address.

WALES & NORTHERN IRELAND

A great deal of the temporary work available in Wales over the summer is related to the tourist industry in some way. The towns that offer the best possibility of finding work of this kind are Porthcawl, Tenby, Swansea, Aberystwyth, Rhyl, Llangollen, Llandudno, Cardiff, Newport and Rogerstone. If you have some knowledge of riding there are also numerous riding schools and trekking centres in more remote locations. Apart from the well known tourist resorts and hotels, there are a few summer events that may need extra hands, such as the International Eisteddfod in Llangollen, Anglesey Agricultural Show, and the Royal Welsh Shows in Builth Wells.

Large manufacturing firms may also be a source of temporary work: in particular, Tetra Pak (who make cardboard milk and juice cartons) in Wrexham, the Driver and Vehicle Licensing Agency in Morriston, and Avana Bakeries and RF Brookes in Rogerstone. It is advisable to apply early to these firms as they sometimes keep waiting lists.

Opportunities can also arise with the larger government departments. Unless you are offered live-in conditions, accommodation is not easy to find.

Unemployment is very high in Northern Ireland and many of the Irish come looking for summer jobs over the Irish sea. In addition to the few employers in this chapter, there are some Irish organizations that need unpaid helpers and these are listed in the Voluntary chapter.

Business and Industry

BENSON GROUP PLC: Ludlow Road, Knighton, Powys LD7 1LP (tel 0547-528534).
OFFICE WORKERS. £3-3.50 per hour. To work 37 h.p.w. Applicants should have specialist skills, e.g. marketing, engineering, computing, etc. Staff needed from 1 June to 15 September. M.p.w. 1 week. Applicants must be available for interview. Applications from March to The Works Manager at the above address. (O)

Children

DEESIDE LEISURE CENTRE: Alyn & Deeside District Council, Queensferry, Deeside, Clywd CH5 1SA (tel 0244-812311).
PLAYLEADERS (30) to organize games and activities for children aged 4-15. Wages approx. £50 p.w. for senior leaders; approx. £35 p.w. for junior leaders. Hours 1.30-4.30pm, Mondays to Fridays. M.p.w. 5 weeks between the end of July and the end of August. Applications to Ms E. Hollingworth at the above address.

Holiday Centres and Amusements

BLUE WELL RIDING CENTRE: Ffynnonlas, Llanllwni, Dyfed SA39 9AY (tel 0267-202274).
KITCHEN HELP. Approx. 5 hours per day with ample free time. Free B. & L. Duties include preparing and serving basic meals, washing up, and keeping kitchen and dining room clean for up to 20 people. Ideal for student. Must be car driver and non-smoker. Also vacancies to help with horses. M.p.w. 3 weeks between March and September. Applications to Lesley Gibbins, Proprietor, Blue Well Riding Centre. (O)

FIELD STUDIES COUNCIL: Dale Fort Field Centre, Dale, nr Haverfordwest, Dyfed SA62 3RD (tel 0646-636205).
DOMESTIC ASSISTANTS (4). £55 p.w. To work from 7am-12.30pm and 5-7.30pm, $5\frac{1}{2}$ days p.w. Free B. & L. Min. age 18 and should be interested in field studies and the environment. Will have opportunity to be involved in the Centre courses. Required from February to November. M.p.w. 3 months. Applications a.s.a.p. to the Bursar, Field Studies Council. (O)

GLEN RIVER YMCA NATIONAL CENTRE: 143 Central Promenade, Newcastle, Co Down, BT33 0EU, Northern Ireland (tel 03967-23172). INSTRUCTORS (8-10). To work up to 3 sessions per day. Experience or qualifications in one of the following is required: mountaineering, canoeing, orienteering or archery, environmental studies and working with young people. DOMESTICS/HOSTS (5). Must be hard-working, sociable and responsible. COOKS (2-3). Basic cooking/catering qualifications necessary. All staff are given expenses of £18 p.w. and work a 6 day week in most cases. Hours are variable. B. & L. is provided free of charge. M.p.w. 4 weeks between 26 June and 23 August. Instructors and day camp staff must attend a staff training programme from 26 June to 2 July. All staff must be prepared to support the Christian ethos of the centre. Applications, from fluent English speakers only, should be sent a.s.a.p. to the Programmes Manager, at the above address. (O)

LLANDUDNO PIER: Llandudno, Gwynedd LL30 2LP (tel 0492-76258). BAR STAFF (4). Wages at standard 'Licensed Non-residential' rates. To work a basic 39-hour week, plus o/t. Applicants should be aged over 18. CATERING and RETAIL STAFF (12). Wages as above. To work a basic 39-hour week plus o/t. Applicants should be aged over 16. CASHIERS (6), AMUSEMENT ATTENDANTS (6). Wages by arrangement. To work around 50 h.p.w. Applicants should be aged over 18. CHILD ATTENDANTS (8). Wages by arrangement. To work around 50 h.p.w. Applicants should be aged over 16. No B. & L. available. M.p.w. 8 weeks between April and October. No previous experience necessary, as training will be given. Applicants must be available for interview. Applications to Mr M. Blore, General Manager, Llandudno Pier.

TRANS-WALES TRAIL RIDES: Pengenfford, Talgarth, Brecon, Powys LD3 0EU (tel 0874-711398). GENERAL DOMESTIC ASSISTANTS (2). £60 p.w. Approx. 40 h.p.w. 1 day off p.w. which may be carried forward. Free B. & L. suitable for females only. Age 18-25 years. Duties include helping in kitchen, bedmaking and cleaning. Smart responsible assistants of high moral standard required who are prepared to speak English clearly to foreign guests. M.p.w. 3 months between 1 April and 30 September. Applications during March and April to Mr and Mrs Michael Turner, Trans-Wales Trail Rides. (O)

YOUTH HOSTELS ASSOCIATION: Plas Rhiwaedog, Rhos-y-Gwaliau, Bala, Gwynedd LL33 7EU (tel 0678-520215). ASSISTANT WARDENS(2). £70 p.w. plus free B. & L. To work 7.30am-noon and 5-10.30pm plus 5-11.30pm twice a week. Two days off every 5-6 days. To assist wardens in day-to-day running of youth hostel, which involves general cleaning (toilets, dormitories, etc.), preparation and serving of meals and some reception and book work. Training is given on site but some catering/cleaning experience would be useful. The hostel is situated 2 miles outside Bala and since buses are infrequent, own transport would be an advantage. Min. age 18 and must be able to live and work with other people. M.p.w. 3 months between 1 June and 31 August. Those interested must be available for interview, including those from the EC who are also welcome to apply. Applications from January to Janice Cadywould, at the above address. (O)

YOUTH HOSTELS ASSOCIATION (Wales): 4th Floor, 1 Cathedral Road, Cardiff CF1 9HA (tel 0222-396766).
ASSISTANT WARDENS (up to 25). Approx. £65 p.w. plus free B. & L. To work approx. 45 h.p.w., varying daily by rota, with usually 2 days off p.w. Hours may vary, the main working periods being in the morning and evening. Duties include catering and domestic work. Preferred age group 18-30. Previous catering, hotel/guest house experience an advantage. M.p.w. $2\frac{1}{2}$ months between Easter and the end of September.The period of work may vary from hostel to hostel. Those interested must be available for interview. Applications (with an s.a.e. or IRC) from the end of January to Melanie Posyer, at the above address. (O)

Hotels and Catering

AMBASSADOR HOTEL: Grand Promenade, Llandudno, Gwynedd LL30 2NR (tel 0492- 76886).
WAITERS/WAITRESSES (2). Wages by arrangement. Good conditions and hours. Free B. & L. Must be over 17 years of age. M.p.w. 2 months from Easter to October. Applications to Mr D. T. Williams, Proprietor, Ambassador Hotel. (O)

ARLINGTON HOTELS: c/o Hotel Diplomat, St Mary Street, Cardiff CF1 5RG (tel 0222-396455).
BAR STAFF, WAITING STAFF, KITCHEN ASSISTANTS, CHAMBER STAFF. Wages by arrangement. To work 40 h.p.w. plus possiblity of o/t. Accommodation available. To work the summer period. Min. age 18. Experience preferred but not essential. Applications to M. Taybi, Area General Manager, at the above address. (O)

BLACK LION HOTEL: New Quay, Dyfed SA45 9PT (tel 0545-560 209).
GENERAL ASSISTANTS (2). Wages as per Catering Wages Act. Flexible hours

but adequate free time. Must be energetic and adaptable. Min. age 18 years. M.p.w. Easter and/or summer vacation. Applicants from the EC welcome. Applications, with photograph, to Mrs T. Hunter, Black Lion Hotel. (O)

BROAD HAVEN HOTEL: nr Haverfordwest, Pembrokeshire SA62 3JN (tel 0437- 781366).
WAITING/CHAMBER STAFF. Must have pleasant appearance and manners, and cheerful personality.
KITCHEN ASSISTANTS. Must have ability to cook simple bar snack menu. Wages and hours specified on application. To live in. Must be available to stay for at least 3 months from July to September. Applications, with photographs, to Mr K. R. Ball, Manager, Broad Haven Hotel.

CARDIFF MOAT HOUSE: Circle Way East, Llanedeyrn, Cardiff CF3 7XP (tel 0222-732520).
SILVER SERVICE WAITING STAFF and ROOM ATTENDANTS. £3 per hour. Hours of work depend on level of business. M.p.w. 2 months between June and October. Min. age 18. Write or telephone the Personnel Manager, at the above address.

THE COURT HOTEL: Lamphey, Pembroke, Dyfed SA71 5NT (tel 0646-672273).
GENERAL ASSISTANTS (2) £90-110 p.w.
BREAKFAST COOK (1). £90-120 p.w.
Both positions involve 5 days work p.w. Hotel experience helpful. B & L is available at £20 a week. M.p.w. 6 weeks, between Easter and the end of September. Some full-time positions are also available. Applications from February onwards to Mr or Mrs Lain, at The Court Hotel. (O)

THE MARINER'S INN: Nolton Haven, Haverfordwest, Pembrokeshire, Dyfed SA62 3NH (tel 0437-710469). A friendly residential inn, set beside the sea.
BAR STAFF (2), WAITING STAFF (3), GENERAL ASSISTANT (1). To work 10am-2pm and 4.30-11pm, on split shifts.
CHAMBER STAFF (1). To work 10am-2pm on split shifts.
From £2.20 per hour. O/t is available. Min. age 20. M.p.w. 3 months, from June to September. B. & L. is sometimes available. Applications from Easter to Mr C. T. Quinlan, at the Mariner's Inn. (O)

PORTH TOCYN HOTEL: Abersoch, Gwynedd LL53 7BU (tel 075 881-3303).
GENERAL ASSISTANTS (10), ASSISTANT COOKS (4). Wages according to Catering and Wages Council. To work a $4\frac{1}{2}$-day week, in split shifts. Free

B. & L. Intelligence and sense of humour required. Cooking experience would be useful but is not essential. Use of tennis court and swimming pool. M.p.w. 6 weeks between April and November. Applications with s.a.e. to Mrs Fletcher-Brewer, Porth Tocyn Hotel.

THE RISBORO HOTEL: Clement Avenue, Llandudno, Gwynedd LL30 2ED (tel 0492-876343).
BAR STAFF (2). £130 p.w. To work a basic 50-hour week in split shifts per 5-day week. Should have previous experience of bar work.
RESTAURANT STAFF (4). To work in restaurant and banqueting room. £125 p.w. plus good tips. To work 10 sessions per 5-day week. Applicants should be energetic and pleasant young people with some previous experience.
ROOM ASSISANTS (3). £100 p.w. To work 36 hours over a 6-day week. O/t available. No accommodation available. Period of work from May to September. Applications to Colin A. Irving, Risboro Hotels Ltd, at the above address. (O)

ROYAL HOTEL: King Edward Street, Barmouth, Gwynedd LL42 1ABV (tel 0341-280383).
BAR STAFF (2), WAITING STAFF (2), CHEF, CHAMBER STAFF. Wages to be arranged. To work 40 h.p.w. Own room provided. Min. age 18 years. Period of work from 20 May onwards. Applications to J.S. and C. Ingham, Royal Hotel.

ROYAL GATE HOUSE HOTEL: North Beach, Tenby, Dyfed SA70 7ET (tel 0834-2255).
WAITERS/WAITRESSES (3). To work shifts of 7.30-10.30am and 6-9pm, plus some lunchtimes of noon-2pm. To work 6 days p.w. Min. age 18. Silver service experience preferred, but not essential.
CHAMBER STAFF (4). To work 8am-1pm, 6 days p.w. Min. age 18. Experience preferred.
BAR PERSON (1). To work shifts of 10.30am-3pm, and 6-11pm. Also shifts of 11am-7pm and 7pm until closing in the residents' bar. To work 6 days p.w. Min. age 18. Experience essential.
SECOND CHEF (1). To work shifts of 10am-2pm, and 5-9pm, 5 days p.w. Min. age 18. Some experience preferred, but training will be given.
RECEPTIONIST (1). To work from 8.30am-3.30pm, or 3.30-11.30pm, 6 days p.w. Training can be given. Must be able to type.
Wages as per the Catering Wages Act. Some accommodation is available. Period of work May/June onwards. Applications to Mr G. T. R. Fry, at the above address.

ST. BRIDES HOTEL: St. Brides Hill, Saundersfoot, Dyfed SA69 9NH (tel 0834-812304).
WAITERS/WAITRESSES (2). From £75 p.w. Silver service experience preferred.
BAR STAFF (1). From £75 p.w. Previous experience necessary.
CHAMBER STAFF (2). From £55 p.w. No experience required. Approx. 38 h.p.w. 6 days p.w. Free B. & L. Age: 30 and under. M.p.w. 8 weeks, between April and October. Applications from 1 January to Mr Martin Whitehead, General Manager, St. Brides Hotel. (O)

TYN-Y-COED HOTEL: Capel Curig, Betws-y-Coed, Gwynedd (tel 069 04-331).
GENERAL ASSISTANTS (4). £90 p.w. plus B. & L. To work 5 days p.w. on split shifts. Min. age 18 years. Applications to G. F. Wainwright, Tyn-y-Coed Hotel.

Outdoor

JOHN BROWNLEE: Kilroot, Newtownbutler, Co. Fermanagh, Northern Ireland (tel 036 573-410).
FRUIT PICKERS (4-6). Wages at pce. w. rates. Free accommodation at farm. Period of work September/October. Applications to Mr John Brownlee, Kilroot. (O)

Sport

CANTREF TREKKING CENTRE: Brecon, Powys LD3 8LR (tel 087 486-223).
PONY TREKKING GUIDES (2). Wages on application. Hours according to length of treks. To work 6 days p.w. O/t (if any) paid. B. & L. available. Min. age 18 years. Must be experienced rider and able to get along well with people. Period of work 1 June or 1 July to 1 September. Applicants must be prepared to work the specified length of time. Interview essential. Applications, enclosing s.a.e., from March to M. Evans, Cantref Pony Trekking Centre.

EAST TARR FARM AND RIDING STABLES: St. Florence, Tenby, Dyfed (tel 0834-871274). Modern mixed farm incorporating riding and trekking centre, located 2½ miles from the seaside resort of Tenby.
GROOMS (2). £65 p.w. To work 7 hours per day, with Saturdays free. Must be able to ride to a reasonable standard and be qualified to take charge of rides and treks. Accommodation provided.
DONKEY ATTENDANT. Wage and hours as above. Working on beach in

Tenby. Knowledge of horses and donkeys useful.
B. & L. on farm provided at £15 p.w. Min. age 17 years and must be willing
to work hard. M.p.w. 2 or 3 months between April and October. Applications
with references may be sent not before 1 March to Mrs H. Williams, East Tarr
Farm. (O)

ERISLANNAN MANOR: Clifden, Co. Galway, Ireland (tel 095-21134).
TREK LEADERS (2). £40 p.w. plus free B. & L. Hours: 8.15am-5pm, $5\frac{1}{2}$ days
p.w. (Saturday afternoons and Sundays free). Must be over 18 years old, and
have riding experience and knowledge of First Aid. Period of work April to
October, or beginning of July to end of August. Applications from February
to Mrs Brooks, at the above address. (O)

HIGH TREK SNOWDONIA: Tal y Waen, Deiniolen, Caernarvon, Gwynedd
LL55 3NA (tel 0286-871232). High Trek is a small company which offers guided
walking holidays in Snowdonia.
TREK LEADER (1). £80 p.w. plus B. & L. Must have MLTB certificate and
a full driving licence.
TREK ASSISTANTS (2). £50 p.w. with free B. & L. for 5 days p.w., including
2 nights camping. To help with driving, portering rucksacks up mountains,
domestic chores, etc. Should have a full driving licence and walking experience
would be helpful.
All staff must be very fit and must have a strong interest in the outdoors and
countryside. Must also have a flexible nature and be able to do anything from
paper work to portering loads. M.p.w. 6 weeks between Easter and October.
Those interested must be available for interview. Applications should be sent
as early as possible to Mrs Mandy Whitehead, at the above address. (O)

MONTGOMERYSHIRE DISTRICT COUNCIL: Severn Road, Welshpool,
Montgomeryshire (tel 0938-2828 ext 290).
POOL ATTENDANTS. Must have at least Bronze life-saving medal.
SUMMER SCHOOL PLAYLEADERS to coach school age children in sporting
activities.
Wages £3.38 per hour: hours by arrangement (mostly in daytime). To work
over the summer holidays. Applications to the personnel Department, at the
above address. (O)

MOUNTAIN VENTURES LTD: Bryn Du, Ty Du Road, Llanberis, Gwynedd
LL55 4TY (tel 0286-870454).
WATER SPORTS INSTRUCTORS (2). Wages negotiable. RYA qualification
and/or experience desirable.

ACTIVITY GROUP LEADERS (4) needed in outdoor pursuits centre. Wages negotiable according to experience. All staff work a 5-day week with some weekends. Accommodation is available. Applications to the above address. (O)

PGL YOUNG ADVENTURE LTD: Alton Court, Penyard Lane (874), Ross-on-Wye, Herefordshire HR9 5NR (tel 0989-764211). Over 2,500 staff needed to assist in the running of activity centres in the Brecon beacons and Black Mountains.
INSTRUCTORS in canoeing, sailing, windsurfing, pony trekking, hill walking, fencing, archery, judo, rifle shooting, fishing, motorsports, arts and crafts, drama, English language and many other activities. Min. age 18.
GROUP LEADERS to take responsibility for small groups of children and ensure that they get the most out of their holiday. Min. age 20 years. Previous experience of working with children necessary.
Pocket money from £30 p.w. Full B. & L. provided. Vacancies available for short or long periods between February and October. Requests for application forms to the Personnel Department, PGL. (O)

SHARE: Discovery '80' Ltd, Smiths Strand, Lisnaskea, Co. Fermanagh, Northern Ireland (tel 03657-21892/22122). Share is a registered charity that runs a residential activities centre to encourage contact between disabled and able-bodied people.
OUTDOOR ACTIVITY INSTRUCTORS (4). Wages depend on qualifications but range from £40-80. To work 39 h.p.w. over 5 days. RYA or BCU qualifications would be useful. Min. age 16. Applicants must be willing and capable of working with people of all ages. Free B. & L. provided. M.p.w. 2 weeks between April and October. Applications, at any time of year, to Mrs R. Johnston, at the above address. (O)

SHROPSHIRE OUTDOOR EDUCATION CENTRE: Arthog, Gwynedd LL39 1BX (tel 0341-250455).
OUTDOOR INSTRUCTORS. Wages according to qualifications. RYA, ML or BCU qualifications useful, teaching certificate a bonus. Interested applicants without qualifications may be taken on, on a voluntary basis. Hours equivalent to 5 days p.w., but long hours. Free B. & L. provided. Activities include mountaineering, canoeing, sailing, walking, etc. Applications to the Shropshire Outdoor Education Centre, at the above address. (O)

TYN-MORFA RIDING CENTRE: Rhosneigr, Anglesey (tel 0407-810279).
TREK LEADERS or ASSISTANTS (2) to escort rides on the beach. Wages negotiable, according to age and experience. Hours: 8am-5pm. To work 6 days

per week. Free B. & L. in caravan. Applicants should be aged 18 or over, able to ride well, and responsible enough to take charge of rides. Season begins mid-May. Applications from 1 May to Mr A. J. Carnall, Tyn-Morfa Riding Centre.

WEST OF IRELAND CAMPS: 18 Guildford Lawn, Ramsgae, Kent CT11 9AY (tel 0853-592518). A Christian organization founded in 1919, running camps for boys and girls aged 8-16 years.
INSTRUCTORS: SAILING (1), HILL WALKING and ABSEILING (1), CANOEING (1), WINDSURFING (1). Wages for all positions are negotiable. Hours can be variable as positions are residential. Accommodation in tents provided. Period of work 1 July to 20 August. Qualifications and Christian commitment required. Interviews are preferred. Applications at any time to Peter J. Pugh, West of Ireland Camps, at the above address. (O)

YOUNG LEISURE ACTIVITY HOLIDAYS LTD: Rock Park Centre, Llandrindod Wells, Powys LD1 6AE (tel 0597-822021). Residential holiday centre for children and adults.
COACHES/INSTRUCTORS. £90 p.w. Residential staff work all hours; day staff work 9.15am-4.30pm. Must have appropriate qualifications for canoeing, sailing, gymnastics, etc.
ASSISTANTS. £60 p.w. Hours as above. Min. age 18 years (preferably over 21). College/university training of 3 years needed. Free B. & L. Students of Physical Education particularly welcome as most activities involve sport. M.p.w. from Easter to the end of August. Applications (with s.a.e.) a.s.a.p. to Mrs E. Higginson, Young Leisure Activity Holidays. (O)

VOLUNTARY WORK

Archaeology

CANTERBURY ARCHAEOLOGICAL TRUST LTD: 92A Broad Street, Canterbury CT1 2LU (tel 0227-462062).
EXCAVATION VOLUNTEERS (20) required to work 40 h.p.w. over 5 days. Approx. £7.50 per day for meals. Cheap campsite space is provided. Min. age 18. Good English is essential as well as good health and the ability to work in all weathers. M.p.w. 2 weeks between May and September. Applications between March and May to Jane Elder, Secretary to the Director, at the above address. (O)

DORSET NATURAL HISTORY AND ARCHEOLOGICAL SOCIETY: Dorset County Museum, Dorset DT1 1XA (tel 0305-262735).
Information about excavations in Dorset may be obtained from the above address. Please send s.a.e.

NORTH YORKSHIRE COUNTY COUNCIL: Planning Department, County Hall, Northallerton, North Yorkshire (tel 0609-780780 ext 2331).
Up to 25 volunteers are needed to assist with the excavation and conservation of local North Yorkshire archaeological sites. Period of work June-September. Min. age 17 years. Previous similar experience desirable. Details available after February from Mary Larkin at the above address.

Children and Youth Activities

BIRMINGHAM YOUNG VOLUNTEERS: 24 Albert Street, Birmingham B4 7UD (tel 021-643 8297).
BYV needs volunteers to help with summer adventure camp holidays for disadvantaged children. Food and accommodation provided. Those living locally in West Midlands preferred. Volunteers should have an interest, and preferably experience, in working with children. Volunteers helping on this scheme should be aged at least 17 years. Each volunteer needed for one week only. There are also opportunities to undertake training and become involved in the fund-raising, social and management acivities of the adventure camps. Applications to the Co-ordinator at the above address.

CHILDREN'S COMMUNITY HOLIDAYS: 34 Mount Charles, Belfast BT7 1N2 (tel 0232-245650).
Children's Community Holidays requires house staff to help in the running of its residential holidays for children aged between 8 and 15 years. The holidays are aimed at bringing together children from Protestant and Catholic traditions, and to provide holidays for children from deprived and difficult backgrounds. Expenses are paid on a day by day basis. Min. age $16\frac{1}{2}$ and applicants must have interest in this type of work. Free accommodation provided. M.p.w. 10 days between 1 July and 31 August. Applications should be sent to the Administrator from 31 March, at the above address. Applicants need not be available for interview, but references are required.

CHILDREN'S COUNTRY HOLIDAYS FUND: 42/43 Lower Marsh, Tanswell Street, London SE1 7RG (tel 071-928 6522; fax 071-401 3961).
This charity provides holidays in the country or at the seaside, for disadvantaged London children, aged between 5 and 13 years. Some children stay with families whilst others attend camps. Volunteers are needed to act as supervisors at 10 day camps during July and August. Applicants must be fond of children, with a sense of fun, and a willingness to ensure that the children enjoy their break away from the inner city. In return, CCHF provides free travel, B. & L., plus a small allowance. For further information contact the above address.

THE CHURCH ARMY: Independents Road, Blackheath, London SE3 9LG (tel 081-318 1226).
The special Summer Evangelism activities of the Church Army involve Beach Missions and Holiday Clubs. Accommodation provided. Applications from committed Christians to Ray Milnes. 'Summer Evangelism', Church Army, at the above address.

CLAN: 40 Warren Road, Stirchley, Birmingham B30 2NY (tel 021-459 3723).
This organization provides short holidays together with associated leisure activities for children aged 7-13 who would not normally benefit from a change in their daily environment. Week-long and weekend camps are held at a number of hostels at attractive sites in the Midlands between July and September and there are also day trips. Min. age for volunteeers is 16 years. Free B. & L. Travelling expenses from within the UK will be paid. Blankets are provided but sleeping bags may be brought if preferred. Experience an advantage but not essential. Applications and further details (enclosing 9" x 4" s.a.e. or IRC) from the above address. (O)

COMMUNITY ACTION PROJECTS: Goodricke College, University of York,

Heslington, York YOl 5DD (tel 0904-433133).
Volunteers are needed to work on week-long camps for underprivileged children. Two weeks of these camps are solely for 14-16 year olds and consist of an adventure-type holiday. Volunteers need a willingness to join in with all activities and to befriend the children. The work is demanding but rewarding. Camping accommodation with the children. Min. age 18 years. Help needed from mid-July to end of August. Applications from beginning of April including s.a.e. or IRC to Liz Thomas, Community Action Officer. (O)

COTSWOLD COMMUNITY: Ashton Keynes, nr Swindon, Wiltshire SN6 6QU (tel 0285-861239).
This is a rural, therapeutic community providing care, treatment and education for severly emotionally disturbed boys, aged 9-18. Volunteers are needed throughout the year for periods of 4 to 12 months. Free B. & L. provided plus £20 p.w. Volunteers must work 5 days p.w. (very full days). Min. age 20 years. Some previous child care experience helpful. EC applicants welcome. For further information contact Mr John Whitwell, Principal, Cotswold Community. (O)

DUNCAIRN PLAYSCHEME: 300A Limestone Road, Belfast BT15 3AR. Also THE PHEONIX CENTRE: Lurgan, BT66 6AT.
VOLUNTEERS required to help run playschemes for children in Lurgan and Belfast. The work involves leading children aged between 8 and 15 in constructive activities, going on outings, supervising swimming, games, etc., in the afternoons and evenings. B. & L. provided from 20 July to 11 August. Skills in music, arts, drama, etc. an advantage.

THE INTERNATIONAL FLAT: 20 Glasgow Street, Glasgow G12 8JP (tel 041-339 6118).
VOLUNTEERS (6) to help on inner city playscheme for children of various ethnic and cultural backgrounds for 3 weeks during July. Hours: 9.30am-4.30pm Monday to Friday. Min. age 18 years. Experience of working with children preferred, and skills such as arts, games, etc. useful. Self-catering accommodation provided. The International Flat is also a social and educational centre for children, women and overseas students' wives. Applications from 30 April to Mrs Gandhi, Community Worker, The International Flat.

LONDON CHILDREN'S CAMP: 105 Bevan Street West, Lowestoft, Suffolk NR32 2AF (tel 0502-569226).
Offers 3 holidays of 11 days' duration on the Suffolk coast for boys and girls who would not otherwise have a break from the capital. Twenty leaders are

required each period to work with 100 children aged 9-14 years. £20 pocket money per camp. Free time on alternate evenings. Free B. & L.; sleeping bags essential. The site is by the sea and there are opportunities for all sports. Min. age 18 years. Experience welcome but not necessary. Two referees required. Fluent English essential. M.p.w. 2 weeks between mid-July and end of August. Applications (the earlier the better) from December to Mr Dave Randoll, at the above address.

MANSFIELD OUTDOOR CENTRE: Manor Road, Lambourne End, Essex RM4 1ND (tel 081-500 3047).
Mansfield Outdoor Centre is situated close to the Hainault Forest, in 60 acres of open country. It is a branch of Mansfield House University Settlement which is a registered charity. The Centre, as well as organizing leisure activities, aims to encourage social interaction amongst the young, disabled and disadvantaged within a Christian framework.
Helpers are needed to work $37\frac{1}{2}$ h.p.w. 5 days p.w. including some weekends. Experience of outdoor activities, such as climbing, canoeing, archery, etc. required as well as experience of working with young people. Travel and expenses to be discussed, and necessary activity and youth work training will be given. B. & L. is sometimes available, free of charge. Volunteers needed all year round. Applications a.s.a.p. to Mr Graham Head, Warden, at the above address. (O)

SCRIPTURE UNION: 120 City Road, London EC1V 2NJ (tel 071-782 0013).
Scripture union is an organization which arranges Christian holidays for young people, and which needs volunteer activity instructors for one week during the summer. Volunteers would be resident on site for this period of time, and should be prepared to work long hours. Age: 18 + years. Qualifications and/or experience in outdoor activities, sports, working with the disabled, First Aid and Life Saving, are welcomed. Some B. & L. is available, for which a charge is made. Work is available between the beginning of July and the end of August. An interview is not necessary. Contact the Activities Administrator, at the above address, for an application form.

STRATHCLYDE REGIONAL COUNCIL: Mearns Primary School House, 218 Ayr Road, Newton Mearns, Glasgow (tel 041-639 7160).
Ten leaders for summer playschemes are needed in the Glasgow area. This is a good opportunity for trainee teachers, social workers, etc. to get pre-qualifiying experience of working with children in an informal setting. Three to five leaders are needed daily. Please note that all leaders work voluntarily, and no payment is possible. More details from Mr J. Heriot, at the above address. (O)

TADWORTH COURT CHILDREN'S CENTRE: Tadworth, Surrey KT20 5RU (tel 0737-357171).
Requires volunteer workers to help with holiday and other schemes for physically and mentally handicapped children. Free lodging and food allowance. Min. age 18 years. Experience with handicapped children an advantage. M.p.w. 4 weeks. Further details from the Administration Department at the above address. (O)

Conservation and the Environment

BRITISH TRUST FOR CONSERVATION: Noah's Ark, Newtown, Isle of Wight PO30 4PA (tel 1983-78576).
VOLUNTEERS (up to 4) to assist with conservation tasks and working holidays over the summer. To work 4 days p.w. No pocket money paid; cost of B. & L. approx. £5 per day. Min. age 17. No previous experience necessary. For further details send £1 (or IRC) for information sheets to the above address. (O)

BTCV (BRITISH TRUST FOR CONSERVATION VOLUNTEERS): Room VW, 36 St. Mary's Street, Wallingford, Oxfordshire OX10 0EU (tel 0491-39766). Volunteers aged 16-75 required to take part in over 550 Natural Break conservation working holidays throughout the country, lasting 1-2 weeks, all year round. The practical conservation work undertaken on projects includes hedge-laying, tree-planting, dry-stone walling, fencing and pathwork, for example. Costs are around £30 per week, to cover membership of BTCV, training in conservation skills, food and basic accommodation in village halls, Volunteer Centres, cottages, etc. Working day lasts from 9am to 5pm, but there is at least one day off per week. For a free brochure send a 42p stamp to BTCV at the above address.

CATHEDRAL CAMPS: Manor House, High Birtswith, Harrogate, North Yorkshire HG3 2LG (tel 0423-770385). Registered Charity No.286248. VOLUNTEERS to work in groups of 15-25 people undertaking maintenance, conservation and restoration of cathedrals and their surroundings all over the country. Hours normally 8.30am-5.30pm, $4\frac{1}{2}$ days p.w. The camps take place from July-September; each camp lasts one week. A contribution of approx. £25 is asked to go towards the cost of the camp and board and lodging. Min. age 16 years. Most are aged 17-25. For further details and an application form, contact Shelley Bent, 16 Glebe Avenue, Flitwick, Bedfordshire MK45 1HS (tel 0525-712697).

DERBYSHIRE INTERNATIONAL YOUTH CAMP: Derbyshire Youth House, Mill Street, Derby DE1 1DY (tel 0332-45538).
One-week youth camps are held between July and August, based in a residential school near Derby City. The projects undertaken include conservation and environmental work in the county parks, and community work on a summer playscheme within the city. A variety of activities are available during the evening, ranging from outdoor pursuits, through to arts, crafts and drama events. Age: 16-21 years. Applications from January to the Derbyshire International Youth Camp, at the above address.

DYFED WILDLIFE TRUST: 7 Market Street, Haverfordwest, Dyfed SA61 1NF.
VOLUNTARY ASSISTANT WARDENS (6 per week) required for Skomer Island, a National Nature Reserve off the Welsh coast. Work involves meeting day visitors, census work, general maintenance and recording, etc. To work 7 days p.w. for a minimum of 1 week between Easter and 30 September. Self-catering accommodation is available free of charge. Min. age 16 and volunteers should have an interest in natural history. Foreign students are welcome. Applications from September to Mrs J. Glennerster, Islands Booking Officer, at the above address. (O)

FESTINIOG RAILWAY COMPANY: Harbour Station, Porthmadog, Gwynedd, North Wales LL49 9NF (tel 0766-512340).
Volunteers are required to help in the maintenance and running of the 150 year old narrow gauge railway. A wide variety of work is available in the Traffic and Commercial Department, Locomotive Operating Department, Mechanical Department, and the Civil Engineering Department. The Active Parks Department needs skilled and unskilled assistance with improving the appearance of the station surrounds and picnic areas. Qualified and experienced electricians and builders also needed. Training given where necessary. Min.

age 16. All volunteers must be fit. Limited self-catering hostel accommodation for regular volunteers, for which a small charge is made; food is extra. Camping space and list of local accommodation also available. Applications to the Volunteer Officer, at the above address. (O)

THE NATIONAL TRUST: Volunteer Unit, PO Box 12, Westbury, Wiltshire BA13 4NA (tel 0373-826826).
Organizes 'Acorn' and other projects for outdoor conservation work on National Trust land throughout England and Wales in spring and summer. Volunteers pay £30 p.w. min. to help cover the cost of B. & L. and are responsible for their own travel (although timings are supplied). Accommodation varies from village halls to barns to hostels; volunteers supply bedding or sleeping bags. Projects vary between 12 and 20 volunteers and are for a min. of 1 week, but 2 or more camps may be joined if dates do not overlap. Min. age 17 years; overseas visitors 18 years. Application forms and information on specific projects available in January from Mrs B. A. Sims, at the above address. (O)

ROYAL SOCIETY FOR THE PROTECTION OF BIRDS: The Lodge, Sandy, Bedfordshire SG19 2DL (tel 0767-680551).
Voluntary wardens are required to work on several RSPB reserves throughout England, Scotland and Wales to assist with their day-to-day running. Accommodation provided. Min. age 16 years. Applicants should be interested in the countryside. Further details of these posts are available from Sandra Manners, RSPB, at the above address.
In addition voluntary wardens are required to work on Operation Osprey in Loch Garten Reserve, Strathspey, Scotland, which runs from 30 March to 31 August. Work is on a 24-hour rota system, with every third day off. The work involves guarding the breeding ospreys and recording their activities, plus helping visitors to the reserve. A volunteer cook is also required each week, cooking on a day on/day off basis with the resident caterer, to prepare meals for between 15 and 18 volunteers and staff. Accommodation provided in tents or caravans at a cost of £10 including meals; volunteers must provide bedding. Min. age 18 years. Applicants should be interested in conservation. Knowledge of ornithology useful. Min. 1 week. Applicants to apply a.s.a.p. to Richard Thaxton, RSPB, Grianan, Nethybridge, Inverness-shire PH25 3EF (tel 047 983-694).

RUTLAND RAILWAY MUSEUM: Ashwell Road, Cottesmore, Oakham, Leicestershire LE15 7BX (tel 05572-813203 for site; 0780-63092/62384 for information).
This Museum, a steam railway centre, is a voluntary organization, and also

registered as an educational charity. It is situated in rural East Leicestershire, within easy reach of Stamford, Leicester, Grantham, Nottingham and Northampton. Volunteers are needed between Easter and September, and are welcome to choose their own period of work. Free accommodation may be arranged on site, otherwise Bed and Breafast accommodation is available at local rates. Work is varied, but is mainly comprised of locomotive (steam and diesel) restoration and servicing, coach/wagon painting and woodworking, and also site development and maintenance. Applications welcomed at any time to the Honorary Secretary, at the above address. (O)

SCOTTISH CONSERVATION PROJECTS: Balallan House, 24 Allan Park, Stirling FK8 2QG (tel 0786-79697).
LONG TERM VOLUNTEERS (4) to provide support for practical conservation work. No wage, but accommodation may be available. Duties include attending Action Breaks and Operation Brighwater projects, as well as tool, equipment and vehicle maintenance. Period of work from June to September. Applicants should be aged 17-70: no previous experience is necessary but those with an interest in conservation preferred.
VOLUNTARY LEADER to lead Action Breaks. Food and accommodation are provided. The job includes organizing work amongst volunteers, distributing tools, equipment, vehicles and food, and taking responsibility for the well-being of volunteers. Period of work from March to November. Applicants should be aged at least 23, hold a clean driving licence, and have experience of working with volunteers and of lowland footpath construction, rhododendron clearance, and marram grass planting.
Applications to Nancy McEwen at the above address. (O)

SUNSEED TRUST: 10 Timworth, Bury St Edmunds, Suffolk IP31 1HY (tel 0284-728863).
Sunseed Trust is a registered charity undertaking various research projects into things such as drought-resistant trees, erosion control, organic gardening, etc. Two gardeners/writers/general hands are required to work as long as possible. Full B. & L. provided plus £10 p.w. pocket money. Duties may include preparing exhibitions, mailing lists, news releases, building repairs, organic gardening, etc. No qualifications are necessary. Working for the Sunseed Trust may lead to similar work in Spain or France in the future. Applications to the above address.

THISTLE CAMPS: National Trust for Scotland, 5 Charlotte Square, Edinburgh EH2 4DU (tel 031-226 5922).
Thistle Camps are voluntary projects lasting one or two weeks which help the

National Trust for Scotland in the conservation and management of the rich variety of countryside, castles, gardens, little houses and historic sites in its care. Projects in 1992 will include sand dune stabilization on the Isle of Iona, footpath construction and repair at Crathes Castle near Aberdeen and Brodick Castle on the Isle of Arran, building and plumbing work on the Isle of Canna, and woodland management at Killiecrankie in Perthshire. The Thistle Camps programme also incorporates the very popular work parties on Fair Isle, Britain's most remote inhabited island, where volunteers work alongside the islanders repairing buildings, maintaining the airstrip and helping with all kinds of farm work, such as fencing, drystone dyking, and haymaking. Min. age 16 years. An experienced leader and/or a Trust Ranger Naturalist supervises all practical work. All camps include time off for recreation and exploration of the local area. Camps are usually located in Trust Base Camps or similar hostel-type accommodation. All food is provided but volunteers help with cooking, washing-up, cleaning and all other chores. Volunteers pay for their own travel to a pick-up point near the camp location, plus £18 per camp as a contribution to food costs. Thistle Camps take place between March and October; in addition, similar conservation projects are organized at weekends throughout the year by local Conservation Volunteer groups. For information on the full 1992 programme apply early to the above address. Foreign applicants should apply as early as possible (March/April) to ensure a place on the camp. (O)

WORKING WEEKENDS ON ORGANIC FARMS: 19 Bradford Road, Lewes, Sussex BN7 1RB.
VOLUNTEERS are needed to spend time working on organic farms, gardens and smallholdings around the UK: organic farming avoids the use of artificial fertilizers and pest killers, and can be labour intensive. Accommodation and food are provided. Once participants have spent two weekends working, it is possible to arrange longer stays. Applicants must have a genuine interest in furthering the organic movement. Applications welcomed from students/individuals of any nationality. For further information send a 9" x 4" s.a.e. to the above address. (O)

Hospitals and Medical Research

THE DULWICH HOSPITAL BROADCASTING/VOLUNTARY SERVICES: East Dulwich Road, London SE22 8JP (tel 081-693 3377).
Volunteers are needed to help with the hospital radio service. Work would include collecting requests from patients, as well as assisting on the radio programmes themselves. Daytime help preferred. Min. age 18 years. Meal allowance paid. No accommodation available. Applications to Vic Short, Voluntary Services Organiser.

NORTHGATE HOSPITAL: Northgate Street, Great Yarmouth, Norfolk (tel 0493-856222 ext 463).
Small numbers of university graduates required to work as Voluntary Assistants within the Patients' Amenity Services and Recreational Activity Programmes in 4 small hospitals that include psychiatric, mentally handicapped and geriatric wards. No pay, but meals provided. Some accommodation may be available for foreign university students. Applicants must be resident in the UK, or else overseas university students with a good command of English. Applications to Mr B. E. Callan, Director of Amenity and Voluntary Services, Anglian Harbours NHS Trust. (O)

ST. PANCRAS HOSPITAL: 4 St. Pancras Way, London NW1 0PE (tel 071-387 4111 ext 368; 24 hour ansaphone).
Volunteers (men and women) are needed to befriend the elderly long-stay patients on the geriatric wards, helping them with leisure activities, outings and entertainments. Anyone who enjoys the company of old people is welcome. M.p.w. 4 weeks. Local fares and meals paid. No accommodation provided. Min. age 18 years. Also volunteer drivers needed to help with outings in a special bus, and to help in the geriatric Day Hospital and Stroke Unit. Contact Angela Casey, Voluntary Services Organizer. (O)

UNIVERSITY COLLEGE HOSPITAL: Gower Street, London WC1E 6AU (tel 071-387 9300 ext 8055).
Volunteers are needed to help on the wards, take patients out in wheelchairs and deal with a wide variety of jobs while regular volunteers are away on holiday. Hours are 10am-9pm. Min. age 18 years. It is most useful if volunteers can help for at least 6 weeks. Unfortunately no accommodation is available. Kindness, adaptability and fluent English are the main qualifications needed. Enquiries to Mrs Lesley Borzoni, Voluntary Service Co-ordinator, at the above address.

Physically/Mentally Disabled

THE ASSOCIATION FOR ALL SPEECH IMPAIRED CHILDREN: 347 Central Markets, Smithfield, London EC1A 9NH (tel 071-236 2632/6487).
VOLUNTEERS (40-90) to help on Activity Weeks/Holidays organized for speech and language impaired children and young people. Volunteers act as constant companions to a child or young person aged 6-20 for one week: the work involves participation in outdoor pursuits such as canoeing, abseiling, walking or beach activities. Lodging is provided. Period of work from the end of July to the end of August. Applicants should be aged 18 with good spoken English. Applications to the Volunteer Department at the above address. (O)

ASSOCIATION FOR SPINA BIFIDA AND HYDROCEPHALUS: Five Oaks House, Ben Rhydding Drive, Ilkley LS29 8BD (tel 0943-609408).
VOLUNTEER CARE WORKERS. To work with children and young people on holiday at the centre. Staff needed throughout June, July and August. Min. age 18. Experience of working with the disabled would be an advantage but is not essential. Applications to Sarah Peek the above address. (O)

BEANNACHAR: Banchory-Devenick, Aberdeen AB1 5YL (tel 0224-861825).
Beannachar is a training community for mentally handicapped teenagers and young adults. Volunteers are needed for household, workshops, garden and farm during the summer, and also long-term volunteers at any time of year. Free B. & L. plus pocket money. Long hours, 6 days p.w. Min. age 19 years. Must have lots of enthusiasm and a positive attitude. Applicants from abroad must speak reasonable English. M.p.w. 2 months between June and September, 6 months for long-term volunteers. Applications anytime to Ms E. A. Phethean at the above address. (O)

BREAK: 20 Hooks Hill Road, Sheringham, Norfolk NR26 8NL (tel 0263-823170).
Volunteers required at two centres on the Norfolk coast providing holidays and general short-term care for handicapped children and adults. Approx. £20 p.w. pocket money and travel expenses within the UK. To work 40 h.p.w. on a rota basis. Free B & L. Duties consist of helping with all needs of guests' care and recreational programme and essential domestic tasks. Demanding work requiring well-adjusted, stable staff. M.p.w. 6 weeks. Longer periods, up to 6 months, possible. Centres open all year round. Applications to Mr G. M. Davison, Director, at the above address. (O)

THE CAMPHILL VILLAGE TRUST: Delrow House, Hilfield Lane, Aldenham, Watford, Herts WD2 8DJ (tel 0923-856006).
This organization runs over 30 working communities throughout Britain for mentally handicapped adults and children, based on anthropolsophy as founded by Rudolf Steiner. Voluntary helpers are required for the household, workshop or on the land during summer; otherwise m.p.w. 12 months. Free B. & L. provided. Min. age 20 years. Foreign applicants welcome. Details on application to Miss Ann Harris, Secretary to Delrow House. (O)

CARE for people with a Mental Handicap: Central Office, 9 Weir Road, Kibworth, Leicestershire LE8 0LQ (tel 0533-793225).
RESIDENTIAL SOCIAL WORKERS (10-20) to assist at communities for mentally handicapped adults in Devon, Sussex, Kent, Leicestershire, Lancashire,

Shropshire and Northumberland. Pocket money of £25 p.w. To work 40 hours per 5 day week. Free B. & L. Min. age 18 years. M.p.w. 6 weeks throughout the year. Applications at any time to the Communty Director, CARE.

CECIL HOUSES: 2/4 Priory Road, Kew, Richmond, Surrey TW9 3DG (tel 081-940 9828).
VOLUNTEERS for work including care of the elderly, domestic work and organizing social activities. Pocket money of £20 p.w. plus free shared B. & L. To work 39 hours over 7 days on a shift basis. Period of work by arrangement. Min. age 18. Applications should be sent to the above address. (O)

THE DISAWAY TRUST: 2 Charles Road, Merton Park, London SW19 3BD. About 42 volunteers are needed during July and September for 8-10 days to help physically disabled people on holiday. A contribution towards travel, accommodation and entertainment is required (about half of actual cost). No special qualifications or experience needed. Foreign applicants welcome, but no travelling expenses available. For further details, including information on dates and locations, contact the Project Coordinator. (O)

HELP THE HANDICAPPED: 147a Camden Road, Tunbridge Wells, Kent TN1 2RA (tel 0892-547474).
VOLUNTEER CARE ASSISTANTS to provide one-to-one care for physically disabled people on holiday. No pocket money paid, but B. & L. provided. Holidays usually last for one week and take place between late May and September. Applicants should be aged between 18 and 60 and need a sense of humour, a strong back, great patience and a sense of responsibility. Experience of similar work an advantage but not essential. A charge of £50 is normally made to helpers for holidays in the UK; there is also a holiday in Spain, for which the charge is £125. Advice can be given on raising this by sponsorship. Applications to the Holiday Organizer at the above address. (O)

HOLIDAY HELPERS: 2 Old Bank Chambers, Station Road, Horley, Surrey RH6 9HW (tel 0293-775137).
VOLUNTEER HOLIDAY HELPERS to help disabled or elderly people who can only take a holiday if they can find someone to go with them. Helpers are expected to provide their own spending money: all other holiday costs are met by the person they are helping. These holidays may be taken at any time of year. Jobs only suitable for those resident in the UK. For further information contact, the Project Coordinator, at the above address.

INDEPENDENT LIVING ALTERNATIVES: Fulton House, Fulton Road, Empire Way, Wembly, Middlesex (tel 081-902 8998 ext 270).

VOLUNTEERS required to help disabled people live independent lives in their own homes by living with them for four to six months. The job involves helping them perform simple activities, such as getting dressed, going to the toilet, washing, driving, etc. Volunteers receive £50 p.w. plus free accommodation, usually in the London area. No particular qualifications are required, but a driving licence would be an advantage. Vacancies arise all year round. Applications should be sent to Tracey Jannaway at the above address. (O)

THE LEONARD CHESHIRE FOUNDATION: Leonard Cheshire House, 26/29 Maunsel Street, London SW1P 2QN (tel 071-828 1822).
The Leonard Cheshire Foundation runs Homes for handicapped adults (mainly physically disabled) throughout the UK. Voluntary workers are required in some Homes to assist with the physical care of residents and their social activities. Period of work from 3-12 months. Free B. & L. Pocket money £25 p.w. min. No travel expenses provided. Application form from the Secretary to the Personnel Adviser, The Leonard Cheshire Foundation. (O)

MENCAP HOLIDAY SERVICES: 119 Drake Street, Rochdale, Lancashire OL16 1PZ (tel 0706-54111).
Organizes an annual programme of holidays for children and adults with a mental handicap. The holidays take place throughout England and Wales, and include adventure and guest house holidays for the more able, and special care holidays for those who are profoundly/multiply handicapped. Volunteers, who must be over 18 years of age, are responsible for organizing activities such as mime, arts and crafts, swimming, outings and free play sessions. Previous experience an advantage, but not essential. The work is long and hard. Free meals and accommodation provided, plus up to £20 assistance with travelling expenses. Period of work 1-2 weeks from Easter until September. Leaflet available from the above address.

 VOLUNTEERS NEEDED

Independent Living Alternatives promotes independence for people disabled. Full time volunteers are required to provide physical support, such as helping an individual to dress, wash, go to the toilet and also, with housework, shopping etc. Volunteers receive £50 pw plus free accommodation (no bills), usually in the London area. No experience is necessary, as all training is provided, but a driving license would be an advantage. Volunteers must be able to speak English and are expected to stay for four to six months. Vacancies arise all year round. Contact **Tracey Jannaway** at: **Independent Living Alternatives, Fulton House, Fulton Road, Empire Way, Wembley, Middx HA9 0TF. 081-902 8998 ext 270.**

NORTHUMBRIA CALVERT TRUST: Kielder Water, Hexham, Northumberland NE48 1BS (tel 0434-250232).
This is a purpose-built holiday centre for disabled people, their family and friends. The Northumbria Calvert Trust is a registered charity and welcomes people with all disabilities, whether physical, mental or sensory.
ACTIVITY INSTRUCTORS (10). To work from 9am-6pm, and one night 6-11pm. Experience/qualifications in sailing, canoeing, climbing or horse riding is useful, as is a driving licence.
DOMESTIC HELP (2). To work 8am-4pm.
BAR PERSONS (2).
All staff work 5 days p.w. on a weekly/7-day rota basis. Min. age 18. B. & L. is provided free of charge. M.p.w. 4 weeks between 1 May and 10 October. Interviews are generally necessary but this may depend on circumstances. Applications from 1 February to the Director at the above address. (O)

QUEEN ELIZABETH'S FOUNDATION FOR THE DISABLED: Lulworth Court, 25 Chalkwell Esplanade, Westcliffe-on-Sea, Essex SS0 8JQ (tel 0702-431725).
VOLUNTEERS aged 18 years upwards are required for 1-2 weeks to help give lively informal holidays to severely physically disabled people at Lulworth Court — a holiday home on the seafront at Westcliffe-on-Sea. Work involves assisting nursing staff to look after guests, many of whom are confined to wheelchairs and need complete help with all aspects of personal care as well as escorting on outings, shopping and theatre trips. The work is fun but demanding, requiring some heavy liftng. A sense of humour certainly helps. Volunteers are needed all year round. Full B. & L. is provided free of charge, and volunteers are given £15 p.w. towards travelling and other expenses. Overseas volunteers are welcome for 1-2 weeks providing they have a working knowledge of the English language. Further details available from the Holiday Organizer, at the above address. (O)

RADAR (Royal Association for Disability and Rehabilitation): 25 Mortimer Street, London W1N 8AB (tel 071-637 5400).
Each year the Association draws up a list 'Volunteers for Holidays' giving details of organizations and various clubs which organize holidays for disabled people. Volunteers are needed to help on these holidays, giving personal assistance to the disabled holidaymakers. Holidays are for a min. of 1 week. Free B. & L. are ususally provided. Min. age for volunteers is normally 16 years. Further details from the Information Department. (O)

RITCHIE RUSSELL HOUSE: Churchill Hospital, Headington, Oxford OX3 7LJ (tel 0865-225482).

VOLUNTEERS to either provide one-to-one care for disabled adults on their holiday during the summer, or to provide regular help in the residential unit at Ritchie Russell House throughout the year. Duties on the holidays include washing, feeding, dressing, etc. Within the unit, duties include helping for up to 3 hours with the morning, afternoon or evening sessions (no personal care involved). Min. age 17. No special qualifications required, but experience of working with the physically disabled an advantage. Applications to Barbara Martin, Voluntary Services Organizer, at the above address.

SHAD (HARINGEY): Winkfield Resource Centre, 33 Winkfield Road, London N22 5RP (tel 081-365 8528).
VOLUNTEERS (12 at any one time) to help with the activities of SHAD (Support and Housing Assistance for people wiht Disabilities), which enable tenants with physical disabilities to live in their own homes in London. Volunteers act as the tenants' arms and legs under their instructions. Volunteers receive £43 p.w., free separate accommodation, all expenses and support and training. Work is on a rota basis: volunteers can expect a minimum of 4 days off a fortnight and regular long weekends. The work takes place around the year: volunteers must be prepared to stay for at least 4 months. Applicants from EC welcome. A driving licence would be an advantage but is not essential. Applications to Sue Denney at the above address.

SHAFTESBURY SOCIETY: The Shaftesbury Society Holiday Centre, New Hall, Low Road, Dovercourt, near Harwich, Essex CO12 3TS (tel 0255-504219). Volunteers required to help with holidays for the physically handicapped with such personal matters as washing, dressing, toilet and feeding. Also some laundry, bed-making and dining room duties. Min. age 16 years. Applicants should be sympathetic to the Christian aims of the Society, willing to work long hours and undertake possibly distasteful tasks. Free B. & L. provided; expenses may be offered for travel within the UK. Period of work 1 or 2 weeks between April and October. All enquiries to the Volunteers' Secretary at the above address. (O)

SHARE: Discovery '80' Ltd, Smiths Strand, Lisnaskea, Co. Fermanagh, Northern Ireland (tel 03657-21892/22122).
Share is a registered charity that runs a residential centre, which through varied outdoor activities aims to encourage contact between disabled and able-bodied people. All ages, from primary school children to senior citizens, are welcomed at the Centre. General volunteers (about 6) are needed to assist disabled guests as well as helping with domestic duties and outdoor activities. They will receive £10 p.w. pocket money for 5 days work. Free B. & L. is provided. Min. age

16. M.p.w. 2 weeks between April and October. Applications, at any time of year, to Mrs R. Johnston, at the above address. (O)

ST. EBBAS: Hook Road, Epsom, Surrey KT19 8QT (tel 03727-22212 ext 251). VOLUNTEERS needed to help with mentally handicapped adults in day services, clubs, drama, music, physiotherapy and sports, including swimming and horse-riding. Accommodation available for 2 people and meals are provided. To work 30 h.p.w. Min. age 16. Period of work June-October. Applications to Voluntary Services, at the above address.

THE SUE RYDER FOUNDATION: Headquarters and Sue Ryder Home, Cavendish, Sudbury, Suffolk CO10 8AY.
Provides homes for sick and disabled people of different ages throughout Britain. Homes are run informally, so the hours are irregular and often long. A great deal of the work done by temporary helpers is domestic, but assistance is also needed for routine office work, etc. Volunteers with qualifications or experience in law, building, languages, secretarial duties, nursing, domestic science, cooking, occupational therapy and physiotherapy, are especially welcome. People with a strong sense of vocation, disciplined and in excellent health are required. M.p.w. acceptable is 2 months; those able to work longer are given preference. Written references are taken up by the Foundation and a Doctor's certificate is essential. (O)

WINGED FELLOWSHIP TRUST: Angel House, 20-32 Pentonville Road, London N1 9XD.
Residential volunteers are needed all year round to help the permanent staff at their centres in Essex, Nottingham, Surrey, Merseyside and a new centre at Netley Waterside House in Southampton. Volunteers will become the arms, legs, companions and friends of the guests, and look after all their daily needs. There will also be some domestic chores such as kitchen work and general cleaning. Min. age 16. Free B. & L. M.p.w. 1 week. No special experience necessary, but a caring and sympathetic attitude, and stamina, is needed. Applications, at any time, to the Volunteer Organizer, at the above address. (O)

WOODLARKS CAMP SITE TRUST: Tilford Road, Lower Bourne, Farnham, Surrey GU10 3RN (tel 0252-716279).
The Trust provides camping facilities for organizations interested in running summer camps for physically handicapped people, particularly children. Camps last 1 week and a small fee is usually paid by helpers to the camp leader to cover the cost of food, etc. All camping equipment is provided including blankets. Teams of voluntary helpers are organized by the camp leader to assist

campers. Anyone interested should write, enclosing s.a.e., to the Honorary Secretary, Kathleen Marshall House, at the above addess.

Social and Community Schemes

ASHRAM COMMUNITY SERVICE PROJECT: 23-25 Grantham Road, Sparkbrook, Birmingham B11 1LU (tel 021-773 7061).
Volunteers are needed to share full-time in the life of this multi-racial Christian residential community and to help on related schemes. The work is mostly manual including cooking, gardening, working with animals, occasional supervision of children and some simple maintenance work. No special qualifications are necessary though horticulturalists and people with building skills are especially welcome. Also people with experience of, or with a long-term intention to, work with people with learning difficulties. B. & L. provided at a charge to be arranged. Help required throughout the year. M.p.w. 2 weeks. Further information available from Ute Jaeckel, Project Coordinator, Ashram Communtiy Service Project. (O)

COMMUNITY SERVICE VOLUNTEERS: 237 Pentonville Road, London N1 9NJ (tel 071-278 6601).
Arranges projects for young volunteers to work in close contact with people in need, including children, adolescents, adults with mental or physical handicaps and the elderly, in homes, hospitals, hostels, with social services departments, in community centres, etc. Volunteers must commit themselves for full-time service for a minimum of 4 months and be aged between 16 and 35. They are placed wherever their help is needed in the UK, and work alongside professionals. No one is rejected. B. & L. provided, plus pocket money and some travelling expenses. CSV also places overseas volunteers aged 18-35 with good English, who are able to meet British visa requirements. Overseas volunteers work on the same projects as UK ones, and receive the same benefits, pocket money, etc. There is a £395 placement fee for foreign visitors. Further details from the above address. Applications must be submitted at least 6 weeks prior to starting date.

EDINBURGH CYRENIANS: 20 Broughton Place, Edinburgh EH1 3HX (tel 031-556 4971).
The Cyrenian Trust provides two facilities that are primarily for young adults who are otherwise homeless, and who have experienced a variety of difficulties which they are seeking to overcome. Both the city centre hostel and that based on an organic farm in West Lothian are run on community principles; those who are living there take a large measure of responsibility for the life of the

whole community. Residential volunteers, of a similar age to residents, live alongside residents sharing the life and work of the community. Support and regular training is provided by non-residential staff. Volunteers receive full B. & L. plus £22 p.w. pocket money, holiday, clothing and leaving grants, and access to a time-off flat. Min. commitment 6 months. No similar experience required. Vacancies all year round. For further information and application form, contact the Administrative Secretary at the above address. (O)

GLASGOW SIMON COMMUNITY: 133 Hill Street, Garnethill, Glasgow G3 6UB (tel 041-332 3448).
VOLUNTEERS (8) to live in small group homes with long-term homeless men and women, or to join outreach projects. Pocket money of £15.70 p.w. plus full B. & L. provided. To live in one of 5 projects 5 days a week; separate accommodation provided for days off. Positions available at any time; minimum stay 6 months. Min. age 18. Applicants should be able to treat homeless people as equal human beings and must be able to cope with stressful work. For further details contact the above address. (O)

THE GRAIL CENTRE: 125 Waxwell Lane, Pinner, Middlesex HA5 3ER (tel 081-866 2195/0505).
The Grail Centre in North London is a small centre for courses, conferences and workshops. The subjects range from prayer and spirituality to arts and crafts, from complementry medicine to ecological issues. Grail volunteers assist the resident community of women with domestic work, gardening and estate management and conservation, maintenance, cooking and administrative and office work. No specific qualifications are required, but skilled people are especially welcome. Applicants should be in good health and aged 19 and over, and have at least a basic knowledge of spoken English. They should be able to cope with the demands of community life and the pressure of non-stop visitors. Volunteers are requested to stay a minimum of 3 months, although an occasional concession is made in the summer for those whose vacation does not allow that. B. & L. provided plus £15 p.w. pocket money. Applicants should write to the Volunteers Co-ordinator, at the above address, 3/6 months ahead of the time they propose to work, and should submit a detailed letter, photograph and s.a.e. or IRC. The Grail can support only 12/15 volunteers each year. (O)

GREAT GEORGES COMMUNITY CULTURAL PROJECT: The Blackie, Great George Street, Liverpool 1 (tel 051-709 5109).
Opportunities for anyone over 16 to try alternative education and the arts together with some sport, recreation and welfare in an inner-city context: including youth work, crafts and games; regular workshops with local

youngsters; staging exhibitions and events; and projects from cookery to classical dance, from photography to fashion. Share cooking, cleaning, administration, and some rebuilding work. Endless opportunities to learn and unlearn, to teach and to create. Wonderfully long hours. Stamina, a sense of humour, and a sleeping bag required. Accommodation provided. Volunteers are expected to stay for at least 4 weeks and to contribute towards food costs if they can. Volunteers are welcome throughout the year and particularly over the summer, Christmas and Easter holiday periods. Further information from the Duty Office at the above address.

HOTHORPE HALL LTD: Hothorpe Hall, Theddingworth, Leicestershire LE17 6QX (tel 0858-880257).
Volunteers are needed throughout the year to work as general domestic and kitchen assitants at this Christian conference centre. Duties will include making beds, cleaning, serving meals and washing up, plus gardening and decorating when time permits. Full board and accommodation provided. Pocket money £15 p.w. To work 6 days p.w., approx. 40 h.p.w. Min. age 18 years. No qualifications required besides good spoken English. Staff should also be committed Christians. M.p.w. 4 weeks max. 1 year. Application forms available from Mr R. Stapleton, Director, Hothorpe Hall. (O)

HOUSE OF HOSPITALITY LTD: Grace and Compassion Convent, Paddockhurst Road, Turners Hill, Crawley, West Sussex RH10 4GZ (tel 0342-715672).
House of Hospitality is an interdenominational charity based in a Catholic religious community, running homes for the elderly. It has six residential houses, a nursing unit and sheltered flats in southern England. The aim of the convent is to provide care based on love, with respect for each person's dignity and freedom, in order to ensure their maximum possible independence. Volunteers are needed to participate in working holidays in the community, with duties including household and office work, and nursing care. Hours vary with individaul arrangements, but are generally 4/5 hours daily, with one free day p.w. B. & L. available for charge of approx. £25 p.w. Volunteers are also invited to join the lay community (Shalom) of the convent. These receive £26 p.w. pocket money, with full B. & L. Hours are full-time, with one free day p.w. Shalom members share the prayer life of the sisters, as well as the work. Residents and volunteers of any religious denomination, or none, are welcomed. All volunteers share in the family life of the houses, bringing with them the 'outside world' to the residents. M.p.w. for working holidays is 3 days. M.p.w. for Shalom members is one year. Interviews are generally necessary for all

applicants. Applications should be sent, at any time, to Sister Caitlin (working holidays) or Sister Patricia (Shalom), at the above address. (O)

THE IONA COMMUNITY: The Abbey, Isle of Iona, Argyll PA76 6SN (tel 06817- 404).
An ecumenical Christian Community sharing work, worship, meals and recreation with guests visiting the Macleod and Abbey centres on Iona, and Camas, the more basic outdoors centre on nearby Mull. On Iona volunteers work in the kitchen, Coffee House, shop and office, help with driving, gardening, maintenance, housekeeping and with the guest programme (particularly with children) including arts and crafts activities. At Camas jobs include working with groups of young people, instructing in outdoor skills (e.g. canoeing and abseiling) and cooking. Volunteers are needed for a minimum of 6 weeks between March and October and receive full B. & L., travelling expenses and pocket money. Volunteers should be in sympathy with the Christian faith and the ideals of the Iona Community. Recruitment begins in December. For details write to the Voluntary Staff Coordinator, Iona Abbey. (O).

OTTO SCHIFF HOUSING ASSOCIATION: Central Offices, Osmond House, The Bishops Avenue, London N2 0BG (tel 081-209 0022).
Runs residential homes in North West London for frail and elderly Jewish refugees of Nazi persecution. Voluntary workers are required to assist with the physical care of residents and social activities. Free B. & L. Pocket money £15.25 p.w. M.p.w. 6 months to 1 year. Further information from Mary Copsey, Head of Care, Otto Schiff Housing Association.

PETRUS COMMUNITY LTD: 82 Holt Road, Liverpool L7 2PR (tel 051-263 4543).
Petrus is a registered charity which provides accommodation and support for homeless, single people in Liverpool. Residential voluntary workers are required to help on various projects, which involves a mixture of domestic, welfare and administrative work. Volunteers receive approx. £30 p.w. plus free B. & L. Time off is based around weekends: a weekend on duty is followed by a weekend off duty and so on, and this also allows for days off in the week. Volunteers, however, are expected to work longer hours if necessary. No special qualifictions are required, but applicants must be aged 18-30, enthusiastic, committed and of a tolerant nature. M.p.w. 3 months, at any time of year, although sometimes short term cover is required due to unforseen vacancies. Foreign applicants are welcome. A phone interview may be sufficient but Petrus prefer prospective volunteers to visit the projects. If this is not possible a one month trial period

operates. For further information contact Ms Rita Lomax, at the above address. (O)

SERVICE 9, BRISTOL'S VOLUNTEER BUREAU: 66 Gloucester Road, Bishopston, Bristol BS7 8BH (tel 0272-247929).
Can supply information on a wide range of voluntary work opportunities in greater Bristol during the summer months. Many organizations pay travel and lunch expenses but there is no B. & L. available, so it is essential that volunteers are living in Bristol. For more details visit the jobshop. Volunteers from Bristol can be placed throughout the year in a variety of voluntary work situations (mostly part-time) throughout the city. Details from Service 9. (O)

SIMON COMMUNITY: PO Box 1187, London NW5 4HW (tel 071-485 6639).
Volunteers are needed to work in a night shelter and residential houses, living and working with homeless people from London. Many have severe problems and are unable to find any other accommodation. No previous experience is necessary but acceptance, tolerance and empathy are qualities expected. The work can be both physically and mentally demanding. B. & L. plus £12 p.w. pocket money are provided. Hours of work vary; 40 hours off p.w. Volunteers are needed for a minimum of 3 months at any time of the year. Applicants from any country will be considered if they have a good knowledge of English. Applications to the above address. (O)

TOC H: 1 Forest Close, Wendover, Aylesbury, Buckinghamshire HP22 6BT (tel 0296-623911).
Toc H runs short-term residential community service projects during the year, which vary in length from one weekend to 3 weeks. Projects undertaken include working with needy children, people with a disability or learning difficulties, the elderly, conservation and manual activities, and study/SCUS (discussion) weekends. The projects provide those who take part with opportunities to learn more about themselves and the world we live in. Foreign applications welcome, particularly from EC countries. Ages: 16 or over. The Toc H programme is published twice a year on the Mondays nearest to 1 March and 1 September. A copy may be obtained from the National Projects Office at the above address. Applicants are advised to apply early. Annual recruitment is 500+. (O)

Workcamps

ATD FOURTH WORLD: 48 Addington Square, London SE5 7LB (tel 071-703 3231).
This is an International Movement whose purpose is to combat extreme poverty

and social exclusion by means of projects of action, research and influencing public opinion. Volunteers are required for summer workcamps mainly for manual work. Workcamps last for two weeks. Min. age 18 years. Medium and long-term volunteers are also recruited and trained to work with the Movement. Further information from the above address.

BASECAMP OUTDOOR CENTRE: Marthrown of Mabie, Mabie Forest, Dumfries DG2 8HB (tel 0387-85493).
Volunteers (up to 10) to assist on work parties to carry out conservation and site-work projects, or work with young people. The centre works with youth clubs, probation and social services, and alternative-to-custody groups. No wage but free B. & L. Min. age 18 years. No experience necessary, but must enjoy working in outdoor environment. M.p.w. 1 week between June and September. Applications from March to Mr Jon Barrett, Director, Basecamp.

CORRYMEELA COMMUNITY: 5 Drumaroan Road, Ballycastle, Co. Antrim BT54 6QU (tel 026 57-62626).
Corrymeela is an interdenominational Christian community committed to the work of reconciliation in Northern Ireland and beyond. 20 to 25 volunteers a week are needed over the summer to work with families and children, in manual work camps, work-study programmes, youth groups and special needs groups, etc. The hours are not fixed. 1 day off a week. Min. age 18. Should have reasonable levels of skill in the following areas: music, arts and crafts, drama, recreation, canoeing, cooking and housekeeping or any skill that would be relevant to the Community's programmes. Need an openness to people of all backgrounds, plenty of stamina and a sense of humour. B. & L. available at approx. £22 p.w., although there is no charge for 3 weeks. M.p.w. 2-3 weeks between July and August. For more details about the Community write to the Volunteer Coordinator, at the above address. (O)

INTERNATIONAL VOLUNTARY SERVICE (British branch of Service Civil International): 188 Round Hay Road, Leeds LS8 5PL (tel 0533-549430).
International Voluntary Service organizes about 60 workcamps in Britain each year as well as sending volunteers to workcamps in over 20 other countries. Volunteeers work for two to four weeks in an international team of 10-20 people, sharing domestic and social life as well as the work. The projects include work with children, work with people with physical or mental disabilities, solidarity work with people of other countries, and manual work, often connnected with ecology or conservation. The projects are not holidays. The work can be hard and demands commitment. Most workcamps are between June and September. Volunteers pay a £75 registration fee (£65 for students, £60 unwaged) and their

own travel costs, and must be 18 or over. Free B. & L. is provided on the project. **IVS can only accept applications from people with an address in Britain.** Write for more information to the address above, enclosing £4 for the listing of summer workcamps (available from April). Enquiries from January will be put on a mailing list to receive the listing when it is ready.

QUAKER INTERNATIONAL SOCIAL PROJECTS (QISP): Friends House, 173/177 Euston Road, London NW1 2BJ (tel 071-387 3601).

QISP runs 15-17 short-term (1-3 weeks) voluntary projects in Britain and Northern Ireland each year. The projects take place in the summer and at Easter. Half the volunteers come from abroad. The project work includes enviromental, manual and women-only projects, working with children (on playschemes or holidays), study projects, working with children or adults who have mental or physical disabilities, or working in psychiatric hospitals (not nursing).

Special experience is not usually required. Volunteers with disabilities are welcome to apply and are placed where facilities allow. Min. age for most projects is 18; 16 for special youth projects. The food and accommodation (usually basic) is free during the project. Volunteers pay for their own travel to the project (although help with travelling expenses is sometimes available) and pocket money. A small registration fee is also charged. Volunteers from abroad are accepted, but must apply through the organiztion in their own country. Volunteers who are unemployed may apply for a travel subsidy. Volunteers from abroad are accepted, but must apply through the organization in their own country. There are opportunities for projects in other countries once volunteers have completed a project in the UK. For further details contact the above address. (O)

UNITED NATIONS ASSOCIATION (WALES): International Youth Service, Welsh Centre for International Affairs, Temple of Peace, Cathays Park, Cardiff, South Glamorgan CF1 3AP (tel 0222-223088).

Volunteers required for international voluntary projects in Wales for social, manual, playscheme and environment projects. Usually 6-8 hours work per day, 5 days per week. Free B. & L. Min. age 17 years. Pay own travel costs. Work period varies according to project but usually 2-4 weeks. Camps arranged between June and September. Registration fee from £25. (British volunteers are also sent to projects overseas; registration fee from £55.) Project 'leaders' are always required. They are trained over a weekend in April, pay no fee, and have travel expenses reimbursed. Volunteers resident outside the UK must apply through the workcamp organization in their own country. Applications from April (enclosing s.a.e.) to the International Service Officer at the above address.

AU PAIR
HOME HELP
AND PAYING GUEST

A popular and relatively inexpensive way for an overseas visitor to stay in Britian is to take up a position as an au pair. In lieu of the hard-to-obtain work permit, a letter of invitation from the organizing body or from the family concerned will suffice, providing it indicates what arrangements have been made for the bearer's support and accommodation. The government prohibits non-West European nationals from entering Britain as au pairs, unless they can show that they can be financially self-supporting. Most positions are for a minimum of six months and a maximum of two years, though some shorter summer placements are available. Only unmarried women aged 17-27 may participate.

AARON EMPLOYMENT AGENCY: Suite C, The Courtyard, Stanley Road, Tunbridge Wells, Kent TN1 2RJ (tel 0892-546601).
NANNIES, DOMESTICS. £80-150 p.w. live-in positions. To work approx. 40 h.p.w. with 2 days off. Must have some experience or qualification.
AU PAIRS. Foreign students who come to the UK to live with an English-speaking family to learn the language. Age 17-27 years. £30 p.w. for 30 h.p.w. childminding and light household duties.
Positions available throughout the year. Usually large numbers of vacancies available. M.p.w. 6 weeks. Canadian, Australian and EC applicants welcome. Applications at any time to Richard or Sue, at the above address.

ANGLIA AGENCY: 70 Southsea Avenue, Leigh-on-Sea, Essex SS9 2BJ (tel 0702-471648). Member of FRES.
AU PAIRS and DOMESTICS for short term summer and longer term posts in the UK. Paying Guest stays arranged everywhere for individuals, families and groups. Enquiries (enclosing s.a.e. or IRC) to Jill Corbet, Anglia Agency.

AT YOUR SERVICE AGENCY: 163A Brent Street, London NW4 4DH (tel 081-203 6885/6862).
AU PAIRS, NANNIES AND MOTHERS' HELPS placed in the UK and

abroad. Open to UK and EC applicants. A commitment of 6-12 months is preferred but there are opportunities for 3 month placements. Experience with children is useful. Age: 17-27. Rates of pay depend on experience and qualifications. Applications to Sandra or Helen, at the above address. (O)

AU PAIRS OF SURREY: Buddenbrook, 15 Stewards Green Road, Epping, Essex CM16 7BX (tel 0378-560180/0992-560180).
AU PAIRS. £30-35 p.w. plus B.& L. for a maximum of 30 h.p.w. Applicants must be female and from Western Europe (but not the UK). Non-smokers preferred. M.p.w. 3 months, with a maximum of 2 years. Should be aged 18-27. Positions are available throughout the year. Applicants should send an IRC to Mrs Christine Martin, at the above address, for further information.

AVALON AGENCY: Thursley House, 53 Station Road, Shalford, Guildford, Surrey GU4 8HA (tel 0483-63640).
Au pair positions between June and the end of September or for 6 month min. periods throughout the year. £130-165 per month depending on experience, possession of driving licence, etc. To, work 30 h.p.w. with light housework. Also placements as *aides des familles* (10): £200-250 per month, for 40 h.p.w. Positions available for EC passport-holders (except Spanish and Portuguese). Free B. & L. Childcare experience not essential. Age: 18-27 years. Applicants must be single and childless. Write for application form and further details to P. A. Penfold, Avalon Agency. (Applications to be written in English.)

MRS E. S. BONN: La Maison du Coin, St. Ouen, Jersey, Channel Islands.
STUDENT to work at a family shooting lodge in the Scottish Highlands for a friendly family including a 17-year old daughter. Work involves light housework and simple cooking. Should be a driver and animal lover. Hours to be arranged. 6 days p.w. Period of work from the end of August to the beginning of September. Plenty of opportunities to go climbing and walking in the beautiful countryside around. Applications (not before 1 May) to Mrs E. Bonn at the above address. Interviews necessary prior to engagement. (O)

MRS BROOKS: Erislannan Manor, Clifden, Co. Galway, Ireland (tel 095-21134).
AU PAIR to live with family. £40 p.w. with hours of work by arrangement. Free B. & L. available. Must be fond of children, able to cook, and be prepared to help in the coffee shop. Period of work July and August. Interview not necessary. Applications from February to Mrs Brooks, at the above address. (O)

CONTINENTAL AU PAIRS: 33 Channel View Road, Brighton BN2 6DR (tel 0273- 677993).

AU PAIRS (50+). Placements with British families for foreign girls. Pocket money of £25-30 p.w. plus free B. & L. in own room, usually with TV. To work 30 h.p.w. Duties include light housework and care of children. Usually 5 days work a week with weekends free. M.p.w. 8 weeks between May and September. Applicants should be aged 17-27. Applications to Mrs K. Smith at the above address. (O)

EDGWARE AU PAIR AGENCY: 19 Manor Park Crescent, Edgware, Middlesex HA8 7NH (tel 081-952 5522). Places girls in London, the Home Counties and throughout the West Midlands. Can also arrange placements in all major European countries and the USA.
MOTHER'S HELPS, NANNIES. Highest wage paid to those with qualifications or experience in childcare. Live-in positions available.
AU PAIRS. Live in as part of a family and are given pocket money. Positions available all year round. M.p.w. 4 weeks at Easter or 10 weeks in the summer. Applications two months before wanting to start work, to Lorraine Bass, at the above address. (O)

EURAUPAIR: Girton house, 31 Tiln Lane, Retford, Nottinghamshire DN22 6SN (tel 0777-704449). Agency placing overseas au pairs with British families.
AU PAIRS. £120 per month min., plus free B. & L. To work 5-6 hours per day, 5-6 days p.w. Applicants must have basic English, and a willingness to fit in with family life. Openness, flexibility and a cooperative personality are also needed. Duties varied, but mostly light housework, babysitting, childminding, ironing, and so on. M.p.w. 1 month, with vacanies occuring all year round. Applicants must have a work permit for UK. Applications to Euraupair, at the above address. (O)

EUROYOUTH LTD: 301 Westborough Road, Westcliff, Southend-on-Sea, Essex SS0 9PT (tel 0702-341434; fax 0702-330104). Member of FIYTO and FRES.
AU PAIR positions arranged in all parts of Britain throughout the year. Min. length of stay 3 months.
Also arranges paying guest stays with or without courses (riding, tennis, judo, surfing, sailing, language, painting) for individuals and groups in Southend-on-Sea. Stays without courses available in various towns and villages of Essex and in London throughout the year.
Write enclosing s.a.e. for details to Euroyouth, at the above address.

GIRLS ABOUT TOWN AU PAIR AGENCY: 15 Maxim Road, Grange Park, London N21 1EY (tel 081-364 0034; fax 081-364 0354).

AU PAIRS. £25-30 p.w. To work 5 hours daily, with afternoons free and 3-4 evenings per week babysitting.
DEMI PAIRS. £15 p.w. To work 3 hours daily with afternoons free and 2-3 evenings per week babysitting.
Free B. & L. provided. Positions available all year round. M.p.w. 2 months. Applicants from the EC welcome. Write to Barbara Feller including s.a.e. or IRC for a full application form.

HELPING HANDS AU PAIR & DOMESTIC AGENCY: 10 Hertford Road, Newbury Park, Ilford, Essex IG2 7HQ (tel 081-597 3138).
DEMI-PAIRS. £12+ p.w. for 3 hours housework, 6 days p.w. 2 evenings babysitting p.w.
DEMI-PAIRS PLUS. £17+ p.w. for 4 hours housework, 6 days p.w. 2 evenings babysitting.
AU PAIRS. £30 p.w. for 5 hours housework, 6 days p.w. 3 evenings babysitting p.w.
AU PAIRS PLUS. £40+ p.w. for 6-7 hours housework, 6 days p.w. plus looking after children.
Free B. & L. The majority of families live in London suburbs and nearby counties, Essex (which includes seaside towns), and country areas. Applicants should be aged 18-27, in good health and adaptable. Willingness to undertake housework and childcare essential. M.p.w. 6 months although there are some vacancies of 3/4 months during the summer. Vacancies available throughout the year. Applicants from EC countries and mothers' helps from Canada, are welcome. Write, enclosing an IRC, to Helping Hands Au Pair & Domestic Agency.

INTERNATIONAL CATHOLIC SOCIETY FOR GIRLS: St. Patrick's International Youth Centre, 24 Great Chapel Street, London W1V 3AF (071-734 2156 and 071-439 0116).
The English branch of the Association Catholique Internationale des Services de la Jeunesse Feminine is specially engaged in au pair placement of young applicants in England and on the Continent. Min. age 18 years. Min. length of stay 9+ months (September-June/July) or 6+ months (January-June/July). Applications enclosing s.a.e. or IRC to the above address. (O)

INTER-SEJOURS: 179 Rue de Courcelles, 75017 Paris, France (tel 1 47 63 06 81).
Au pair posts for French girls throughout the UK; also in France, Germany, Italy, Spain and Baleares islands for English or French girls. Wages approx. £28 p.w. To work 5 hours per day, 6 days p.w. Duties include housekeeping,

looking after children and baby-sitting 2/3 evenings p.w. Free B. & L. Work is available throughout the year, minimum period 6 months (3 months over the summer). Age 18-25 years. Paying guests arrangements also made. Applications anytime to Mme Pierrot, Inter-Sejours.

JOLAINE AU PAIR & DOMESTIC AGENCY: 18 Escot Way, Barnet, Hertfordshire EN5 3AN (tel 081-449 1334; fax 081-449 9183).
Arranges au pair, demi-pair, mother's helps and demi-plus positions in England throughout the year, short or long term. Demi-payant positions are arranged for periods of 3-12 months and mean that the girl pays approx. £12 p.w. and works about 2 hours per day and 2 evenings p.w. plus babysitting, in exchange for the experience of living with an English family. Also offers paying guest service to students or visitors to England. Cost from £71 p.w. per person, group bookings possible. All ages welcome. Applications anytime, enclosing s.a.e. or IRC, to the above address. (O)

THE LONDON AU PAIR AND NANNY AGENCY: 4 Sunnyside, Childs Hill, London NW2 2QN (tel 071-435 3891).
AU PAIRS (50). £32 p.w. plus free B. & L. To work 30 hours per week (5/6 hours per day), with 1 day free. Age: 18-27. Applicants must have a basic knowledge of English, and experience of caring for young children is an advantage. Should also be prepared to help with housework, and preferably be non-smokers. M.p.w. 7 weeks, with work available between June/July and August/September. Interviews unnecessary unless applicants already resident in UK. Applications in March/April to Mrs M. Dyer, at the above address. (O)

MRS J. MARBER: 27 Ham Farm Road, Ham Common, Richmond, Surrey TW10 5NA (tel 081-546 9457).
AU PAIR required for an adult family. Duties to include light housework, ironing, washing up and walking the dog. Own bedroom and bathroom provided. Period of work April to October. To work 30 h.p.w. (5 hours over 6 days). Position most suitable for a female student from EC aged between 17-25, with a good knowledge of English. Good public transport is available in the area. Applications, including a recent photograph and s.a.e. or IRC, to Mrs J. Marber at the above address.

MRS M. MISIRLIZADE: 44 Blenheim Drive, Oxford OX2 8DQ (tel 0865-513788).
MOTHER'S HELP to look after girl aged 9 and boy aged $6\frac{1}{2}$ and help with housework, from the beginning of July until first week in September, including accompanying the family on holiday, with all expenses paid. Knowledge of

French language an advantage. Salary negotiable. Applications to Mrs Misirlizade, at the above address.

MONDIAL AGENCY: 32 Links Road, West Wickham, Kent BR4 0QW (tel 081-777 0510; fax 081-777 6765).
Arranges placement of Western European nationals, including Austrians and Yugoslavians, in England, and British nationals, in France, Spain and Austria. The agency stresses that it can place only au pairs who can stay for at least 6 months. Min. age 18 years. Also arranges paying guest positions. Applications enclosing s.a.e. to Mrs J. K. Talbot, Mondial Agency. (O)

NORFOLK CARE SEARCH AGENCY: 19 London Road, Downham Market, Norfolk PE38 9BJ (tel 0366-384448; fax 0366-385226).
DOMESTIC NANNIES and MOTHERS' HELPS. £80-150 p.w. plus full B. & L. To work an 8-10 hour day. Min. age 18. Positions available throughout the year. Enquiries, enclosing s.a.e., to Mrs V. A. Parker, Proprietor, Norfolk Care Search Agency.

NORTHERN NANNIES RECRUITMENT AGENCY: 10 Leeds Road, Leeds, West Yorkshire LS8 5LD (tel 0532-488424). An agency specializing in the domestic sector, with vacancies in the South of England, Yorkshire, Lancashire, and the Northeast (as well as abroad).
NANNIES, AU PAIRS, MOTHERS' HELPS, DOMESTICS, etc. Unlimited vacancies available. Wages negotiable. To work approx. 8 hours per day, with two days off p.w. Must be flexible, however. Min. age 18. Experience an advantage, but not essential. All positions include live-in accommodation. Staff required all year round. Apply a.s.a.p. to Beverley Parsons or Yvonne Walker at the above address. (Applicants must be available for interview.) (O)

OPTIONS TRUST STAFF RECRUITMENT: 4 Plantation Way, Whitehill, Bordon, Hampshire GU35 9HD (tel 0420-474261). This is a non-profit making organization, set up and run by a number of disabled people, who employ staff to enable them to live in homes of their own in the community.
PERSONNEL ASSISTANTS (4-10). £80-100 p.w. plus free B. & L. To work approx. 40 h.p.w. with 2 days off. The work involves personal care, domestic duties and driving amoung other things. Min. age 18. Driving licence required but no previous experience is necessary. M.p.w. 6 months, at any time of year. Applications to Mrs V. Mason, at the above address. (O)

OXFORD AUNTS: 2 George Street, Oxford OX1 2AF (tel 0865-249784).
NANNIES/MOTHERS' HELPS to live with families and look after children,

clean, cook, etc. Also positions for cook/housekeeper/companions to elderly people who are sometimes infirm. B. & L. usually available. Applications from foreign students can only be considered if they are already in Britain and have up-to-date references. Applicants from America must have obtained a work permit through BUNAC and those from Canada a working visa. Otherwise applications any time of the year to the above address.

ROCKINGHORSE: 8 Turn Again Lane, Oxford OX1 1QL (tel 0865-794224/728125).
NANNIES. £90-120 p.w. To work 7.30am-6.30pm Monday-Friday. Applicants must have NNEB, NAMCW, PCSC or some recognized teaching certificate.
MOTHERS' HELPS. £60-80 p.w. To work flexible hours, but similar to above. Must have practical experience.
AU PAIRS. £25-35 p.w. To work approx. 4-5 hours daily Monday-Friday. Must have a love of children.
All positions live-in. Vacancies generally occur in Oxfordshire and can vary tremendously. All staff must complete a registration form and supply 3 referees. M.p.w. 4 weeks. An interview is usually needed. Applications to Grainne Lamphee from February/March, at the above address. (O)

SINCLAIRS EMPLOYMENT AGENCY: 7 Longmead Avenue, Bishopstown, Bristol BS7 8QF (tel 0272-420171).
ELDERLY HELPS. £25 per day, to work for 7 days, one month, or longer. No qualifications required, but must use initiative and be capable.
MOTHERS' HELPS. £65-75 per week including B. & L. To work 5 days a week on average, helping mother with children and housework. Must love children and have common sense.
NANNIES. £100 p.w. minimum, or £25 per day. To work 5 days p.w. on average, usually in sole charge of children. NNEB or NAMCW qualification required, or lots of experience.
MATERNITY NURSES. £200 p.w. on average. To work usually for 4-6 weeks at each post. To be in sole charge of new baby. NNEB required, and experience of newborn babies.
B. & L. included with every job at no extra charge. Temporary work is available all year round. M.p.w. one week. Interviews are carried out where possible, but staff are accepted without as long as references and photographs provided. Applications to be sent a.s.a.p. to Shirley Sinclair, Principal, at the above address. (O)

SOLIHULL AU PAIR AND NANNY AGENCY: 87 Warwick Road, Olton, Solihull, West Midlands B92 7HP (tel 021-707 0179). Places girls in London, the Home Counties and throughout the West Midlands. Can also arrange placements in all major European countries and the USA.

MOTHER'S HELPS, NANNIES. Highest wages paid to those with qualifications or experience in child care. Live-in positions available.

AU PAIRS. Live in as part of the family and are given pocket money. Positions available all year round. M.p.w. 4 weeks at Easter, 10 weeks in the summer. Applications two months before wanting to start work to Ray Bushell, at the above address. (O)

SOUTH-EASTERN AU PAIR BUREAU: 39 Rutland Avenue, Thorpe Bay, Essex SS1 2X (tel 0702-01911).

AU PAIRS. To work 5 hours per day, with up to 3 evenings babysitting p.w. To live in as part of the family, and assist with general housework and child care.

AU PAIRS PLUS: To work 40 h.p.w. Duties as above.

Both of these positions should allow time for language study.

Also needed DEMI-PAIRS, MOTHER'S HELPS, NANNIE, DOMESTICS in the UK and abroad.

Vacancies arise all year round for all positions. Wages from £120-350+ per month (dependent on position). Basic childcare experience an advantage. Ages: 17+. Period of work 6 months-2 years, although summer placements are available. M.p.w. 6 weeks. B. & L. almost always available (except for some UK posts where increased wages compensate). Applications at any time, enclosing 2 s.a.e.'s, to the above address.

UNIVERSAL CARE LTD: Chester House, 9 Windsor End, Beaconsfield, Buckinghamshire HP9 2JJ (tel 0494-678811).

Places au pairs with families throughout the UK. £25-30 p.w. 5 hours per day. Age 17-26. M.p.w. 6 months. Also places mothers' helps in all parts of the UK. £50-60 p.w. To work 8-10 hours per day. Free accommodation. Age 18-35. Applications for both au pairs and mothers' helps required at least one month in advance.

VISA PERSONNEL: 27 Margaret Street, London W1.

AU PAIRS (20-30). Wages £140-150 per month plus free B. & L. To work 5 hours per day (approx. 2 hours in the morning, 3 in the afternoon), $5\frac{1}{2}$ days p.w. Au pairs needed to work in the UK mainly, but some overseas work is also available. Applicants must have a basic knowledge of English, and childcare experience would be useful. Work involves living with family, caring for children, taking them to school, etc. Also some light housework. M.p.w. 2-3 months, but preferably longer. Applications a.s.a.p. to the above address. (O)

USEFUL PUBLICATIONS

CENTRAL BUREAU FOR EDUCATIONAL VISITS AND EXCHANGES: Seymour Mews House, Seymour Mews, London WlH 9EP (tel 071-486 5101). Publishes *Working Holidays 1992*, an annual guide to paid and voluntary work opportunities available throughout the year in Britain and around the world. There is a large section on Great Britain which has information on jobs in the following areas: Archaeology, Au Pairs/Childcare, Children's Projects, Community Work, Conservation, Couriers/Reps, Domestic, Farmwork, Leaders & Guides, Monitors & Instructors, Teachers, Workcamps and General. In addition to work opportunities, it gives advice on insurance, work permits, travel, accommodation, etc. The price for *Working Holidays 1992* is £7.95 in bookshops, or £8.99 including UK postage (mainland Europe: £10.50, worldwide: £13).

Also publishes *Volunteer Work*, a comprehensive guide to medium and long-term voluntary work, with information on over 100 recruiting organizations active in Britain or abroad. Although many opportunities are for those with skills/experience, there are some for people with motivation and enthusiasm. Price £3 in bookshops, £4 including UK postage (mainland Europe: £6.50, worldwide: £8).

Another Central Bureau publication is *A Year Between*, which gives details of long-term voluntary projects, work placements and adventure opportunities in Britain and abroad. It is specifically aimed at those taking a year out of education, particularly school-leavers and graduates. Price £6.99 in bookshops, £7.99 including UK postage (mainland Europe: £9.50, worldwide: £12). The above guides are available from bookshops or by post from the Central Bureau.

COUNCIL FOR BRITISH ARCHAEOLOGY: 112 Kennington Road, London SEll 6RE (tel 071-582 0494). For people interested in archaeology and excavations, digs provide an interesting and enjoyable way of spending some time with people of similar interests. Details of excavations are given in the Council's *British Archaeological News*, issued bi-monthly, price £10 for a year's subscription. Having studied the newsletter, students should apply to the director of the particular excavations which interest them. The min. age for all these digs is usually 16 years.

HOBSON'S PUBLISHING PLC: Bateman Street, Cambridge CB2 1LZ (tel 0223-354551).
Published *A year off ... a year on?* in 1991, on behalf of the Careers Research and Advisory Centre. This is a guide to jobs, voluntary service and working holidays for those looking for work while at school or college. It provides information, contacts, names and addresses, ideas—and the student view. The price is £4.95 (plus £2.50 post and packing).

VACATION WORK PUBLICATIONS: 9 Park End Street, Oxford OX1 1HJ (tel 0865-241978; fax 0865-790885).
The International Directory of Voluntary Work is a comprehensive guide to voluntary work, both temporary and long-term. Opportunities in social, manual, office and children's work, agriculture, conservation and teaching are included. It lists many charitable organizations in Britain which welcome summer staff. Price £6.95 plus £1 postage.
Work Your Way Around the World starts in Britain and provides valuable tips about casual work in this country. The chapter on Britain includes detailed sections on fruit and hop picking, tourism and catering, English language teaching, etc. Price £8.95 plus £1 postage.
Vacation Traineeships for Students is a directory of on-the-job training opportunities for all types of career. It includes details of over 7,000 career-related holiday jobs in Britain (and abroad) for students and graduates in construction and engineering, computers and electronics, media and sales, business and management, etc. Price £6.95 plus £1 postage.
The Teenager's Vacation Guide to Work, Study and Adventure is an invaluable book for teenagers up to the age of 17 who are looking for something different to do during their holidays; it covers both Britain and Abroad. Price £6.95 plus £1 postage.

ANY COMMENTS?

We have made every effort to make this book as useful and accurate as possible for you. We would appreciate any comments that you may have concerning the employers listed.

Name:

Address:

Name of employer:
Entry on page:

Comments:

Have you come across any other employers who might merit inclusion in the book? (A free copy of a Vacation Work title of your choice will be sent to anyone who sends in the name and address of an employer subsequently included in the Directory.)